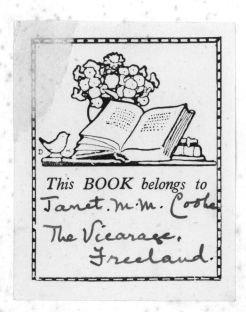

This BOOK belongs to
Janet. M. M. Cooke
The Vicarage,
Freeland.

CHARLOTTE M. YONGE
From a watercolour drawing by George Richmond, R.A.

Fr.   *National Portrait Gallery*

THE ENGLISH MISS
TO-DAY & YESTERDAY

IDEALS METHODS AND PERSONALITIES IN THE
EDUCATION AND UPBRINGING OF GIRLS
DURING THE LAST HUNDRED YEARS

By

ALICIA C. PERCIVAL

GEORGE G. HARRAP & CO. LTD.
LONDON   TORONTO   BOMBAY   SYDNEY

First published 1939
by GEORGE G. HARRAP & CO. LTD.
182 *High Holborn, London, W.C.* 1

Made in Great Britain. Printed by Neill & Co., Ltd., Edinburgh

PREFACE

Nothing shows such subtle variation as men's ideals. This book sprang from a desire to see how theories about the upbringing of girls have altered during the last hundred years—from a desire, in other words, to study the change in the ideals for the educated woman. It does not pretend to be a complete history of girls' education during that period. But even the briefest survey of ideals, a summary of what the girl was meant to become at different times during the century, cannot but involve an account of her much-varied training. Nor can her instructors be neglected, and those forceful personalities whose lives and ideals so much altered the trend of her upbringing. What course would the stream of education have taken if it had not been diverted by the labours of Miss Beale and Miss Buss, of Emily Davies, of the Lawrences of Roedean, of the founders of the Girls' Public Day School Trust, and of the throng of men and women who worked with and after them? Possibly its direction would not now be as different as is commonly imagined; the study of girls' education leads one to believe that we are heading towards an ideal not very remote from that of a hundred years ago. Yet we have not moved merely in a circle, but in a spiral; our ideas having spread continually farther and wider.

The material of the book has come from three sources. That the social life of any period colours its literature is a commonplace; conversely we may say that its literature, especially its fiction, reflects in some degree its social life. Information about the early days of the nineteenth century, when the English miss was usually brought up at home, by a governess, or in a fashionable private school, has been collected largely from novels and from

3

memoirs of the early and middle part of the century. It was found that to extend the survey backward beyond the eighteen-thirties rounded off the retrospective view more satisfactorily than to keep precisely to the hundred years; there is more break between the eighteenth and nineteenth centuries than at the accession of Queen Victoria. In any case, however, it is hard enough to get any idea of continuity in educational development during the early years of the century; this must be my excuse for departing from a rigid chronological line and for taking information about particular subjects where it could be found.

In the second period, the richest in progressive events, most of the material has been taken from the full and excellent lives of the pioneer women, from reports of Royal Commissions and of the Board of Education, and from the jubilee books of various institutions. I can only hope that others will find these documents as enthralling as I did myself.

For the years of this century and for some way farther back I have relied chiefly on personal reminiscences either found in memoirs or told me direct by friends.

I should like here to thank all those through whose information and assistance I have been enabled to write this book. I am specially grateful to Mr H. E. M. Icely, Reader in Education at the University of Oxford, not only for his kindness in correcting the proofs, but for his encouragement, without which the work would never have been begun, and to Miss D. M. Stuart, for her advice, without which it would probably never have been completed. To the late Mr George G. Harrap and to the editorial staff of Messrs George G. Harrap and Co., Ltd., I owe much. I wish to express my thanks also to Miss Helen Moss and Miss Herma Fiedler for helping me with the index.

Finally, I gratefully acknowledge permission received from the following for the use of copyright material:

The Oxford University Press, for extracts from Mr G. M. Young's *Victorian England*, Miss Eleanor Lodge's *Terms and Vacations*, Mrs M. Vivian Hughes' *A London Girl of the Eighties*, Mr G. A. N. Lowndes' *The Silent Social Revolution*, and *Rural Education*, by Mr A. W. Ashby and Miss P. G. Byles; Messrs John Murray, for the extracts from *The Girlhood of Queen Victoria*, edited by Viscount Esher; Messrs Macmillan and Co., Ltd., for extracts from the works of Charlotte M. Yonge and for an extract from Lady Wilson's *Dear Youth*; Miss Margaret J. Gifford, for extracts from *The Diary of an Oxford Lady*; Miss D. M. Stuart and Messrs George G. Harrap and Co., Ltd., for an extract from *The Girl through the Ages*; Messrs G. Bell and Sons, Ltd., for extracts from the works of Mrs J. H. Ewing; Messrs Kegan Paul, Trench, Trubner and Co., Ltd., for extracts from *The Journal of Emily Shore* and from *The Headmistress Speaks*, edited by Miss E. Philips; Messrs Williams and Norgate, Ltd., for an extract from Miss Rachel Davis's *Four Miss Pinkertons*; Messrs Edward Arnold and Co., for an extract from Miss B. Clough's *Memoir of Anne Jemima Clough*; Messrs Longmans, Green and Co., Ltd., for extracts from Dr Sara Burstall's *Retrospect and Prospect*, Miss A. E. Ridley's *Frances Mary Buss*, the Reverend Mother Stuart's *The Education of Catholic Girls*, and Mr T. Rayment's *Modern Education*; the Controller of H.M. Stationery Office, for extracts from the Report of the Consultative Committee (Board of Education) on the Differentiation in Curricula between the Sexes in Secondary Schools and the Report of the Consultative Committee (Board of Education) on the Primary School, and for an extract from the evidence given before the Royal Commission on the Elementary Education Acts; Messrs Sampson Low, Marston and Co., Ltd., for an extract from Miss Frances Gray's *And Gladly Wolde he Lerne and Gladly Teche*; the Hogarth Press, for extracts from Miss Jane Harrison's *Reminiscences of a Student's*

Life and from *Our Freedom and its Results*, edited by Mrs Ray Strachey; Messrs Victor Gollancz, Ltd., for extracts from *The Modern Schools Handbook*, edited by Mr T. Blewitt; Mr A. P. Herbert, the Proprietors of *Punch*, and Messrs Ernest Benn, Ltd., for lines from *Hush, Mrs Hundred, Hush!*

A. C. P.

CONTENTS

ILLUSTRATIONS

PROLOGUE

Miss Jane Harrison tells in her reminiscences that when she was on the Council of the Girls' Public Day School Trust she used to go round to the local prize-givings with certain "'British lions,' whom you could always count on to roar suitably." Irreproachable sentiments were expressed in speeches on well-established lines, and the discourses inevitably ended with that well-worn quotation, "A perfect woman, nobly planned." So tired did she grow of this phrase that she mentally offered a prize of half a crown to anyone who could resist it—but, she adds, "The prize would never have been won."

What was the object of the 'planning,' and what would the perfect woman have been like? If we looked through the centuries for a picture of the ideal woman—or even of the ideal Englishwoman—we should find some curious images. To trace only through the last hundred years, the ideals held up before "Caroline" of 1838 and her namesake of to-day—if these two pictures were set face to face they would hardly be acknowledged as related. And as the finished product varied, so the system of education which was to produce it has been altered beyond recognition.

There had been a time when the development of the girl, though progressing along different lines, reached a much closer level of culture to that of the boy than it did at the beginning of the last century. But from about the sixteenth century education for boys had risen and spread (though not as high nor as widely as might have been hoped by the founders of so many grammar schools), whereas that of girls gradually sank, till by the time of Queen Victoria's accession it was as low as it ever had been.

The cause of the decay was twofold, and becomes apparent from the seventeenth century. The more sober ideal for a woman, connected perhaps wrongly with the Puritans, was that she should be a housewife, and no more—or very little more. The opening of the woman's story in Genesis was neglected, and only the end remembered. In Wyclif's translation the words relating the creation of woman had been: "Make we to hym a help like hym," or, in the version of 1388, "an help lyke to himself." In the Authorized Version was substituted "an help meet for him," and the adjective lost its significance. The very word 'meet' became part of the noun 'helpmate,' and its force was ignored.

It may have been inevitable that a people whose life and language had for a century been permeated by the Bible should have been influenced by the view of women there presented. But, after all, the Hebrews were an Eastern people, and obviously their ideas of women had more than a tinge of the purdah, if not of the harem. There was in the Old Testament an occasional prophetess, a Deborah or a Huldah, but for the most part the women were "in the tent" or ignored altogether. The "virtuous woman" herself is not "sitting in the gate "—she leaves that to her husband, and remains within, giving "meat to her household, and a portion to her maidens." A woman's virtues were domestic, and her position depended on her husband. Even the lovely Ruth was in the eyes of the Mosaic law little better than a chattel; whoever took over the land of the dead man took also his widow. The place of women in the New Testament had, as we see it in the Gospels and Acts, advanced far, but the typical Puritan looked equally to the old dispensation and the new. Nor when from the latter he took the counsel of St Paul was he likely to be more liberal-minded on the subject of women's place in society. Apart from the never-forgotten question of head-covering and all it stood for, he would find good support for his idea that wives should submit themselves to their husbands and women remain silent in churches.

Milton's Eve and her position in Eden illustrate what woman had become:

> He for God only, she for God in him.

She does not even stay after the meal, during which she has waited on Adam and the Angel, but "sat retired." Half-way through Adam's history lesson she goes out.

> Of him to ask
> Chose rather; he, she knew, would intermix
> Grateful digressions, and solve high dispute
> With conjugal caresses.

This is not to say that the English girl of the seventeenth and eighteenth centuries was taught nothing. It was natural and possible for her to take a pride in what she could do, and her craft was housekeeping. And though only one aspect of her mind might be cultivated, reading and writing being regarded as only "dilution of mother-wit," yet the trained housewife of the eighteenth century was not to be despised nor entirely pitied. The Vicar of Wakefield chose his wife,

> as she did her wedding-gown, not for a fine glossy surface, but such qualities as would wear well. To do her justice, she was a good-natured, notable woman; and as for breeding, there were few country ladies who could shew more. She could read any English book without much spelling; and for pickling, preserving, and cookery none could excel her. She prided herself also upon being an excellent contriver in housekeeping; though I could never find that we grew richer with all her contrivances.

But on Mrs Primrose and the class below her a change was to come for the worse. It came with prosperity and the mechanical age. Early in the nineteenth century more money began to reach the middle and lower-middle classes; they inhabited larger houses and kept more servants. The idea grew up that the daughters of the house should not do the work of the cook, the dairymaid,

13

the housekeeper, etc. By the time of *Pride and Prejudice* Mrs Bennet is distinctly superior about Charlotte Lucas when the latter is "wanted for the mince-pies." She remarks, "I always keep servants that can do their own work—my daughters are brought up differently." The Bennets are, on the father's side at least, of pretty good family, but the rot crept downward. The Miss Gunns, tradesman's daughters, in *Silas Marner* cannot but admire Nancy Lammeter's toilette. But their one point of criticism is that, being a farmer's daughter, she has hands roughened by cheese-making.

Later in the century things grew worse.

> Men forget that the continually increasing use of all sorts of machinery for the supply of household wants has completely altered the aspect of our domestic interiors. The rounded life of our grandmothers, full of interest and variety and usefulness, is a thing of the past. Some of us may look back on it with regret, but it can never be recalled. How can women, living in towns where they can buy almost every article in domestic use cheaper than they could make it, unless they reckon their time and eyesight as worth nothing at all, work with spirit at tasks which are obviously futile? It is not in human nature. A hundred years ago women might know little of history and geography, and nothing at all of any language but their own— they might be careless of what was going on in the outer world —ignorant of science and art—but their minds were not therefore inactive. Circumstances provided a discipline which is now wholly wanting, and which needs to be supplied by wider and deeper cultivation.

So wrote Miss Emily Davies, and she explains the hiatus in a girl's life after she has left school but before she marries—a pause of at least three years, often much longer—as a relic of the time when

> our mothers and our grandmothers were accustomed to undergo at home what was in fact an apprenticeship to household management. . . . Down to a comparatively recent period every household was a workshop; spinning, weaving, knitting, sewing, all are gone or going. What has become of the busy hands and brains? The hands are gone into factories; the brains are idle.

This last statement was but a reflection in the cottage homes of what had begun much earlier: gradually, in houses where the tradition had been that they should be taught housekeeping and nothing else, girls ceased to learn housekeeping, and continued to learn nothing else— unless they took to 'accomplishments.' For there had been another path which a woman's education might take. If she were by position excluded from the chores of housekeeping, or by nature averse from them, she could yet fulfil a function in society—that of an accomplished and well-bred lady. Her ideal type was perhaps found in France rather than in England, in the *salons* of Mlle de Scudéry or the Hôtel de Rambouillet, and later of Mme du Deffand and Mme Geoffrin. All the same, eighteenth-century England made a very passable imitation with her fine lady. Witty, alert, not lacking in brains or in cultivation, she played her part in the world of politics—witness Sarah, Duchess of Marlborough, and the Duchess of Somerset—of literature—witness Lady Elizabeth Hastings [1] and Lady Mary Wortley Montagu —or simply as a leader of fashion—witness the Countess of Suffolk and Lady Hervey.

As Richard Holt Hutton put it in the next century:

> The learned women of preceding ages . . . were taught their learning essentially as an accomplishment, as a ladylike craft, something higher than the harpsichord, a kind of intellectual embroidery, not as a study. I mean that they learnt it not for the sake of preparing their minds to grasp truth, but for the sake of polishing their minds so as to shine among distinguished men; for social and literary effect, not for intellectual purposes. I doubt if we had in proportion to the number of educated women nearly so many accomplished women as the eighteenth century. Social intercourse is less prepared for, wit and repartee are less cultivated, even taste and artistic accomplishments probably attain a less exquisite perfection than in the most refined society of the extinct 'French' school.

---

[1] Subject of Steele's exquisite compliment: "To love her was a liberal education."

Hutton is probably too hard on the really intellectual women who flourished during the latter half of the century—Miss Elizabeth Carter, Mrs Montagu, Mrs Inchbald—and on the earlier educationist Mary Astell, but it is worth noting that this distinguished critic does consider the eighteenth century as the age primarily of 'accomplishments,' and he does ascribe this ideal to the French. It is relevant to add the confession of Lady Morgan, who was the author of a successful play, *The Wild Irish Girl*, and several novels, and the first 'woman of letters' to receive a pension as such (1837):

> The strongest point of my ambition is to be every inch a woman. . . . I dropped the study of chemistry lest I should be thought less a woman. I have studied music as a sentiment rather than a science, and drawing as an amusement rather than an art, lest I should become a musical pedant or a masculine artist.

Mrs Barbauld's reply when it was suggested by the Bluestocking Mrs Montagu that she should become the principal of a ladies' college is of the same tenor:

> A kind of academy for ladies where they are to be taught in a regular manner the various branches of science appears to me better calculated to form such characters as the 'Précieuses' or 'Femmes Savantes' than good wives or agreeable companions. . . . The best way for a woman to acquire knowledge is by conversation with a father or brother and by such a course of reading as they may recommend.

She would have had the support in this of Arthur Young—who notes (September 16, 1787): "The conversation of men not engaged in trifling pursuits is the best school for the education of a woman"—and, to go back a couple of generations, of Swift. Swift makes it a point in his praise of Stella that she chose men for her companions, the usual topics of ladies' discourse being such as she had little knowledge of and less relish.

> Yet no man was upon the rack to entertain her, for she descended to anything that was innocent and diverting. . . . Although her knowledge from books and company was much

more extensive than usually falls to the share of her sex,[1] yet she was so far from making a parade of it that her female visitants, on their first acquaintance, who expected to discover it by what they call hard words and deep discourse, would be sometimes disappointed, and say, "They found she was like other women." But wise men, through all her modesty, whatever they discoursed on, could easily observe that she understood them very well, by the judgment shown in her observations, as well as in her questions.[2]

There was, indeed, an eighteenth-century movement which one would have thought must lead to an improvement in the education of women and in their position.

To rest woman's claim to the most liberal culture on her right, real or supposed, to share with man the so-called professions implies a complete misunderstanding of the ground on which *man's* claim is really based. It is not because he is to be a barrister or a surgeon or a merchant, but because he is to be a man, with faculties and aspirations, moral and intellectual, and with social duties requiring enlightenment and guidance for their due discharge that the boy demands, and ought to receive, a liberal culture. So, precisely, is it with the woman.

This, though taken from a lecture delivered by Dr W. B. Hodgson as late as 1864, is only the application of a doctrine pronounced in the previous century—a part of the philosophy of Jean-Jacques Rousseau. Logically followed, Rousseau's theory would go far. If man could claim equality with man simply on the ground of his humanity, if each individual had rights and duties merely because he was a member of the human race, on what ground could woman be excluded from those rights and duties? If all society were organized in a Social Contract, how could woman be denied a place in the State. And if she had such a place, why not train her to fill it? Rousseau

---

[1] But, to judge from the notes which Swift found it necessary to append to Stella's copy of *Paradise Lost*, the standard was not high. We can only imagine that the rest of "her sex" were almost completely ignorant of history, geography, and literature—as, indeed, we might suppose from those papers of *The Tatler* and *The Spectator* which were addressed to the female intelligence.

[2] *On the Death of Mrs Johnson.*

had magnificent schemes for the right education of the boy, so that he might develop first of all into a man, a citizen, and after this into the complete barrister, surgeon, merchant, or what-not. How then did he provide for the girl?

Alas! Rousseau's theory did not carry him so far. Sophie's education is as nothing compared to Émile's, for Sophie has no function, hardly any existence, as herself. This is her upbringing:

> The whole education of women should be related to that of men. To please them, to be useful to them, to become loved and honoured by them; to bring them up when young, to care for them when grown; to advise, to console them, to make life easy and pleasant for them—these are the duties of women at every age, and this is what they should be taught from child-hood.[1]

Moreover,

> They are dependent on what men think of them, on how highly their virtues are valued. By the law of nature women, just as much as children, are at the mercy of the judgments of men; it is not enough that they should be estimable; they must be esteemed; it is not enough that they should be beautiful; they must be pleasing; it is not enough that they should be virtuous; they must be considered as such.

And

> Woman's book is the world about her; if she reads it ill she is at fault or blinded by some passion. Nevertheless, the true mother of a family, far from being a woman of the world, is no less confined to her house than a nun to her cloister.

So we are back again at Milton's Eve and Swift's Stella.

One eighteenth-century reader at least, who had followed Rousseau's thought eagerly, rose from this study of his work bitterly disappointed. There had been a hope of finding woman treated by this new philosopher and his followers as a reasonable creature with a civil existence

---

[1] *Émile*, Book V.

in the State—whether she was married or single. But if the most advanced minds denied her this, what chance was there for her of being anything but a mere 'sideboard ornament' or a 'shirt-and-pudding maker,' treated as either a goddess or a slave? Yet this one cry was raised against such pitiable neglect of half the human race; one voice protested that the whole attitude of both men and women towards different treatment and different virtues for the two sexes was a wrong one.

Mary Wollstonecraft's life makes very sad reading. That she suffered largely for *les défauts de ses qualités* does not make her fate less tragic. Born in humble, even squalid, circumstances, with a good-for-nothing father and a patient drudge of a mother, Mary managed to raise herself so as eventually to become a reader and translator (of French and German books; Italian she found she could hardly manage) for Johnson, the bookseller. She had to go through much before she achieved this: she took in sewing; she worked as a companion, being then treated as "an upper servant"; she kept a small school with her sisters, and later became a governess, expected to teach French and "a heap of rubbish called accomplishments." Mary Wollstonecraft had acquired the elements of her education at a small school in Beverley, from a retired clergyman in Enfield, and out of her father's old books of divinity, philosophy, and poetry when the family were rusticating in Wales. When about twenty-five she wrote *Thoughts on the Education of Daughters*—a plea for greater freedom, both mental and physical, in the upbringing of young girls, more solidity in their training, with less store set on "delicacy." But her most important work appeared some five years later, in 1791, *A Vindication of the Rights of Woman*.

This work was not so much a polemic, in spite of its title, as a plea, a plea for complete equality in every aspect, social and educational, of women with men. She appealed first to her own sex, to exert themselves and to acquire strength of both mind and body. And to men she appealed to assist in the emancipation of their companions, to raise them and educate them.

> Would men but generously snap our chains and be content with a rational fellowship instead of slavish obedience they would find us more observant daughters, more affectionate sisters, more faithful wives, more reasonable mothers—in a word, better citizens.

Woman's education as it then was hindered rather than helped her.

> To render women truly useful members of society they should, by having their understandings cultivated on a large scale, acquire a rational affection for their country founded on knowledge, because it is obvious that we are little interested about what we do not understand. . . . Let woman share the rights and she will emulate the virtues of man.

Mary had worked out a scheme of education including co-education and day schools; she produced a list of subjects suitable for *all* children to learn, and she urged that cultivation of the body should also be encouraged, for "at present fragility is cultivated at the expense of common sense." That women should be trained for some remunerative employments; that intellectual companionship rather than the physical aspect should be emphasized in marriage; that instead of being arbitrarily governed women should be represented in the State constitutional assembly—these were among her more telling proposals.

Some part of what Mary Wollstonecraft said had been set down before by that far-seeing and distinguished woman, whom Swift so unpardonably ridicules, Mary Astell in her *Essay in Defence of the Female Sex*. But the one lived fifty, the other nearly a hundred and fifty, years before the time was ripe for a women's movement along either social or educational lines. Even in Revolutionary France, where she followed and wrote up the course of events, Mary Wollstonecraft had the sorrow of seeing the National Assembly reject the Bill for Female Suffrage. She would have had to wait more than a hundred and twenty years to see such a Bill carried in this country.

The rest of her story and her connexion first with Imlay and then with William Godwin (of *Political Justice*) is well known. She eventually married Godwin, but they continued to live about twenty doors off from each other, feeling that constant cohabitation was apt to strain the nerves, and that in one house they would have had "no peace, no privacy." Their daughter, at whose birth Mary died, was afterwards Mary Shelley. By the time of her death (1797) the protests raised by Mary Wollstonecraft's *Vindication* had died down; the Rights of Woman, like the Rights of Man, were becoming stale cries. Some of her words were remembered, and seventy years later John Stuart Mill, then Member for Westminster, used to quote, "Women always have the worst of it when law is to decide." But her own life ends with the words, caught from her mother, "A little patience and all will be over."

Mary Wollstonecraft's name remains honoured; her appeal was remembered. Modern research has discovered a faint echo of that appeal, a protest that never went beyond the secrecy of a diary or a circle of relatives. "Poor Nellie Weeton," whose diaries have been discovered and edited by Mr Edward Hall, was about fifteen years later protesting helplessly in the same cause. Sometimes it was on her own behalf: "Why are not females permitted to study? . . . Oh, why have I been so chained down in obscurity?" Sometimes it was on more general grounds: "In proportion as the mind of man has been cultivated and become more refined, the intellect of woman has been more appreciated." These words met with no response, were perhaps unheard except by her entirely unsympathetic brother Tom— who probably agreed with their father that "daughters must be either mop-squeezers or mantua-makers"—but they are interesting as evidence that there were other "vindicators" besides "this shining woman," as Mary Wollstonecraft was, to judge by her miniature, so aptly called.

To see how far they were from receiving sympathy it is worth looking at a few of the more general views held over a hundred and fifty years—right up to the beginning of the present century. We have first the very clear indication that the single woman was the woman *manquée*, however fine might be her character and intellect. Elizabeth Carter, one of the most scholarly of the eighteenth-century educated women, was told by her father:

> If you intend never to marry, as I think you plainly intimate in one of your letters, then you certainly ought to live retired, and not appear in the world with an expense which is reasonable upon the prospect of getting a husband, but not otherwise.

In the sixties of the next century Miss Frances Power Cobbe was protesting against the tremendous difficulties put in the way of a girl who wanted to take up any but "that one sacred vocation of matrimony, for which she may lawfully leave a blind father and a dying mother and go to India with Ensign Anybody"; and complaints against a girl's wishing to take up a career have gone on till the present day. In the nineties we have from an old member of Queen's College a protest against the notion that philanthropic work is the exclusive domain of life's failures—perhaps a disadvantage to others besides the philanthropist. And on the lack of any previous training for even the one vocation that was considered respectable for those of gentle birth—teaching—there is the biting comment of Miss Freer, later Honorary Secretary of Swanley Horticultural College: "To have lost money was formerly considered all that was necessary to prepare a woman for earning a salary." This earning of a salary was in itself considered for a long time as degrading, except in special circumstances; for a married woman it might be impossible, as the hard case of Mrs Norton proved. As late as 1870 Miss Beale is asking indignantly, "Why should it be thought dishonourable for a woman to earn money?"

Not only was it regarded as necessary that a woman should be dependent, and undesirable that she should earn, but it was asserted that she was incompetent to keep herself. It was no use trying to educate her, for she had not educable brains. This was not quite a unanimous opinion, but it was pretty generally held during the first half of the century and even beyond. Miss Davies's description of what a woman is considered as capable of profiting by—or the reverse—ends with the often quoted remark that

> newspapers are scarcely supposed to be read by women at all. . . . When *The Times* is offered to a lady the sheet containing the advertisements and the Births, Deaths, and Marriages is considerately selected.

It was not even desirable for a girl to learn to concentrate her attention on one subject at a time, for the reason, given by Mrs Gaskell, that she was always at everybody's call.

> A woman's usefulness depends on her power of diffusing herself and making her influence felt at a number of points at once. . . . You would only make her unhappy by giving her the habit of fastening her intellectual powers on one thing at a time.

The most bitter opponents of the progress of women's education included various newspapers, particularly *The Saturday Review*. Miss Julia Wedgwood, Browning's friend, states that their stock remark on all women's productions was, "It is gratifying to reflect that so much labour, etc., cannot but have produced valuable results to the writer." And—it seems incredible—one of the early Girton scholars states that in 1901 she was asked by her publisher not to put her Christian name on a German grammar that he had accepted, as a woman's name might disadvantageously affect its sale.

There is no need to go on illustrating a prejudice which is well known, and discussion of which becomes in these days rather wearisome. One protest against it, however, made in the middle of the century, is important. During the years 1851 to 1858 John Stuart Mill was, with the help of his wife, writing the *Essay on the Subjection of Women*. It was towards the end of this period that he made his speech in favour of the Married Women's Property Bill—a Bill which was not, in fact, carried till twenty-five years later. But his speech, and the publication of the *Essay*, did much to alter English thought on both the ideal character and the rightful position of women.

What seems most interesting to watch during the century is the changing and development of this ideal character. For education could not alter until the educationists both knew what change they desired in the 'educand' and could convince the parents that this change was for good. But it was equally true that one could not judge the capacity of girls or women to be educated until one had tried out on them some system of education. Therefore progress was bound to be slow. The aim had to advance alternately with the means.

One thing managed to break occasionally the vicious circle of low aims and restricted means: the career of some woman of great intellect or great character. It was said by Miss Wedgwood about life in the forties:

> Difference of sex then bore on intellectual development in the same way that the difference between wealth and poverty does. Individual zeal might in either case overcome common disadvantage, and the distinction of such exceptional achievement . . . was perhaps more striking than anything with which we can compare it to-day. But ordinary women were then shut out from the intellectual opportunities open to ordinary men, and even extraordinary women were then excluded from the employments and dignities accessible to ordinary men.[1]

---

[1] *The First College for Women* (*Queen's College, London*): *Memories and Records of Work Done*, 1848-98.

Nevertheless a few of them forced an entrance, and their lives and education are worth studying briefly before a more general survey is attempted.

Though the opening of the nineteenth century saw a number of schools, day and boarding, already in being, and the establishment of many more of these private enterprises, the education of upper-class girls was in the main a 'home industry.' Therefore it is to descriptions of home and family life that one must look for an account of education in the early part of the century to deduce what was the ideal character of the girls thus brought up. But the early schools cannot be neglected, nor that ever-present figure the governess, with her attempts to direct the character and intellect of her pupils. With the middle of the century, and not unconnected in the first place with the governess, comes the first real attempt at educating women 'seriously'—but the attempt must be justified by a new statement of the ideal, and the serious-ness must be less marked than other more acknowledged feminine qualities. The next effort, however, was not at all on these lines, and we get to those reformers who were anxious to prove, both in schools and in the new depart-ment of higher education, that men and women were not fundamentally different in intellect, and that what could be done by the one could be done by the other. These pioneers may be called the 'equal terms' school of thought. When this idea had gained ground there appeared a sudden desire to try it out, and without adopting the more extreme views about equality those who were interested in education followed up the theory of individual development by giving each girl, as far as possible, such advantages in education as she appeared capable of taking. Somewhat curiously, it was found that this could be done better (and at less expense) in large than in small communities, and the next remarkable thing is the acceptance and growth of public spirit in girls' schools. The foundation of the high schools and the public boarding schools brings us to the end of the century and beyond, but there is a much larger section of the population to be reckoned with, and, inappropriate as their early aims may seem to us, we cannot ignore the elementary schools or primary education. Then, although it did not directly affect forms of education, a great change in ideals arrived with the struggle for new political and economic freedom, culminating with the War. The new ideals were themselves influenced by the post-War theories about the importance of the community. And finally there are the schools of to-day, trying to solve problems old and new. In the end we are left with the question, *"For what* are we educating our girls?" This book is not a treatise in answer to that question, but an attempt to show what answers have in the last hundred years or so been given to it.

CHAPTER I

EMINENT WOMEN

W E shall have cause to remark more than once how often in the nineteenth century practice gets ahead of theory. Whatever may have been the position of women in the social order, Queen Victoria's reign was remarkable for the outstanding women in almost every line of life, from royalty downward, and there has hardly been any century which has produced such magnificent work as that of the pioneers. Admittedly the procession starts farther back with Mary Wollstonecraft, one of the first, as we have seen, to assume that there was by the natural order of things a position in society for women. (This is where she parts company with the Bluestockings, who, on the whole, would allow the social order to continue as it was, but who were conscious of a pleasant superiority in that they and their own circle were exceptions, and to be regarded as such.) It is true that many of the notable women of the nineteenth century made no kind of public protest about women's rights—they had a job of work, and got on with it. Such criticism as they had to face they met with constancy, often suffering severely because there was a double opposition—to their work and to their sex. Some, on the other hand, definitely protested against their inferior position, but the voices were seldom shrill— the term "shrieking sisterhood" is more unkind than true.

Mr G. M. Young acutely defines their type as follows:

> The outstanding Victorian woman is a blend of the great lady and the intellectual woman, not yet professional, and we can graduate the proportions until at the opposite ends of the scale we encounter the limiting instances of the Queen herself and Harriet Martineau . . . in Miss Nightingale, with the emphasis of genius, the kind achieves its balance.

27

One would only add that even if Miss Nightingale did not consider herself a professional—which is doubtful—she certainly made possible a profession for other women.

If we allow the term 'Victorian' to cover the early years of the nineteenth century (just as 'Elizabethan' is permitted for literary purposes to extend over at least twenty years beyond the Queen's death) we may classify the outstanding women into the learned, the competent, the reformers, and the artists. (The 'arts' include poetry, painting, and acting; of outstanding musicians I admit there is little trace until Dame Ethel Smyth appears.) Names readily occur. In the learned or Bluestocking tradition we must except Hannah More as outside the period; but there are Harriet Martineau, Maria Edgeworth, and George Eliot, while among those who are less generally known but remarkable in their own spheres the succession runs from Mary Somerville to Hertha Ayrton. Of the women whom for want of a better title I have labelled 'competent' the outstanding example is the Queen herself, with Florence Nightingale as great or greater in her own line. In this group too comes Miss Beale, of Cheltenham, who has perhaps met with less recognition than she deserves—education being ever a Cinderella among causes. It is difficult to draw the line between these workers and the reformers, but I have taken the word 'reformers' as chiefly applicable to those whose primary object was to attack some social evil and whose constructive work grew from this. Such were Elizabeth Fry, Josephine Butler, and Octavia Hill. And among those whose expression came through art there are Helen Faucit, the Shakespearean actress and critic (but, alas! no art is so ungrateful as the player's as far as the guerdon of posthumous praise is concerned); Lady Butler, the artist; among novelists the Brontës; and in the field of poetry Elizabeth Barrett Browning, Emily Brontë, and Christina Rossetti.

Of such types were the greatest women of the century.

What was their training? Was such a woman a phenomenon unaccounted for by tradition or education, or
was her upbringing of such a kind that we should expect
it to fit her for the great part she was to play? Was she
great because of or in spite of her education?

It would be hard enough to come to a conclusion even
had they all enjoyed (or suffered) a training of remotely
the same kind, but if we take any half-dozen 'samples'
we find no two alike. Their experience ranges from the
governess to the boarding school, from father's tutorship
to the free, read-as-you-please ideal of Lamb's "Bridget
Elia."

To begin with royalty. The Duchess of Kent's strict
discipline for the daughter who was to become Queen is
well known, but the influence which seems to have been
strongest on the young girl was that of Baroness Lehzen.
She was the daughter of a Lutheran pastor, and had
looked after the Princess from the age of five. We can
judge of Queen Victoria's affection for her governess
from her journal. At the age of sixteen she wrote:

> *Dear good* Lehzen takes such care of me, and is so unceasing
> in her attentions to me, that I shall never be able to repay her
> sufficiently for it but by my love and gratitude. . . . She is the
> *most affectionate, devoted, attached* and *disinterested* friend I
> have, and I love her most *dearly*.[1]

And at the time of her coronation, after mentioning her
mother's presence, she adds:

> There was another most dear being present at the ceremony
> in the box immediately over the Royal Box, and who witnessed
> all; it was my dearly-loved, angelic Lehzen, whose eyes I
> caught when on the Throne, and we exchanged smiles.

Her education after she reached beyond the intellectual
capabilities of Baroness Lehzen was under the supervision of the Reverend George Davys, afterwards Dean
of Chester, who collected a team of specialists to teach

---

[1] The passages from Queen Victoria's journal are reprinted by permission from *The Girlhood of Queen Victoria*, published by John Murray.

penmanship, arithmetic, French, German grammar, dancing, drawing and watercolours, singing, and, later, Italian. He himself concentrated on religious knowledge and history. A number of books are referred to in the Princess's journal, many on theological or historical subjects. (The journal at this time, one must remember, was written for perusal by the stern mother whose whole life was devoted to training her daughter.) Here are typical entries:

> *Friday, 28th August* (1835). At ½ past 11 came the Dean till 1. I read first in the Old Testament, then in Clarendon, and finished with the *Spectator*. At 1 we lunched. I read after luncheon in the Bishop of Chester's *Exposition of the Gospel of St Matthew*. It is a very fine book indeed. Just the sort of one I like; which is just plain and comprehensible and full of truth and good feeling. I have given up reading Smith's *Theology*. It is more a book to refer to than to read all through.
>
> *Thursday, 9th February* (1837). Read to dear Lehzen out of the newspapers Lord John Russell's very able and judicious speech on bringing in the Irish Corporation bill; and out of the Irish History. Read in *Bajazet* and wrote my journal. Lehzen dictated French to me. Played and sang. Read in Raumer's *Koniginnen*. Read in Clive's life while my hair was doing. At 6 we dined. Read in *Bajazet*. Sang, and Mamma also. Stayed up till 10. Read in School Shakespeare while my hair was undoing.

To estimate her progress she underwent an examination by the Bishops of London and of Lincoln, who pronounced her to be thoughtful and well grounded. At the age of eleven, when she had undergone a previous examination, her mother wrote that she was "not aware of the station she was likely to fill." Sir Walter Scott, having dined at Kensington Palace, had thought otherwise, and, indeed, as Miss Sitwell points out, English history could not have been taught beyond George III and left an intelligent princess ignorant in 1830 of the probabilities of the case. Later on science, as well as history, was allowed to appear on the programme, for in

1833 "came Mr T. Griffiths to lecture on Physics," the plan of the lecture including "Alchymy," or transmutation of metals, results of chemical action, conductors and non-conductors of heat; and three days later "came Mr Walker to lecture" on the properties of matter, which included cohesion, capillary attraction, and mechanical powers.

Lord Esher comments on the German trend in the Queen's education, natural enough when one remembers the Duchess of Kent's family, and it is probable that after Lehzen the most powerful influence in her life before her reign began was her Uncle Leopold, King of the Belgians. But after she became Queen one cannot omit that curious figure Lord Melbourne and his moulding of her as yet only partially formed mind. There are the long pre-Cabinet councils, generally faithfully recorded in the journal, and there are the evenings at Windsor, so trying to Mr Creevey and others, when the young Queen looked at drawings in the portfolios and chattered to "Lord M.," who invariably sat beside her. Melbourne was her most trusted adviser in affairs of State until the growth of that stronger and lasting influence—Albert's.

To turn from the restrictions of Kensington Palace to the freedom of Earlham is like leaping forward a century instead of going backward thirty years. Elizabeth Fry, née Gurney, seems to have had little education beyond being one of a large family, eleven all told, who were left motherless when Catherine, the eldest, was about seventeen. Certainly Kitty Gurney was remarkably successful in her efforts to bring up her younger brothers and sisters as the most delightful and united of families, though it was for character rather than for intellectual ability in the usual sense that they were notable. Their influence and that of their relations by marriage (who included Fowell Buxton and Samuel Hoare) was far-reaching both in philanthropy and in finance, and if their characters can be said to have been trained in any way, it was by a remarkable blend of liberty and discipline. The liberty was found in the country upbringing, in the comfortable circumstances, and in the wide views of the "gay Quakers" (as opposed to the "plain Quakers"); the discipline in belonging to a deliberately exclusive sect, in the give-and-take of a large family, and in the constant writing of a diary. On the side of freedom and self-development we have all the coming and going of which *The Gurneys of Earlham* gives such a vivid picture, the guests ranging from princes of the blood to 'travelling'—*i.e.*, preaching—Friends; there is the music and dancing, the effect of which Elizabeth discusses so seriously in her journal when she thinks of becoming a "plain Quaker": is it "throwing me off my centre?" (The latter is an admirable expression often used in the Quaker self-examination of the Gurneys' diaries.) There are the trips to London also, the plays and the operas, the visit to Mrs Siddons, and the companionship of that novelist and "Sibyl" Amelia Opie. On the side of discipline come the really high standards both of conduct and of intelligence among the family and their friends, and that valuable instrument of self-examination and self-education the journal. The writing of a diary we shall find again and again in nineteenth-century upbringing, whether like that of Queen Victoria, already mentioned, or of Augustus Hare (whose mother wrote so severely that if he did not put in his faults she would know that he was concealing something) for perusal by an elder, or whether it was what a small school-girl of to-day would call an 'own book.' One short example will suffice of the straightforward self-criticism that pervades Elizabeth Gurney's book: "I must not mump when my sisters are liked and I am not."

Whether it is her natural strength of character or the result of stern journal-keeping, Elizabeth after her "conversion," when she begins to teach her "imps" and to converse with a girl friend who knows much more than she herself does of books and "characters in history," is able to set herself to work at the age of eighteen or so to repair the neglect of her younger days. We hear of her reading Hume, of French, and of grammar. The last is read for half an hour, though to the modern mind "reading" seems a queer term to apply to a study of grammar. She wishes "hartily" to write and speak English better—a wish that is fulfilled so far as fluency and expression go, though spelling remains a stumbling-block. (Did Joseph Fry look over his wife's *Observations on the Visiting, Superintending, and Government of Female Prisoners* before publication a quarter of a century later?) In any case, she was then within two years of her marriage, and once she became mistress of that very hospitable house in Mildred Court, in the City, and mother of a constantly increasing family, it is to be doubted whether she ever had time to catch up in the knowledge of "characters in history."

It is just worth noting, with regard to Elizabeth Gurney's education, that she was considered both delicate and, in that brilliant family, the "stupid one." (A recent biographer has pointed out that Beatrice Potter, later Mrs Sidney Webb, in her youth met with the same criticism—"the only one of my children who is below the average in intelligence." Probably, as with Elizabeth Fry, this was due to ill-health.) Moreover, in the family circle, closely united as they all were, she was rather the 'odd man out,' as she came between the two elder and the four younger sisters, who formed different little groups. Of the brothers the eldest, John, was of a particularly independent character (he even resisted the family habit of keeping a journal, being the only one not to do so), and the others were some years younger than Elizabeth (though later Samuel was particularly devoted to her). Perhaps this gave a certain feeling of loneliness and an independence of character which were essential for her development.

Helen Faucit, renowned in her own day for her acting, not only of Shakespearean parts but in the plays of Browning, Bulwer-Lytton, and other contemporary dramatists, had also, through illness, much time on her hands in her youth. She went to a small school at Greenwich, but her delicate health made it necessary for her to be sent to the seaside, where "in the lonely days by the seashore," she writes, "I had almost unconsciously learnt by heart all the scenes in which my favourite heroines figured." Her imagination, however, was busy before this. In her letters, which are primarily studies of Shakespeare's female characters, but which contain a good deal of autobiographical material, she remembers how on their walks to Lee Churchyard she and a German friend would gaze with fascinated horror into a vault which they imagined as the setting for Juliet's awakening. She also tells how the few girls who constituted the school got up some scenes from *Cymbeline* as a surprise for their 'governess' on her birthday. Later, during her solitary days, she read fairly widely, mostly the poets, Milton, Byron, and "modern drama"; and she talks of a kind instructor who "taught me the value of the different metres in blank verse and rhyme." It was the best possible training for her particular kind of imagination; she lived in the lives of the characters she was to impersonate, and though after a youthful attempt to play Juliet at fifteen she went back to study for three more years, when she actually took up stage work, her successful progress was continuous, until the "conditions of the stage," as her husband, Sir Theodore Martin, put it, "made it impossible for her to continue."

The upbringing of the Brontë family has been too often and too well described to need much comment. There were few restraints other than their circumstances (which in all conscience were barriers strong enough) and Aunt Branwell's insistence on plain needlework. One cannot doubt that the life at Haworth Parsonage was exactly calculated to develop the exultant pride of Emily, the undismayed independence of Charlotte, and the gentle persistence of Anne. We know how their intellects were made keen by mutual sharpening, and how eagerly they absorbed every scrap of political or imaginative literature that came their way, wresting it from the outside world and sharing it with one another. (Mrs Gaskell tells how Maria at seven years old would shut herself up with a newspaper, and coming out would retail everything to the others: "Debates in Parliament and I don't know what all," said her informant.)

'Group genius' is the rather tiresome and indefinite term that has been used to express the quality which five of this remarkable family possessed in greater or less degree—a vitality which showed itself in the powerful, though not attractive, personality of the father, in the uncontrolled art and life of the son, and in the intellectual and spiritual vigour of the three daughters. A life which might have deadened and stultified a family of ordinary girls allowed the best, perhaps the only, development possible for the Brontës. Indeed, any experiment at schooling away from their home and the background of the moors seems to have been a misery and, with the exception of Charlotte's ordeals at Cowan Bridge and in Brussels, nothing but unproductive misery.

Perhaps the greatest lack in their education came not on the intellectual but on the social side. Charlotte felt this particularly, and it is possible that a more normal upbringing would have enabled her to draw characters more in the round, and to tell a story without such bitterness and despondency as one feels there lies behind her books. But the early years come once only, and one good thing excludes another. You cannot have both solitude and a life of continuous social stimulus, both the family and the boarding school—and there is little doubt that for the Brontë girls fate chose wisely.

To turn to another North Country woman, this time

from Northumberland, Josephine Butler, *née* Grey, was brought up as one of a large family—six daughters and three sons. "My sister Harriet and I were a pair," she writes, and her later letters show how this very close intimacy—really that of the 'double cherry'—continued through their lives.

> We were never separated except for a few days occasionally, until her marriage and departure from her own country for Naples . . . we were one in heart and soul and one in all our pursuits. We walked, rode, played, and learnt our lessons together.

She adds that "the characteristics which stand out in my memory are her love of free outdoor life, of nature, and of animals"—characteristics, it would seem, of both sisters. They were brought up, first under a "strict governess," and then for two years at a school in Newcastle. Josephine Grey says little in her autobiography about her own attitude to study, but mentions that the sister "hated lessons," and does not speak of any particular delight or progress of her own on the academic side. In 1852 she married George Butler, who then held a tutorship in the University of Durham, and who after some years in Oxford became Vice-Principal of Cheltenham College, and in 1866 Principal of the Liverpool College. We shall have occasion to remember that the Northern towns, Liverpool and Manchester in particular, were favourable to the cause of women's education. The University Extension Lectures were started in four Northern cities as a course of lectures chiefly "for ladies." Their organization was at first in the hands of the North of England Council for Promoting the Higher Education of Women, of which body Mrs Butler was president from 1867 to 1873. She only resigned because the struggle in which she had become engaged, against legalized prostitution, made it impossible for her to give the time and energy which she knew to be necessary to educational work.

It is difficult to gather, from the scanty account of her education, where Mrs Butler acquired the training which enabled her to write not only so much and so effectively on behalf of her cause (from her early pamphlets, of which *Une Voix dans le Désert* was translated into most European languages, to Bible studies published shortly before her death in 1906), but also biographies of figures which had inspired or interested her. Such is that on St Catherine of Siena, which earned Mr Gladstone's praise, and on Jean Frédéric Oberlin, pastor and agriculturist. The intellectual power which gave her such influence over men like F. W. H. Myers and Goldwin Smith seems to have developed chiefly by contact with other trained minds—she accepted for herself the standards of her father and husband. She was devoted to the former, as her memoir of *John Grey of Dilston* shows.

> My father was a man with a deeply rooted, fiery hatred of all injustice. The love of justice was a passion with him. Probably I have inherited from him this passion. . . . He had no grudge against rank or wealth, no restless desire of change for its own sake, still less any rude love of demolition; but he could not endure to see oppression or wrong of any kind. "You cannot treat men and women exactly as you do one-pound bank-notes, to be used or rejected as you think proper," he said in a letter to *The Times* when that paper was advocating some ill-considered changes, beneficial to one class, but leaving out of account a residue of humble folk upon whom they would entail great suffering.

Similarly her whole autobiography, besides her *Recollections of George Butler*, shows how deeply she was devoted to her husband and respected his judgment, and how much his approval of her work meant. Yet perhaps in her early training she owed as much to her mother as to any later influence.

> Living in the country, far from any town, and, if I may say so, in the pre-educational era (for women at least), we had none of the advantages which girls of the present day have [in 1896]. But we owed much to our dear mother, who was very firm in

requiring from us that whatever we did should be thoroughly done, and that in taking up any study we should aim at becoming as perfect as we could in it without external aid. This was a moral discipline which perhaps compensated in value for the lack of a great store of knowledge. She would assemble us daily for the reading aloud of some solid book, and by a kind of examination following the reading assured herself that we had mastered the subject. She urged us to aim at excellence, if not perfection, in at least one thing.

Elizabeth Barrett also had the advantage of learning from a much-loved father. Whatever strain came into their relationship later, her devotion to him is shown by the dedication of her collected poems, published in 1844, when she was thirty-eight years of age. She speaks of "an existence which has been sustained and comforted by you as well as given," reminds him that when she was a child and wrote verses he was her public and her critic, and adds:

> Somewhat more faint-hearted than I used to be, it is my fancy thus to seem to return to a visible personal dependence on you, as if indeed I were a child again; . . . to satisfy my heart while I sanctify my ambition, by associating with the great pursuit of my life its tenderest and holiest affection.

The mention of "verses" may be a reference to her "epic," entitled *The Battle of Marathon*, written when she was eleven years old, of which the proud father had fifty copies printed. The subject reflected not so much the young poet's classical taste, pronounced though this was, as her study of Pope, but she herself says, "The love of Pope's Homer threw me into Pope on one side and Greek on the other, and Latin as a help to Greek." The classics she was certainly taught by her father, who, despotic as no doubt he was, had a singular pride in his clever eldest child, and encouraged both her learning and her writing. There is probably more than a hint of him in the father of Aurora Leigh. That a prototype was not lacking for the aunt, Miss Leigh, who brought up Mrs Browning's heroine so carefully, we may guess from the remark of a stern grandmother who came to stay with the Barretts. The old lady did not approve of "these readings and writings," and used to say she "would rather see Elizabeth's hemming more carefully finished off than hear of all this Greek."

There is no mention of school in Elizabeth Barrett's life, nor any of governesses, though it seems incredible that there should not have been governess or tutor in so large and wealthy a family. At any rate, they seem to have had no influence in forming the mind of the poetess. But from about 1828 to his death in 1848 her chief tutor in classics was the blind scholar Hugh Boyd. He guided her study, and her poem *Wine of Cyprus* alludes, in terms conversational rather than poetical, to her readings with her instructor. But she must have worked chiefly on her own.

> We lived at Hope End, a few miles from Malvern, in a retirement scarcely broken except by books and my own thoughts, and it is a beautiful country and was a pleasant retirement in many ways. . . . There I had my fits of Pope and Byron and Coleridge, and read Greek as hard under the trees as some of your Oxonians in the Bodleian, gathered visions from Plato and the dramatists, ate and drank Greek and made my head ache with it.

That she really studied and was something more than a dabbler is shown by her attempt at a translation of *Prometheus Bound*. She afterwards declared it "should have been thrown in the fire" and withdrew the publication, substituting, however, another version. Professor Oliver Elton remarks, "She read the poets honestly from Homer to Gregory Nazianzen," and her articles for *The Athenæum* on "Greek Christian Poets" contain a number of translations of these. (Miss Barrett elaborates the idea that the early Christians kept alive the lamp of Greek poetry.) But in a letter to Richard Horne, one of her literary friends, she has an illustrative passage about her reading:

39

So you think I never read Fonblanque or Sydney Smith—or Junius perhaps? Mr Kenyon calls me his "omnivorous cousin." I read without principle. I have a sort of unity indeed, but it amalgamates, instead of selecting—do you understand? When I had read the Hebrew Bible from Genesis to Malachi right through . . . and the Greek Poets, and Plato right through from end to end, I passed as thoroughly through the flood of all possible and impossible British and foreign novels and romances with slices of metaphysics, laid thick between the sorrows of the multitudinous Celestinas. It is only useful knowledge and the multiplication table I have never tried hard at.

This is not the attitude nor the education of a scholar, as Elizabeth Barrett was herself aware, for it lacks mental discipline, but it produces a remarkably cultivated and appreciative mind. She very truly adds:

We all generally err by *reading* too much and out of proportion to what we *think*. I should be wiser, I am persuaded, if I had not read half as much—should have had stronger and better-exercised faculties. . . . The fact is that the *ne plus ultra* of intellectual indolence is this reading of books.

It must be remembered, of course, that Elizabeth's secluded and invalid life, considered necessary since her 'delicacy,' caused either by a cough or an accident at the age of fifteen, was conducive to a great deal of reading, and her education would naturally tend to make her 'full' rather than 'exact.'

The Mr Kenyon referred to in the above letter was a distant relative from the West Indies, and of considerable wealth. In an earlier century he might have become a 'patron of the arts.' But by this time the arts no longer accepted such direct patronage, though their followers, even such as Wordsworth and Coleridge, were not averse from being entertained, and Mr Kenyon was less aristocratically termed "a feeder of lions." Elizabeth, though she did not require feeding, was emphatically a lion—and remained so all her life. There is a very fair description in *Aurora Leigh* of the lionizing public who accept the heroine rather because what she has written is written by a woman than because it is good in itself. Elizabeth Barrett was not of the type to protest about equal political rights for women, but as an author she expresses herself with some severity:

> Please to recollect that when I talk of women, I do not speak of them . . . according to a separate peculiar and womanly standard, but according to the common standard of human nature.

But she would never have got her public to agree with her.

There was more power and perhaps more detailed knowledge, though not of the Greek poets, in Miss Martineau. Harriet Martineau's childhood was an unhappy one, whether we ascribe that unhappiness, as does her early biographer, to an unsympathetic family and a stern mother, or whether it was due, as her brother roundly states, to "inert digestion." But from the day when, at the age of seven, she was overwhelmed by the glory of *Paradise Lost* she was not stinted of the education which was to mean so much to her. Mrs Martineau had never had the benefit of a good education herself—a fact which was to her disadvantage in the literary and cultured clique of Norwich, to which Mrs Barbauld was an occasional visitor. She was determined that her daughters should acquire something beyond the usual female accomplishments of making straw bonnets and silk bags —which pursuits are referred to in Harriet's letters. When Harriet was about twelve Mr Perry, the head of a local boys' school, was converted to Unitarianism. This change involved the loss of so many of his scholars that he offered places to girls, and for two years Harriet, who had been grounded in Latin by her brother, attended with her elder sister. She was taught Latin, French, and English composition according to the rules of rhetoric. After the final collapse of the school she continued to work at home with masters, till she was sent to stay with

an aunt who kept a school at Bristol. Here she fell under
the influence of Lant Carpenter, a Unitarian minister,
and her interest in his personality and doctrines caused her
to apply herself to studying the Bible and philosophical
treatises. Her first works, encouraged by her brother
James, were philosophical in substance, and were published anonymously in *The Monthly Repository*, the
Unitarian organ. They caused another brother to offer
her the encouraging, but at the time not very practicable
advice to "give up darning stockings and take to
Literature." Her next attempt was in a competition of
the British and Foreign Unitarian Association—three
essays, designed to convert Roman Catholics, Jews, and
Mohammedans respectively. Harriet, again anonymously,
won all three prizes.

At the age of twenty-seven Harriet Martineau thus set
down her aim in life: it was to be "a forcible and elegant
writer on religious and moral subjects so as to be useful
to refined as well as unenlightened minds." A later
resolve was "to think and learn and to speak out with
absolute freedom what I have thought and learnt."
To this end she resolved to discipline herself by strict
rules of study and behaviour and "the cultivation of my
intellectual powers with a view to instruction of others by
my writings."

This single aim she pursued all through life, by articles
and by tales illustrating the philosophical or economic
faith she held. Almost to the end she wrote—leaders in
The Daily News, articles in *The Westminster Review*, and
an autobiography to be published after her death. Sheer
character and the "almost unrivalled innate powers of
her mind," rather than encouragement and education,
gave Miss Martineau her position, and

> She had every excuse for supposing that if women were fit
> to do the work of men there would be no serious obstacles in
> their path, for her own career seemed to prove the case beyond
> the possibility of doubt.

The best summary of the education of Florence Nightingale is contained in a letter of Mrs Gaskell's, written from the Nightingale household, where she was staying in 1854, when Florence was thirty-three:

These two girls had a governess for two and a half years—from 7 to 9½ with F. N. Then she married, and they'd another, whom they did not like, so then Mr N. took his girls in hand, and taught them himself. He is a *very* superior man; full of great interests, took high honours at college—and worked away at classics and metaphysics, and mathematics with them; especially F. N., who, he said, had quite a man's mind. She does not sound to have been wayward—only carried away by a sense of the "Father's Work" that she ought to be about. . . . Now she is 33, Florence takes up one thing at a time and bends her whole soul to that. Music was it once. When they were 17 and 18 Mr and Mrs N. took them to Italy before they were presented. And F. worked at music; the scientific part; and for the time cared for nothing but music. She has never cared in the least for art. Then again the study of the truth as disguised in the myths and hieroglyphics of Egyptian religion as the root of other religions took hold of her; (you will see the exquisite beauty of her ideas on this head when you get her letters) and for a year and a half in Egypt and in Athens she was absorbed in this. Now all this is swept away. . . . She never reads any book now. She has not time for it, to begin with; and secondly she says life is so vivid that books seem poor.

Miss Nightingale was at this time Superintendent of the Ladies' Hospital in Harley Street (originally connected with the Governesses' Benevolent Institution), and had gone that year to take superintendence of the cholera patients in the Middlesex Hospital, but her great work was yet to come. Nevertheless she had by this time escaped from the cage of social and domestic life that had held her for so many wearisome years, and her family was beginning to believe, as she herself had been convinced for nearly twenty years, that she had a mission as yet unknown. The enthusiastic Mrs Gaskell writes of her work in the epidemic: "She is so like a saint."

Miss Nightingale had been brought up in a family Whig by politics, Unitarian by tradition, and distinctly wealthy. Her standard was such that she remarked of their summer home, which contained fifteen bedrooms, "But surely you don't consider Lea Hurst a *big* house." She also said once, looking at the rows of windows at Embley, where they spent most of their time, "I am thinking how I should like to turn it into a hospital, and just how I should place the beds." Her education and that of her sister was probably typical of that of their wealthy contemporaries. There was the usual fancy-work, use of the globes, and copying of elegant extracts or moral sentiments to acquire a beautiful Italian, ladylike handwriting. French also she knew so well that at ten she began her life's story in that language. But when her father, whose literary and philosophical tastes had been inherited by his younger daughter, along with her mother's capability and 'push,' took charge the range of subjects was much widened. He taught them Latin, Greek, mathematics (Florence was always very competent where figures and book-keeping were concerned), history, and Italian. They read with him Tasso, Ariosto, and Alfieri. By the age of sixteen they were reading Homer, Cicero, and Plato. He also read *The Times* aloud in the evenings; Florence hated this. Her sister bore it placidly and got on with her drawing, which shows that the 'wireless mind,' which enables its possessor to work to a background of sound, already existed. Florence is said to have been a very steady worker, to have filled multi-tudinous notebooks with translations and analyses, and to have written essays on set themes. Yet there was little manifestation of the swan which the ducks (her mother's own metaphor) were rearing. She doubtless found a number of poor and sick folk whom, as the squire's daughter, she was able to help, but the idea that she was an outstanding nurse from childhood's days appears to be exaggerated. On the contrary, she says,

> My greatest ambition was not to be remarked. I was in mortal fear of doing something unlike other people. I was afraid

of speaking to children because I was sure I should not please them.

And she reproaches herself in her journal for dreaming, not doing. Yet, like Elizabeth Fry, she seems to have been the member of the family to whom anyone turned in emergency or illness.

Most of her biographers stress the cultural and social distinction of the Nightingale environment, and later on Florence puts down "desire to shine in society" as one of her temptations. The family had travelled in Italy, Switzerland, and France, and had everywhere introductions which led the girls eventually into the most brilliant Paris society, even to the *salon* of Mme Récamier. Yet Florence always took her pleasures seriously, and in her journal, besides the descriptions of what was historical and "artistic" (and, in spite of Mrs Gaskell's remark, she *did* sketch), a particular interest is shown in the social condition and political crises of Italy in 1838–39. Again, during her travels in Egypt and in Athens, besides traces of a genuine interest in Egyptian mythology, there are references in her diaries to the conditions of the Arabs, to the work of Sisters of Mercy, to the American missionaries in Athens—subjects which caused her sister a good deal of surprise and distress when they came into her letters home. And it was on the way back from this journey in 1850 that she was able to stay for a fortnight in the Deaconesses' Institution at Kaiserswerth, to which she returned the next year for three months as an apprentice. This was the nearest she had got to a hospital training before she became Superintendent: when some years back she had suggested going to learn the work of a nurse at Salisbury Hospital it had "terrified Mama . . . as if I had wanted to be a kitchenmaid." It was her parents' horror at this plan that caused her to write despairingly, "I shall never do anything," and to put the question to Dr Howe, the philanthropist (husband of the author of "Mine eyes have seen the glory of the coming of the Lord"), "If I should determine to study nursing and devote my life to that profession, do you think it would be a dreadful thing?" Dr Howe did *not* think so, but the majority of Florence's acquaintance, and particularly her family circle, did.

Similar in travel and tutorship to Florence Nightingale's, yet very different in outlook, was the upbringing of the woman who so nearly became the first elected female R.A.—Lady Butler. Elizabeth Thompson, as she was when in 1874 her *Calling the Roll after an Engagement in the Crimea* became the picture of the year, was the elder sister of Alice (Mrs) Meynell. Each girl at a very early stage had made up her mind in what art she was going to excel. Elizabeth from the age of five specialized in pictures of movement, particularly in battle paintings. The two sisters had the quite exceptional advantage of being taught by a father himself of good education and ample means. (His fortune, like that of Mr Moulton Barrett, came from the West Indian sugar plantations.) His strong influence on his daughters is recorded in Alice Meynell's poem *A Father of Women*, in which she acknowledges, "Our father works in us." He determined that they should have the chance of learning anything that would be useful to them, irrespective of their sex, and their education included swimming, billiards, and pistol-shooting. It was not, however, the usual boy's classical education that he gave them, but something nearer to what a rich father might provide for his daughters to-day—including modern languages and history. The former they acquired partly by travel. As Lady Butler writes to her sister:

> What a happy chance it was that our parents should have been so taken with the Riviera di Levante as to return there winter after winter alternately with the summer spent in gentle Kent or Surrey.

History they learnt by hearing their father read while Elizabeth at least was busy using her pencil, like

FEMALE SCHOOL OF ART (QUEEN SQUARE), 1868

By courtesy of "The Illustrated London News"

Parthenope Nightingale. Yet she had "exacting home lessons" (such is the account of her brother-in-law, Wilfrid Meynell, in *The Art Annual* of 1898) to counter-balance the unusual freedom of her leisure hours, when she was allowed to ramble about the countryside, and for three years during which the family was settled in the Isle of Wight the girls lived the usual full social life. Elizabeth, however, took up art seriously, attending the "never-to-be-forgotten" South Kensington school, where she was soon admitted to the advanced 'Life Class' instead of having to work her way there through the course of two or three years. But this did not mean any scamping of the artist's discipline, and for years she studied in Florence—not leaving her copying of the frescoes even in the hot summer—and in Rome, where she had great difficulty in finding a studio, and this even though her mother was chaperoning her.

A young lady working by herself! A thing unknown—no one would let me a studio, so we ended with the makeshift you remember in our apartment.

She sent pictures to the Academy for three years before the one that made her name; and *The Daily Telegraph* critic said in 1874, "To the general public Miss Thompson is as new as the Albert Memorial at Kensington." "This honest, manly Crimean picture," as it was termed, was followed next year by *Quatre Bras*, and among her other well-known and highly praised works were *Balaclava*, *Dawn at Waterloo*, *The Camel Corps*, and *The Remnants of an Army*. She married Colonel Butler, A.D.C. to the Queen, and with him was stationed or travelled in Egypt, Palestine, the Sudan, Brittany, and the Cape. Her success as a painter was so great that she was able to say later with some complacency, "I rejoice to know that my best works are nearly all in public galleries or in the keeping of my Sovereign."

The childhood of these eminent women is a subject which might be indefinitely pursued. We might investigate George Eliot's boarding schools at Nuneaton and Coventry; her school-life began when she was five years old. We might follow Mary Arnold, later Mrs Humphry Ward, born in Tasmania and educated first at Miss Clough's new and advanced school at Ambleside, and then at the Rock Terrace School for Young Ladies, described somewhat bitterly in *Marcella*. (And we can hardly wonder that it was remembered as a place of "sulks, quarrels, and revolts" when we read the account of getting up at 6.30 in the dark winter mornings, of the cold ablutions and dreary meals, and of days in bed with senna tea and gruel, when seclusion was tried as a cure for the tantrums.) We could study Dorothea Beale's experience at school in France and her work at home teaching her young brothers Latin, Octavia Hill's enlightened upbringing by a parent who thought she and her sisters should be qualified to earn their own living, or Christina Rossetti's single-minded devotion to her mother. We could go even farther back to Mary Somerville's self-education in Latin, Greek, and mathematics. To spread the net more widely, among the less well-known there is Frances Ridley Havergal, author of children's hymns, whose elder sister "undertook this charming little pupil," and who never had a regular governess; there is Hertha Ayrton in the London school of her aunt, Mrs Hartog; there is Mrs Swanwick (Nelly Sickert) at the Girls' Public Day School at Notting Hill Gate. The list is of infinite variety.

And when we come to the end of our randomly selected Victorian women, what can we make of their education? Is there any common denominator, or are there even constant factors—and how do they affect the educational products? The first question seems to draw a negative answer; there was no single consciously used method, and there was not even a single ideal, for, as we shall see, this ideal was gradually changing and developing. But a few factors may be traced, prevalent if not constant.

We have noticed the recurring tension between discipline and liberty in the education of many of these girls, taking various forms. Often the discipline lies in parental restraint of some kind—the strait path traced by the Duchess of Kent for England's future Queen, the strong pressure of the Nightingale family, accentuated by the nervous illness of Florence's sister; illness, too, is a discipline in the case of Elizabeth Barrett. But for these women there was the compensating advantage of easy circumstances, and for at least two of them all help in the way of instruction and mental freedom. Harriet Martineau had to contend with poverty, with a restrictive mother, and later with deafness, all of which constituted a harder discipline than any so far mentioned, but on the other hand she was allowed the liberty of thought and education characteristic of the sect to which she belonged.

It would seem that Unitarianism made for the growth of the female mind; at least it is remarkable how many of the most brilliant women of the century were connected with this creed—also with one another.[1] Certainly the influence of their religion was very strong in the lives of the most able Victorian women, whether it produced the ethical and argumentative strain of Harriet Martineau or the devotional inspiration of Christina Rossetti and of Alice Meynell, the strong piety of Josephine Butler and Elizabeth Fry or the devoted energy of Florence Nightingale.

Another formative influence often found is that of a dearly loved or much-respected older man. This is frequently a relative, brother, husband, or friend, but not

[1] Indeed, one is continually coming across links between the notable women of the mid-century. Mrs Gaskell numbered among her friends Florence Nightingale, Charlotte Brontë, and Miss Fox, the daughter of Harriet Martineau's publisher. Hilary Bonham Carter, a cousin of the Nightingales, went to the school kept by Miss Rachel Martineau; she herself was a friend of the Brownings. Barbara Leigh Smith, afterwards Mme Bodichon, niece by marriage to Mrs Nightingale, was the Rossettis' "invaluable Barbara," and she was a pioneer in educational work which brought Emily Davies into contact with her.

always, for there is Elizabeth Barrett's tutor, Mr Boyd, and there is "dear Lord Melbourne." The Victorian paterfamilias has not had a good 'Press' in this century, but the fathers of Dorothea Beale and of Elizabeth Thompson, the brother of Harriet Martineau, and the husbands of Josephine Butler, Elizabeth Fry, and, of course, of Elizabeth Barrett, undoubtedly counted very considerably in the development of these lives. Besides, the support of George Butler, of William Gaskell and Joseph Fry, gave their wives a position and a power which they could hardly have attained otherwise—their contented homes and numerous offspring were the seal of that respectability which made them acceptable to their own age. It enabled them to appeal to the solid and respectable elements in the British public, as well as to the religious and enthusiastic. A father's backing too was a sign of respectability, as well as a formative influence; it made a great difference to Dorothea Beale after her setback at Casterton, and we have seen in her dedication what Elizabeth Barrett felt. There *were* girls for whom this backing was absent—Miss Nightingale is the outstanding example—but Victorian fathers do not seem to have withstood their daughters' plans (apart from the peculiar views on marriage held by Mr Barrett and the selfishness of the Reverend Patrick Brontë) to the extent that their mothers did. The pressure of the latter was often very delicate. But Harriet Martineau was well established in the world of letters before she freed herself from the restrictions of her mother, Anne Clough devoted herself to hers till past her own middle age, and Christina Rossetti lived with Mrs Rossetti up to the latter's death, which did not occur till within a few years of Christina's own.

One more element we find contributing to the development of many great women of the century. Just as there is a balance in their lives between discipline and freedom, so there is between solitude and the social life, 'social' being used almost in the Rousseauesque sense—'connected with mankind.' Of course, the community unit of the Victorian woman was generally the family. It was not only in brilliant families such as the Gurneys of Earlham or the Brontës of Haworth Parsonage that home life formed a great part of education. There was much to be learnt from living in a family, whether you were one of the eldest, like Dorothea Beale, or of the youngest, like Octavia Hill. (Mrs Joseph Wright, commenting on the unselfishness of a friend, quotes the reply: "That's no credit to me; I was one of sixteen.") But many outstanding women had also, for some cause or other, an opportunity for solitude, during which the inner life and character were perhaps most firmly established. It might be through illness, as with Elizabeth Barrett; delicacy, as with Elizabeth Gurney or Helen Faucit; deafness, as with Harriet Martineau; or it might be deliberately cultivated, as by Emily Brontë, with her long walks over the moor, and by Christina Rossetti in her devotional meditations. But, whether by accident or design, the loneliness which has so often formed a part of great lives is found in these.

Such then are a few of the elements in a Victorian girl's upbringing—the delicate balance of freedom and restriction; of community life and solitude; the influence of father, husband, brother, or friend; the strong religious motive. It will be worth while, when we have traced the course of education down to the present day, to see how many of these survive, or what their substitutes are in the education of a daughter of to-day.

CHAPTER II

HOME EDUCATION AND THE YOUNG LADY

CATHERINE MORLAND was not, so Miss Austen informs us, in her early days "in training for a heroine," for she only began to improve in this direction at fifteen. We may therefore conclude that her upbringing was not abnormal for a girl of her period and position; she was a clergyman's daughter, and no one knew more about clergy families than Miss Austen. Catherine is described as quite mediocre in propensities and abilities, one of ten children who were in general very plain, and until the age of fourteen rather wild and noisy. She was luckier, perhaps, than some of her contemporaries in enjoying an active physical life, for she was apparently allowed to indulge in her love of "cricket, baseball, riding on horseback and running about the country." As for her lessons, which "she shirked whenever she could," she was taught writing and accounts by her father and French by her mother. Poetry was also learnt by heart, but not with that love which one would expect of the heroine of the later chapters of *Northanger Abbey*. However, from her reading between the ages of fifteen and seventeen, we learn which were "the works that heroines must read to supply their memories with those quotations which are so serviceable and so soothing to the vicissitudes of their eventful lives" —those of Pope, Gray, Thomson, and above all Shakespeare. From these Catherine learnt several useful tags, among them that a young woman in love always looks

> . . . like Patience on a monument
> Smiling at grief.

Like the Bennet family, the Morlands were brought up without a governess (at least, there is no mention of

Her prayers said, she soon is drest,
Not caring what "becomes her best."
Her aim is of a nobler kind—
By study to improve the mind,
To turn the leaf of history o'er
And arts and sciences explore.

*From " The Elegant Girl, or Virtuous Principles the True Source of
Elegant Manners"*

one), but one hopes without the result expected by Lady Catherine de Bourgh, who had thus rebuked Elizabeth:

"Your mother must have been quite a slave to your education."

Elizabeth could hardly help smiling as she assured her that had not been the case.

"Then who taught you? Who attended to you? Without a governess you must have been neglected."

"Compared with some families, I believe we were, but such of us as wished to learn never wanted the means. We were always encouraged to read, and had all the masters that were necessary. Those who chose to be idle certainly might."

"Aye, no doubt; but that is what a governess will prevent, and if I had known your mother I should have advised her most strenuously to engage one."

Lady Catherine would also have supplied her, for she goes on to talk of several young persons who have been delightfully situated through her means, and of Lady Metcalfe's gratitude at finding one of them "a treasure."

But the day of the governess as such, as distinct from the *dame de compagnie*, had not fully come, and there must have been a number of girls like Catherine and Elizabeth who continued such education as they had 'on their own.' Alas! it is not easy for a young girl fresh from the school-room, and often with the scrappiest of mental training, to persevere with any course of reading. Too many must have deserved Mr Knightley's censure on Emma—who by this time had reached the age of twenty-three.

Emma has been meaning to read more ever since she was twelve years old. . . . The list she drew up when she was only fourteen—I remember thinking it did her judgment so much credit that I preserved it some time, and I dare say she may have made out a very good list now. But I have done with expecting any course of steady reading from Emma.

With 'accomplishments' the case was rather different, though the word was capable of several interpretations. Mr Bingley in a rare moment of irony explains that he never heard a young lady spoken of for the first time without being informed that she was very accomplished: "they all paint tables, cover skreens and net purses." But more generally it was assumed that

> a woman must have a thorough knowledge of music [which presumably meant ability to perform on 'the instrument'], singing, drawing, dancing, and the modern languages to deserve the word; and besides all this she must possess a certain something in her air and manner of walking, the tone of her voice, her address and expressions, or the word will be but half deserved.

Here is the accepted ideal; it is only the tiresome and hypercritical Darcy who insists on "the improvement of her mind by extensive reading."

It is, in fact, in the arts of sketching and piano-playing that Jane Austen's heroines show themselves best educated. Elizabeth is capable of sitting down "easy and unaffected" to play for a party's delectation. Eleanor Tilney is really interested in sketching, and Catherine catches the taste. Mary is the only plain one of the Bennet family, and has on this account worked hard for knowledge and accomplishments. She is drawn as a figure of fun, but it is not her playing and singing or the fact that she "reads great books and makes extracts" which Miss Austen is ridiculing, but the "vanity and pedantry which would have injured a higher degree of excellence than she had reached." So low does Miss Austen rate Mary's artificially cultivated accomplishments that from a remark she made after *Pride and Prejudice* was written we learn that Mary eventually married "no higher than one of her Uncle Philip's clerks."

Yet even among the really intelligent young women book-learning counts for very little. There is only one reference to Elizabeth's settling down to a book, and even then she soon abandons it for conversation, and when this is curtailed by the exigencies of card-playing—she goes to bed. In fact, throughout the conversation of Miss Austen's heroines there is hardly a word which denotes that they have read anything more informative than *The Mysteries of Udolpho*, except a little eighteenth-century poetry, Scott, and Shakespeare. No book of history, travel, or *belles-lettres* need ever have been opened, and this is the more curious when one remembers Jane Austen's own amusing and delightfully partisan *History of England*, written for and in the schoolroom. However, her letters show the same tendency: *new* fiction is referred to, but of the classics there is not much trace. Her wit, like that of her best characters, is not "the forced products of another man's brain," but the "natural sprouts" of her own.

Jane Austen's heroines belong to an earlier age than is covered by the last hundred years; Catherine Morland, indeed, goes back into the eighteenth century and the early Romantic Revival, for, though her history was published in 1818, she had remained for six years in the drawer of a Bath publisher. But the standard of home education, though naturally it varied tremendously with the home, does not seem to have risen as a whole during the first half of the century. However anxious the mother was to do the best for her children, a serious and steady education at home was a difficult matter because of the inevitable hindrances of family life. There was bound to be cause for such distress as that felt by one of Miss Yonge's more studious girls whose parents belong to the 'close' society of a cathedral town. A governess has to be engaged, because

> At Southminster our time is so taken up that poor Sarah gets neglected, and it is very trying to an eager, diligent girl to prepare lessons and have them continually put off, so we thought of indulging her with a governess to bring her on in some of the modern languages and accomplishments that have grown rusty with us.

Even in Oxford, in the house of a university professor, there are comings and goings, and grown-up people's affairs must take precedence of a child's lessons. Mrs Jeune, wife of the Master of Pembroke College, writes thus about her family, of whom the eldest, a daughter, is about ten years old:

1849. *July 22nd.* Since being here we have determined on relinquishing our governess and trying the plan of educating our children ourselves, my husband purposing to take a large share in it himself, the advantage of which will, I think, make up for some irregularity which will be unavoidable from visitors, etc. . . . I believe we are very hard to please, and no female, scarcely, would teach as my husband would consider *well*; the system he would follow and that pursued by females generally, almost universally—are so totally different.

Margaret appears to be not unintelligent, and her parents encourage her in intellectual progress. Before she is in her teens she is presented on her birthday with "a beautifully bound volume of Campbell," and "her father and my joint gift was a superb Milton, all which delighted her little heart." (But her uncle sends her an umbrella, "most opportune this wretched weather"— May 6th!) Later a good-natured professor adds "a work of his own on Geology." She has at twelve years of age attended a course of lectures on this subject and industriously made notes. The class, it is interesting to find, is chiefly composed of women (1851). A lecture on Modern History—the Reign of the Conqueror—is also mentioned.

Nevertheless, although Mrs Jeune comments that "Her father draws out Margaret's powers of mind more than any governess would do," she is found, four months after the plan is begun, saying that she must "resume the children's lessons"—which had presumably been broken off because of the company they had been entertaining. Later on the parents are discussing the possibility of sending the children to school in France,

unless the governess plan which we have now taken up succeeds wonderfully. We now think of a daily governess, masters for what she fails in, and a French nursery governess, as they call themselves, but who in fact is to be the girls' maid as well—but our plans are so easily upset that I do not know how it will end.

It ends in their sending the two elder girls, when they are about thirteen and fourteen, to a school in Paris, well recommended, with a good garden, twenty-five girls, mostly French, and the mistress, Mlle Nieman, a nice, sensible person who will consent to make an alteration in the diet (but we are not told, much as we should like to know, in what this alteration consisted) for 300 francs p.a. The plan is rather deprecated by Mrs Jeune's acquaintance on religious grounds. One friend is greatly disturbed at the possibility of their choosing a Roman Catholic school, and another exclaims, "Oh, to think of sending your little girls to impious Paris!" (The mother adds, "So like Mrs W.!") To some extent they are justified in their expectations of worldliness, and Mrs Jeune is shocked that, with the exception of their once going to church, the Sunday appears wholly disregarded. Margaret explains that Sunday and one other day are their times for—dominoes!

However, the little girls are at first well and happy, and they improve in their studies. The only drawback, mentioned several times, is the lack of exercise and fresh air. This, as we shall see, is such a common complaint in private schools at this and a much later period that one wonders whether the Paris school was exceptionally bad or whether the Jeune girls, who were brought up to walk and ride, found it particularly hard. In time their health really does seem to have suffered: we hear that "Meggie has a bad cold, 'as usual,'" and that the younger girl does not eat. Their schooling is brought to an abrupt conclusion, when they have been in Paris less than ten months, by scarlet fever, which Lydia catches at school, and they go to Weston-super-Mare for the invalid to recover. After Margaret is fifteen no further reference is made to a continuous education, though we hear of lessons with a drawing-master and a month or so in London with friends.

The arrangement by which the father of a family was

tutor to his daughters was not unknown, and is in the tradition of the eighteenth-century Bluestockings, who were generally taught in this way down to Maria Edgeworth and Harriet Martineau. This tradition accounted for the knowledge of Latin possessed by a few girls of the period, though it was probably only a smattering, because of the desultory fashion in which their education proceeded. In *Six to Sixteen* Mrs Ewing gives a picture of Major Buller, who, having dismissed an unsatisfactory governess, undertook to carry on the lessons of his daughter and the girl who lived with them.

> Major Buller was so good a teacher that he brought out what intelligence we possessed, and led us constantly to ask questions about anything we failed to understand. In English grammar this led to stumbling-blocks and confusion, and finally to the Major's throwing the book across the room exclaiming : "I never learnt English grammar, and it's quite evident that I can't teach it."
>
> "If you don't know grammar, Papa, then *we* needn't," said Matilda promptly, and being neat of disposition she picked up the book and proceeded to put it away.
>
> "I never said that I didn't know grammar," said the Major, . . . "but what I know I got from the Latin grammar. And, upon my soul," added Uncle Buller, pulling at his heavy moustache, "I don't know why you shouldn't do the same."
>
> The idea of learning Latin pleased us greatly, and Major Buller (who had been at Charterhouse in his boyhood) bought a copy of Dr Russell's grammar and we set to work. And either because the rules of the Latin grammar bore explanation better than the English ones, or because Major Buller was better able to explain them, we had no further difficulties.

But, of course, this state of things only went on "for some months." Then there was a change for various reasons, one being that the very charming and talented woman who was governess to a neighbouring family with whom the girls shared French lessons went away on leave with that family. The girls were next transported to a school, where French conversation and drawing seem to have been the staple food of education, and no more is heard of Latin.

Girls' schools of the nineteenth century, though varying less in curriculum, were no more alike in standard than those of the present day, but, good or bad as they might be, the tradition in favour of home education for girls remained among rich or aristocratic families until the end of the century. In certain cases it has survived up to the present day. Miss Charlotte M. Yonge, discussing in *Womankind* the question of "home, school, or governess," considers it ideal, even for the professional class, none too opulent, that the girls should be educated by the parents. She recommends teaching by "the father if he is a man of leisure, otherwise the mother or elder sister," the parents' teaching to be supplemented by 'technical' assistance (*i.e.*, masters) in music, drawing, languages, and arithmetic. The next best teacher was a good governess supervised by the mother, and she gives rather grudgingly as an alternative "a good school"—boarding school is implied—but adds that expense often puts this out of reach of large families. The size of the family, indeed, tended to make home education the most economical as well as the most desirable proposition. If the family were not large enough to employ a good governess another family might be invited to join (as in the case of the Passover, one is tempted to remember), or a pupil might be invited to live in the house and share the lady's time.

This 'party of pupils' should continue until the girls are fifteen or sixteen, when their characters and habits may be considered settled. They may then with profit and without moral danger be sent to an establishment, presumably of the type that was later called a 'finishing school,' but, as we shall see, great discrimination must be used in selecting it. The girls are not 'out' at this age, but they have generally left the ordinary school or school-room. Georgiana Darcy and Margaret Jeune are examples.

The period which immediately follows schoolroom life

is called 'young-ladyhood,' and may be, Miss Yonge continues, a valuable time to those who are wise enough not to fritter it away. A girl needs the training of home and family life and experience of society acquired in these years before embarking on any course of preparation for what even in the seventies was beginning to be thought of—a profession: learning to nurse, studying art, or taking up housekeeping. Naturally there is at first a reaction from the methodical life of the schoolroom, so a journey abroad, a visit to friends or to town, or a real vacation is recommended for a time; then the girl should set herself to something sensible, a training in real application, for at least two hours every morning. Languages (reading on her own), history, or 'science' (botany or geology, perhaps, is meant), and the keeping up of the accomplishments by teaching the younger sisters are prescribed.

The advantages and disadvantages of the well-filled schoolroom must be taken into account in comparing the effect of home education with the modern school or private tuition. Where six or eight pupils of varying ages and abilities were all being educated by one superintending female—be it mother, governess, or elder sister—there was plenty of scope for individual work on the part of the child. In fact, a girl or boy was forced by the circumstances to acquire independence in working, while enabled to make use of what was 'going on' around. Every one brought up in a Victorian schoolroom has been heard at some time to say, "I never learnt that piece of poetry, but I know it almost by heart through hearing my sister say it." Dates (of English kings) and Answers to Questions could obviously be learnt in this way quite unconsciously, especially by anyone with a good aural memory. (It is one of the mistakes of the present century —the first decades of it at any rate—that we have shamefully neglected the aural memory, and taught through the eye alone instead of making use of both gates.) Moreover, the child could, and did, go at its own pace—given a competent teacher—and there was no reason why the quick pupil should be kept back for the other thirty-five in the class, as in a modern high school. On the other hand, there was no one except the unfortunate governess to be hampered by the need of going slowly for the dull child, and even the governess was not goaded, as the present-day class teacher is all too often, by the necessity of completing a syllabus or pushing an entire form through an examination. Besides, the younger child, being almost continually in the hearing of its elder sisters, was bound to be stimulated by their more advanced work or conversation. The elder herself, on the other hand, was frequently turned on to teach her small brother and sister, and this would both consolidate her own knowledge and test her powers of explanation and exposition. The other side of the picture—the effort needed on the part of the governess to instruct the miscellaneous crowd under her control—we will examine later.

Another means of education which is now almost universally neglected, though its place may occasionally be taken by an intelligent use of the wireless, was the practice of reading aloud. As Mrs Cruse points out, this habit of reading in the family circle had a striking effect on the novels of the nineteenth century—it set a premium on decency. No work of fiction was of much value to a Victorian father that was not of such delicacy that it could be read without bringing a blush to the cheek. Much of Scott's work, both prose and verse, was particularly suitable. The Waverley novels are long (an advantage when one considers the length of winter evenings), high-principled, and of a style, both narrative and descriptive, that gains considerably by being read aloud. Dr Jeune read *Ivanhoe* for a rather curious reason: to stimulate Margaret's imagination, because at ten years old "she seems indifferent to anything which is not *real*, or, as she says, 'true.'"

But, of course, it was not only fiction that the young ladies heard as they bent over their sewing, netting, tatting, or what-not. Poetry was not neglected. Mr Austen—another father of leisure—read Cowper's works to his daughters of a morning (hence it may be that Marianne Dashwood was familiar with his works), and James, his son, is referred to as having read *Marmion* to Jane and Cassandra. Ethel May, in *The Daisy Chain*, also read *Marmion* aloud to the younger members of the family and their convalescent visitor, Leonard, and the conversation which ensued made a deep impression on the lad. Ruskin's father, besides reading the usual eighteenth-century poets and, rather unexpectedly, the popular romantic Byron, was a great exponent of Shakespeare.

Historical works might be read in the same way: Gibbon was instructive, and Motley's *Dutch Republic* made suitable "morning reading" for the young ladies. Miss Yonge advised no novels in the morning except in a foreign language, as an exercise. And, speaking from experience, I maintain that there are few better and easier ways of acquiring familiarity with a foreign tongue than by hearing it read 'in chunks' from a fine reader day after day.

Miss Yonge gives a very fair scheme of what might be termed 'schoolroom work.' She is fighting against that scrappiness in education which one finds both in fact and in fiction, and which is typified by Margaret Jeune and Margery Vandaleur (*Six to Sixteen*). She says:

> During the time of tutelage much must be acquired irrespective of natural taste and ability, while afterwards there is freedom to pursue whatever line is most obvious and agreeable.

In other words, she insists on a general, not a specialized education, and wants it to be not a smattering, but a foundation on which individual tastes can be raised. Her minimum demands are correct writing of English (with grammar), French, Italian, arithmetic (which should include book-keeping; and, as an indication of the

THE GOOD GIRL

Miss Lydia Banks, though very young,
Will never do what's rude or wrong;
When spoken to she always tries
To give the most polite replies.

Observing what at school she's taught,
She turns her toes as children ought;
And when return'd at night from school
She never lolls on chair or stool.

Some children, when they write, we know,
Their ink about them, heedless, throw;
But she, though young, has learn'd to think
That clothes look spoil'd with spots of ink.

Perhaps some little girl may ask
If Lydia always learns her task;
With pleasure I can answer this,
Because with truth I answer, "Yes."

From "The Cowslip," by ELIZABETH TURNER
(1811)

standard, we learn that the pupil should have advanced to practice by the age of twelve), Latin, in preference to German, and enough Greek to read words and find them in a lexicon. (Ruskin also exhorts his readers, man or woman, boy or girl, to learn the Greek alphabet.) She mentions the earliest book of Euclid and some algebra, and history, English, "Ancient," and French. She deals more fully with the curriculum when she is discussing "the Governess," but here emphasizes what might be considered the cultural aspect of a girl's education, which included ability to listen intelligently to a conversation and "to know how to see sights." She illustrates the latter point by explaining that of two girls taken to see a medieval castle or abbey one will by nature be interested in the story of the founder or the historical associations, the other in "the curve of the arch" or the natural surroundings, according to whether the appreciation is "romantic" or "scientific." The distinction may not seem to us very happily named, but it is a real one, and her psychological approach to the development of cultural taste is good.

The other point—the need "to know what people are talking about"—is one often brought up by the wiser parents of our present and the previous generation. The fact is that through altered circumstances, economic and social, comparatively few girls have a chance of listening to the "interesting conversation" of their elders. This may be the result of the parents' having to be away for meals, of fewer house-parties, or of more time given to school affairs; it comes partly from an increased supply of entertainment, professedly suitable "for the young"; it is in part due to the reaction against the dictum "Children should be seen and not heard." But, whatever the cause, there is no doubt that few children *do* hear their elders talk about subjects that are worth discussing, in a cultured fashion. Their own conversation suffers enormously from this lack.

With regard to the accomplishments before mentioned —the guitar-playing, china-painting young lady in a novel is generally either reformed in the end or rewarded according to her frivolity. Plain sewing Miss Yonge regards as of far more importance than these 'accomplishments,' but makes the chilling remark, "Begin nothing of which you have not well considered the end." At a guess I should say that among the middle classes the present generation are as competent at this subject as any Victorian heroine, though less value is now set on 'fine work' and embroidery, delightful as it is to find it. (Miss Jane Harrison states, "Every day I spent hours doing exquisite hems and seams; I cannot to this day make the simplest garment.") In drawing the school-room girl should persist past "the period of drudgery" to discover whether she really has a taste for the subject or not, and the fact is recognized that at one stage ideas are definitely hampered by a newly acquired knowledge of rules. Here Miss Yonge anticipates a modern school of thought which would have the child draw freely while the imagination works strongly but the critical powers are as yet undeveloped. The argument in favour of learning music does not in itself seem an adequate one: "It is the readiest means by which a lady can assist in Divine Service."

Throughout Miss Yonge and her followers have quite a definite aim in mind:

> The philosophy of the world seems to be that Woman is the helpmate, and it is impossible to predict in what line her aid and sympathy may be needed; therefore it is well to give her the germs of many varieties of acquirement in readiness to be developed on occasion.

That "occasion" is a mere euphemism for "marriage" is not to be doubted, but the idea is a large advance educationally on Amelia Sedley or even Catherine Morland.

To show what Miss Yonge thought *could* be learnt by the studious member of a large family with no more advantages than the ordinary masters and a visiting governess let us look at Ethel May, aged fifteen at the beginning of *The Daisy Chain*. There is no specific account of her studies, but the following subjects are casually mentioned in the course of the novel.

Ethel was doing Latin and Greek alongside her brother Norman, who was in his last year but one at a local public school. Her Latin verses are on one occasion "shown up" by an unscrupulous rival of Norman's as his own—and they receive considerable commendation. In Greek she reads Euripides and Thucydides, but finds the choruses of Sophocles hard. This learning of the classics to a parallel standard with a brother is quite often mentioned in Victorian fiction—*e.g.*, in *The Cousins and their Friends*, a story from *Aunt Judy's Magazine*—and it seems to have been a recognized fact in some families. (Dorothea Beale learnt in this way, and herself taught the younger brothers —just like Ethel May.)

French was taught by a master, M. Ballonpré, who objected to being asked questions. Ethel was annoyed, because she could not bear—again like Miss Beale—to learn like a parrot without understanding the principles of the language. She learnt Italian, reading Tasso (teacher not specified; it may have been her elder sister) and Spanish.

In arithmetic we hear of "a most beautiful sum in compound proportion about a lion, a wolf, and a bear eating up a carcase," and there is a reference to cube root. This does not sound very advanced, perhaps because Miss Winter, the governess, "had little liking for the higher branches of mathematics." Ancient geography sounds an odd subject, and presumably did not include "imports and exports."[1] There is no science except botany, and when, two years later, the Mays have a new governess Ethel is teaching *her*, by observation of

---

[1] Dr Butler, headmaster of Shrewsbury, compiled an *Atlas of Ancient Geography*, including Greece and Rome, with classical topography, and the Holy Land.

specimens. There is no reference to history, but *all* Miss Yonge's heroines have a wide knowledge of historical and literary allusions, even including heraldry, and there is a good deal of learning by heart, especially of Shakespeare. The only "lesson" at which Ethel jibs is "an examination" by questions of the general-knowledge type—the schoolroom standby until many years later. These her father roundly denounces: "great nonsense they are!" Ethel, as it is more gently put, "thought it useless, and was teased by it."

Poor Ethel! No wonder she was tried by such childish things. Two years later we read of her relegating her Hebrew grammar to the shelf of the seldom used. She has also been told that girls ought to wait patiently (for what?), "and not be eager for self-imposed duties." But the most bitter pill is that, being engaged in household duties, as the eldest active sister, as well as teaching in the village school, she has no longer been able to keep up with the schoolboy brother, and is told, "We all know that men have more power than women."

Unfortunately, whether through the insufficiency of the teaching, the desultoriness of the time-table, or the lack of interest on the part of the girls themselves (there were not many Ethels), the result of a schoolroom education was sometimes far from being the cultural success envisaged by Miss Yonge. In *A Flat Iron for a Farthing* Mrs Ewing gives a devastating account of its effect on a family of five girls, all of whom have been 'put through' the normal curriculum at no small cost of time and money.

> The laborious and expensive education of their childhood did not lead to anything worth the name of a pursuit, much less a hobby with any one of them. . . . With much pains and labour they had been drilled in arts and sciences, in languages and "the usual branches of an English education." But apart from social duties and amusements the chief occupation of their lives was needlework. I have known many people who never received proper instruction in music or drawing who yet from what they picked up of either art by their own industry and

67

intelligence nearly doubled the happiness of their daily lives. But in vain had "the first masters" made my cousins glib in chromatic passages and dextrous with tricks of effects in colours and crayons. They played duets after dinner, and Aunt Maria sometimes showed off the water-colour copies of their school-room days, which, indeed, they now and then re-copied for bazaars, but for their own pleasure they never touched a note or a pencil. . . .

They were very nice girls, and I do not think they were entirely to blame for the small use to which they put their 'advantages.' They were tall and ladylike, aquiline-nosed and pleasant-looking without actual beauty. It took a wonderful quantity of tarlatan to get them ready for a ball, a large carriage to hold them, and a small amount of fun to make them talkative and happy.

As a mean between these two extremes in fiction here is a picture of Miss Moberly's early days. Miss Annie Moberly, first Principal of St Hugh's College, Oxford (1886–1916), was the seventh daughter of the headmaster of Winchester (later Bishop of Salisbury), and wrote her reminiscences under the title *Dulce Domum*. A later Principal of St Hugh's has written of her:

A great gulf divides our days from those in which the Moberly clan grew up. That era of large mansions, spacious grounds, long families, circles of well-born Church folk, with their privileged position in the educational and the political worlds, we shall see no more. Annie Moberly, to whom Mrs Keble stood sponsor at her christening, received her training not at school, but in the social *milieu* of such people as the Kebles and the Yonges, the Wordsworths and the Selwyns. . . . Mrs Moberly, an Italian scholar and a woman of deep spirituality and charm, read with all her fifteen children every morning, so long as they were at home, for two hours of regular lessons, superintending their preparation again from four to six; a governess supplied the rest of the teaching required. Dr S. S. Wesley was organist of the cathedral and guided their musical doings, while the surroundings of Winchester supplied historical study without end. . . . Annie was deep in her books, played the piano, and unconsciously prepared herself for her future work.

The following extracts from a letter show the education

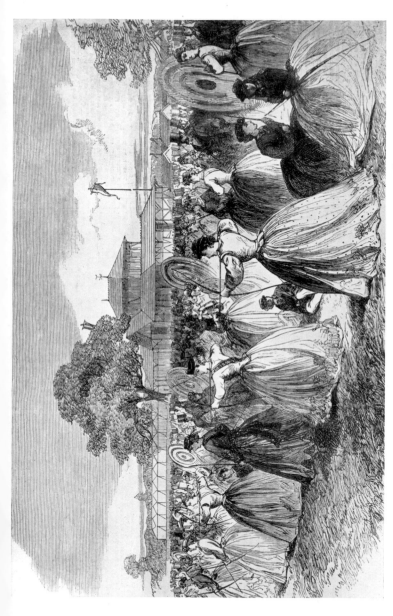

ARCHERY MEETING AT ALEXANDRA PARK, JULY 1864

By courtesy of "The Illustrated London News"

68

of the fifties and early sixties in a less stimulating yet cultured atmosphere. Miss W. became fairly well known as a writer of magazine stories.

We lived simple lives (in a country parish), and after we grew older we had governesses, French and English, and from them had regular and careful lessons. Our books as children were principally ones I cannot well remember: *Line upon Line*, *Peep of Day* (both scriptural), and later Edgeworth's stories, *Little Arthur's History of England*. I grew fond of history, Roman especially, and French—the Napoleonic period—also I loved poetry, and as I grew older revelled in Shakespeare and Shelley. When I was about seventeen or eighteen I read a great deal, dabbled in all kinds of works, as we had a good library; then passed on to the library without, read Huxley and the current magazines with the new thoughts and problems of the day. . . . Then I went to London and studied in the studio of my cousin George Kilburne, from there to another cousin of mine who was working at the National Gallery. I learnt to know all the pictures there, and they were happy days.

It was at this time that the writer made the acquaintance of Dalziel, a proprietor of "many journals," who read and approved of her stories, which turned her to novels and short-story writing. With the funds from this, though rather against the wish of her editor, she betook herself to Germany, where she learnt from a professor and had her stories published as *feuilletons* in German papers —the *Frankfurter Zeitung*, *Karlsruher Zeitung*, and others. Both in England and in Germany story-writing appears to have been well paid. From Mrs Ewing's life also we learn that she was able to "treat" the other members of her family to trips to the sea and abroad.

Miss W. ends her account with: "They were happy, pleasant days then, and in everything thoroughly Victorian." A system of education could hardly desire a better verdict.

An education almost as varied as Ethel May's, if not so profound, is shown in the very delightful *Journal of Emily Shore*—a diary kept from 1831 to 1839, chiefly at a quiet country home. Emily was the eldest girl of a family of five. Her father, the Reverend Thomas Shore, took pupils, many of whom became well known later in the political world, and he 'counted cousin' with Lord Teignmouth and W. M. Praed. He was his daughter's chief tutor, but we find sometimes that "Mamma set us right again." Emily Shore had a passion for natural history, and must have learnt chiefly from her own observation and the study of books—she generally adds the botanical name of a flower when she describes it or mentions finding it. But she is wonderfully observant of other things too. Birds, caterpillars, buildings, processes of manufacture—*e.g.*, printing—are all described with the clearness and precision of which the following extracts are examples:

Amongst the plants which I brought from the bogs on Tuesday was one which had an upright, leafless, undivided stalk, with a pinky bunch of buds at the top. I could find no other specimen, and, as it was only in bud, I could not tell what it was. I gathered it, and this morning one of the buds expanded, and I was able to examine it, and found to my great joy that it was the *Menyanthes trifoliata*, or marsh buckbean, an uncommon plant, and one of the most beautiful of all English flowers. It has but a single undivided stalk, which is thick, succulent, pinkish, or flesh-coloured, and in my specimen rather serpentine. The leaves grow only at the root, and I could not find them. The flowers grow in a spike-like bunch at the top of the stem, each flower with a pink floral leaf at the base of the pedicle; the class is *Pentandria monogynia*. The corolla of each flower is divided into five parts, so is the calyx. The flower is pure white above, pinky underneath; but its great beauty is that the petals are shaggy or feathery above, the featherings being pure white and as delicate as possible. The pistil is extremely short, and so hidden by the feathering that I could not examine it. The stamens are long, their filaments are pure white, and the anthers black and golden orange. The buds are pink. My specimen was about six inches high. . . . I am very proud to have found it. . . .

We found in our walk to-day a large locust, two inches in length, of a light green colour. He had six legs—the two hinder ones were those he leaped with; all the thighs were speckled with minute black spots. The top of his head was of a dark colour, his eyes black, and from above these, out of green roots, sprung two feelers, longer than his whole body, of a clear reddish yellow, speckled with black. On his neck there was something like a saddle; along his back extended a stripe of the colour of a dead leaf. His knees [!] were brown, and his legs downwards from his knees full of little thorny points, and his claws very large. Four little jointed things, like very small legs, came from his mouth; the upper part of his body seemed to be composed of seven or eight broad rings, laid over each other like scales; the under part of the body was green with two milk-white longitudinal stripes. I drew this creature.

We find Emily at about thirteen years old teaching her younger brothers and sisters, and a description of her day is as follows:

Our daily employments vary but little. I rise as soon as I can wake, which is usually as late as half-past seven, and employ myself in doing my Greek and Latin and learning whatever I have to get by heart. After breakfast I feed the birds with breadcrumbs, and from about that time till twelve o'clock I am usually employed in teaching the children and in some of my own lessons. At twelve we go out till dinner; after dinner I amuse myself for half an hour; then I read to Mamma and do my needlework; then we go out again for about an hour and a half; then I and Richard finish our Greek or Latin for Papa, and I read Fuseli's lectures to Mamma. This employs me till tea, after which I and R. do our lessons with Papa, and then we amuse ourselves till bedtime. This is generally the way I spend my time; of course, the coming of visitors sometimes makes a little difference.

Three years later she is instructing Arabella, Louisa, and Mackworth in Greek, Grecian history, and arithmetic on alternate days; also Mackworth by himself in geography and French history, using Mrs Markham's text-book. An editor's note recalls her saying with pleasure of the use of εἰ and ἐάν and ἄν with the different moods, "I do think I shall be able to make you understand it." The editor of her journal also adds that "the time-table . . . was freely varied in favour of open-air investigation." There is also the difficulty even in this studious household of obtaining quiet and concentration.

Emily writes an extremely clever little skit (anticipating Miss Ruth Draper's *Italian Lesson*) on her attempt to read "Sir Joshua's *Discourses*" aloud to the mistress of the house. They are interrupted by the housemaid (twice) and William, by the cook (twice), the nursemaid Mary, another maid, the younger brother, and finally (fatally for the reading) by a visitor, before they have got through half a dozen sentences.

Her taste in literature appears precocious, but she is so natural and unaffected in her journal that one must attribute it to a really advanced intellectual development —there is not the slightest desire to show off. She has a long and delighted account of her first acquaintance with Spenser, taking herself rather seriously.

> Having accidentally met with an extract from his *Hymn of Heavenly Love* . . . I went to Papa's study and read the whole poem, which is most exquisitely beautiful, and perhaps equal to anything Milton ever wrote. . . . I was so much delighted with it that I read another, his *Hymn of Heavenly Beautie*, which in point of poetic excellence perhaps exceeds the other. . . . Papa's copy of his poems is a very old edition printed in the time of Queen Elizabeth, to whom it is dedicated. The illustrations are very curious and the engravings most laughable; the print is small, and the old words make it rather difficult to read.

Five years later she writes:

> I also learnt by heart, by reading once over, all that I did not know perfectly of my favourite poem, Spenser's *Hymn of Heavenly Love*. I remember the delight I felt when I first dived into Spenser's treasures. I was barely twelve years old, and my attention was first led to him by meeting a few verses of this hymn quoted in Bowdler's *Selections*. I think I relished it as much even then as I do now; the greediness with which I devoured *Mother Hubbard's Tale* and some of the eclogues . . .

There are a good many appreciations of Shakespeare's plays, *Hamlet* being her favourite. It would be interesting to know whether he also was read in Mr Bowdler's edition; it sounds, though, as if "Papa's copy" were freely allowed. There are references to various poets, to

Ivanhoe (and a justification of her novel-reading when she is on a visit: "I am sure Papa would not object"), and to *The Pickwick Papers*. But Emily's taste in books lies chiefly in the direction of history. This she studies by making—in the most modern fashion—chronological charts. One she arranged in five columns. The first column had the chronology of the Emperors of the West, succeeded by that of Italy in general; the second the Emperors of the East till the taking of Constantinople; the third Persia; the fourth the caliphs; the fifth was miscellaneous, and included in the latter part the Ottoman sultans. She says, "I first draw out a short chronological abridgement of the preceding day's lesson, then I read a fresh portion—of course, with maps"—which she paints by way of "relaxing my mind." She then carefully reads through a portion of one of the charts she has drawn up, and learns by heart all the dates she thinks necessary.

> All this occupies me till about two or three o'clock; till tea at eight I am employed in taking exercise, in desultory reading, in lying down, and in accidental occupations. After tea I read, in the *Biographie Universelle*, the lives of one or more distinguished individuals mentioned in my English studies of the day, which both keeps up my knowledge of French and impresses the history more strongly on my memory.

That her reading is not superficial can, I think, be seen from her comments. She explains why she greatly prefers Greek to Latin, and she is delighted with her new insight (after reading the Venetian history) "into the different and complex annals of the great families and principalities of Northern Italy, such as the Carrara of Padua, the della Scala of Verona, the Visconti of Milan, of whom I before knew little but the name." She adds quietly, "Really there is hardly any pleasure equal to that of acquiring knowledge." The extracts quoted deal only with her studies and observations of nature; they do not give by any means a full view of Emily's character. It is tragic to learn that this really charming girl died of consumption

73

at the age of nineteen. Her anticipations of her own death are pathetically brave; she is inclined to agree with the general verdict that "one of the principal causes of my illness was overworking my mind with too hard study," but adds, "I cannot bear the idea of living even in sickness without systematically acquiring knowledge."

I have dwelt rather long on Emily Shore's attainments, as there is a natural tendency to believe that all sound education, if not religious learning, ceased among girls from the days of the Bluestockings to the age of the university woman. Whether this were desirable or not has been a matter for controversy; the point is that it is not altogether true. Obviously Emily was an exceptionally brilliant girl, with no other outlet (and apparently no other desire) but study; her story shows, however, that there were Victorian young women who on sheer scholarship could put the modern school-girl to shame. Moreover, it proves the existence of a type drawn or referred to, not always convincingly. I never quite believed in Ethel May's attainments until I read of Emily Shore's.

To turn again to evidence from fiction. Though the young lady's education appears so haphazard—attractive accomplishments, odd bits of knowledge, languages, and docility jumbled together in the attic of her brain—yet there were sometimes principles behind it. Aurora Leigh seems to have been brought up in the early forties, and Mrs Browning explains her aunt's motives in seeing that she learnt what she did. We are not told *how* she was taught, except that, in common with other Bluestockings (but she is complimented later on wearing her blue "so chiefly in her eyes"), she had been taught by her father before he died "the trick of Greek and Latin." The aunt, however, who liked "instructed piety," made her learn first the Catechism, the Collects, and the Creeds—this, of course, is the basis of Miss Yonge's system, and later of Miss Beale's—and, further, the Articles and "various popular synopses" of doctrine. French and German, "tongues, not books," constituted the range of liberal education which her aunt approved of. The mathematics were included, and Aurora

> brushed with extreme flounce
> The circle of the sciences, because
> She misliked women who are frivolous.

The usual *Child's Guide* questions are next mentioned, because of Miss Leigh's taste for "a general insight into useful facts," music—Aurora's "sleights of hand" corresponded to Mrs Ewing's glib chromatic passages (and one must remember the one and a half or two hours' practising time which is mentioned for an average girl)—drawing, sketching, dancing ("the polka and Cellarius"), and, a range I have not often found:

> Spun glass, stuffed birds, and modelled flowers in wax,
> Because she liked accomplishments in girls.

Then follows a harangue against "a score of books on womanhood" that harped on a theme very common among educationists: the wives'

> right of comprehending husband's talk
> When not too deep,

provided they never strayed beyond the conventions, for

> she owned
> She liked a woman to be womanly,
> And English women, she thanked God and sighed
> (Some people always sigh in thanking God),
> Were models to the universe. And last
> I learnt cross-stitch, because she did not like
> To see me wear the night with empty hands
> A-doing nothing.

And the result? Aurora is depicted, avowedly, as an unusual woman (as Elizabeth Barrett Browning herself was unusual), for she continues her own education (when she parts reluctantly with her father's books she gives a biting criticism of Wolff's *Prolegomena*), and, moreover, is able to support herself by her pen in London. But though she is socially lionized, society is still largely of the opinion of Dr Johnson: her work is not so much well

done as wonderful because it is done at all—by a woman.[1]
Her cousin, endeavouring to dissuade her from her
career, prophesies:

> You never can be satisfied with praise
> Which men give women when they judge a book,
> Not as mere work, but as mere woman's work,
> Expressing the comparative respect
> Which means the absolute scorn.

Elizabeth Barrett, herself the companion of Kenyon
and other scholarly men, must have known often enough
this patronizing attitude. Aurora's end is similar to that
of "the Princess." How could it be otherwise?

> Art is much, but love is more.

Any reference to any Victorian novel, broadly speaking,
in which the question of female education is discussed
shows only the one conclusion. It would be easy to
multiply instances; *Shirley* is the best known, but one,
taken at random from *Hopes and Fears*, is typical:

> Phœbe was so notable and joyous in her labours [arranging
> her brother's rooms] that Honor drew the conclusion that
> housewifery was her true element, and science, art, and litera-
> ture only acquired because they had been her duties.

This was, of course, not only a theme of fiction; it was
understood to be (and, though the convention may have
changed, the attitude remains the same to-day) the view
of the parents. It is all very well for Margaret Jeune to
attend lectures on geology and to improve in her studies
—but what rejoices Mrs Jeune's heart is "the homage
which dear Meggie begins to receive at dances, because
she is certainly strikingly superior in looks to most of the
other girls, and has a fine bearing, which distinguishes
her." The really important thing is that H.R.H. (the
Prince of Wales) danced the third dance with her; that
Sir John Lawrance "led her out" the observed and envied
of a great many; and that "the Great London Lion" and

---

[1] "A woman preaching is like a dog walking on its hinder legs; it is
not well done, but you are surprized to find it done at all."

76

African traveller M. du Chaillu "seemed charmed with her"—though, be it acknowledged in favour of accomplishments, he is also able to compliment her on her French. And Margaret herself, not unnaturally preferring the prospect of Commemoration balls to the meeting of the British Association, writes to a friend:

> We shall be over-run by scientifics of all nations who will do nothing but run wildly after 'sections'; I am resolved not to improve my mind in *any* way.

Female education in the home, then, as a rule did not go very deep. *The Spectator's* eighteenth-century comment on its aim was hardly a caricature:

> To make her an agreeable person is the main purpose of her parents, and from this general folly we owe our present numerous race of coquettes . . . taught a fantastical behaviour . . . under pain of never having a husband if she steps or moves awry.

Mrs William Grey in her plea before the Society of Arts in 1871 puts it even more shrewdly. After quoting Mr Fitch's dictum, "The accomplishments which they value are those which promise rather to increase her attractiveness before marriage than her happiness or her usefulness after the event," she explains:

> There is a pretty theory abroad which is always brought forward when women's education is talked about—*i.e.*, that they are educated to be wives and mothers. I do not know a more fallacious one. They are *not* educated to be wives, but to get husbands. They are *not* educated to be mothers . . . to be the mistresses of households. What they are educated for is to come up to a certain conventional standard accepted in the class to which they belong, to adorn (if they can) the best parlour or the drawing-room, to gratify a mother's vanity, to amuse a father's leisure hours; above all to get married.

"Not to *be* wives, but to *get* husbands." It is a poor outlook. And in a general way this was, or had been, true. At best the ideal for the product was adaptability; as a rule the characteristic of the education was scrappiness.

CHAPTER III

THE LADIES' SEMINARY

THE most celebrated pupil of Miss Pinkerton's Academy for Young Ladies in Chiswick Mall left that establishment "when the nineteenth century was in its teens." As Miss Pinkerton, "the Semiramis of Hammersmith," was herself the friend of Dr Johnson and the correspondent of Mrs Chapone, and as the establishment had been "honoured by the presence of the great Lexicographer," who died in 1784, the lady might well at this time have been thinking of retirement. Perhaps Becky Sharp's action in flinging the "Dixionary" from the carriage window gave her the final fillip—though, to be sure, we hear of Miss Pinkerton's some months later giving Mrs Bute Crawley a polite but venomous character of her late articled pupil. Certainly she ought to have found herself well provided for after thirty years, seeing that she charged Mr Sedley £93 p.a. for his daughter's education—a good sum for the time—and Amelia was not even the richest nor the most aristocratic of Miss Pinkerton's young ladies. But, whether the lady retired or not, her fame remained for many generations, so that her name has almost become a generic term for the headmistress of a ladies' seminary.

Amelia may have been surpassed in rank and wealth by the Duke's daughter and the heiress from St Kitts, but she was obviously the embodiment of her schoolmistress's, and perhaps her creator's, ideal. Miss Pinkerton thought her worthy of a letter to her parents, in which she describes her as "a young lady not unworthy to occupy a fitting position" in their polished and refined circle, and stresses her virtues and accomplishments, her industry and obedience, and, above all, her delightful sweetness of temper.

In music, in dancing, in orthography, in every variety of embroidery and needlework, she will be found to have realized her friends' *fondest wishes*. In geography there is still much to be desired; and a careful and undeviating use of the backboard, for four hours daily during the next three years, is recommended as necessary to the acquirement of that dignified *deportment and carriage*, so requisite for every young lady of *fashion*.

Even more interesting than Miss Pinkerton's pane-gyric, because so gratuitous, is Trollope's commendation, which shows how acceptable a type Amelia was.

Readers complain of Amelia because she is absolutely true to nature. . . . She is feminine all over, and British—loving, true, thoroughly unselfish, yet with a taste for having things comfortable. . . . I know no trait in Amelia which a man would be ashamed to find in his own daughter.

One great advantage Miss Pinkerton had over her modern equivalent—she knew exactly the type of girl she was required to turn out, and that after all is half the battle for the 'successful' school. There is no such certainty about the modern parents' requirements—or perhaps it is that the object for which their girls' education is intended to fit them is not so crudely put. For the Victorian, and pre-Victorian, parents, however delicate and prudish they may have been over the means, had no reticence whatever about the aim. It is amazing to the modern mind how frankly this was stated—in novels, in conversation, and even in such an official report as that of the Schools Inquiry Commission, where it is admitted against "solid attainments" that they "are actually dis-advantages to matrimony." To quote the bald observa-tion of *The Saturday Review* in 1864, "The object for which girls are supposed to be brought up is that they may be married." The same thought appears in the rather tiresome *badinage* of Thackeray ("Of what else have young ladies to think but husbands?"); in the outbursts of Charlotte Brontë ("They scheme, they plot,

79

they dress to ensnare husbands"); and in the delicate but equally telling ridicule of Jane Austen when she says of Charlotte Lucas:

> Without thinking highly either of men or of matrimony, marriage had always been her object; it was the only provision

MISS PINKERTON
W. M. Thackeray

for well-educated young women of such fortune and, however uncertain of giving happiness, must be their pleasantest preservative from want. This preservative she had now obtained, and at the age of twenty-seven, without having ever been handsome, she felt all the luck of it.

To be sure, Elizabeth Bennet felt that Charlotte was degrading her sex by accepting Mr Collins on these terms, but that there were many more Charlottes in the nineteenth century than Elizabeths one can hardly doubt.

The aim being so clear, how was Miss Pinkerton to see that her charges were educated to fit? We have

noticed the stress laid on needlework and the accomplishments, whether the girl was taught at home or at school.
Among these must not be forgotten the acquirement of
a 'correct' style of handwriting, sometime called calli-
graphy. (Little Laura Martin, one of Miss Pinkerton's
younger pupils, "was just in round hand.")

The mother of "A London Girl of the Eighties"
explained that when she was a little girl at a school in
Falmouth where they taught very little indeed, they used
to make a great point of penmanship. She had to copy
out elegant sentiments. That was how penmanship
(delightful word!) was often acquired.

Miss Pinkerton is said to have been drawn from Miss
Richmal Mangnall, authoress of the famous *Questions*,
and by good fortune a diary belonging to one of her pupils
has survived. Here we find that "the little ladies" (her
term for the younger girls; the older ones were "the
great ladies") learnt, among other things, ancient
geography, ancient history, and thoughts on education.
"Spelling and dictionary" are also mentioned, and the
punishment for "losing at spelling," as for many other
crimes, was bed.

But a more complete curriculum is given by Hood in
describing "The Grove" school, where "the twenty-four
Young Ladies of Miss Bate" were educated. Their
mixed fare was as follows:

> And thus their studies they pursued—on Sunday,
>   Beef, collects, batter, texts from Dr Price;
> Monday, French, pancakes, grammar—of a Monday;
>   Tuesday—hard dumplings, globes, Chapone's Advice;
>   Wednesday—fancy-work, rice-milk (no spice);
> Thursday—pork, dancing, currant-bolsters, reading;
>   Friday—beef, Mr Butler, and plain rice;
> Saturday—scraps, short lessons and short feeding,
> Stocks, backboards, hash, steel collars, and good breeding.[1]

For the physical training of her pupils Miss Bate, like
Miss Pinkerton, made use of those instruments for many

---

[1] From *Love and Lunacy*, 1838.

years known in schools, of which the backboard was the one most frequently referred to. This was a piece of wood used, as its name implies, for straightening the young lady's back. She wore it crosswise behind the shoulder-blades and under the armpits, or as an alternative she might lie flat upon it for certain hours during the day. The teaching of deportment, to which *The Spectator* made such satirical reference, continued long after the days of Miss Bate, and doubtless the well-trained young lady there did not differ much from the product of Suxberry House, thus described by Miss Edgeworth:

> Miss Fanshaw, an erect, stiffened figure, made her *entrée*; and it was impossible not to perceive that her whole soul was intent upon her manner of holding her head and placing her elbows as she came into the room. Her person had undergone all the ordinary and extraordinary tortures of backboards, collars, stocks, dumb-bells, etc. She looked at Isabella and Matilda with some surprise and contempt during the first ten minutes after her entrance; for they were neither of them seated in the exact posture which she had been instructed to think the only position in which a *young lady* should sit in company. Isabella got up to look at a drawing; Miss Fanshaw watched every step she took, and settled it in her own mind that Miss Harcourt did not walk as if she had ever been at Suxberry House.

It would seem that the worst crime against the girl of the nineteenth century was not the lack of training, or the mistraining, of her mind, but the wreck that was made of her body—that is, if we put aside the misdirection of her spiritual and emotional faculties; but in the ordering of these, as I have implied, Miss Pinkerton had little choice. If the "principles of religion and morality" in her school had *not* been such as were worthy of the establishment visited by "the great Lexicographer," and if Amelia had *not* been right-minded enough, and sweet enough in disposition, or appearance of it, to get herself a husband, the parents would have been outraged, and there would have been no more Academy for Semiramis. But of her pupil's person the schoolmistress had chief control, and the mismanagement of girls at the most important age of physical growth must be held responsible for a large proportion of the ill-health which women of the period enjoyed by tradition, and which often survives to-day among the better-off. Against this, to be fair, one must set the heroic achievements of women like Maria Graham, afterwards Lady Callcott, and later of Gertrude Bell, who have nothing to learn from the modern generation in the way of physical endurance, and who could not have survived their adventures if their health had not triumphed over the fashionable upbringing of the time. But, without generalizing unduly, one may assume that the average fashionable school of the century was more likely to undermine a girl's constitution than to preserve it.

As to the amenities, the following account of what was admittedly an old-fashioned school in the latter half of the century was probably pretty true of earlier private schools:

> The meals were very plain. Bread and scrape for breakfast, unless any of us had brought provision from home such as pork pie or anchovy paste. The bread was just like chaff; it was specially stale as being better for us, and the minimum allowance was two slices. At the beginning of term it was almost impossible to get down the two slices in the time allowed, but later on hunger occasionally demanded more. At eleven in the morning a plate of dry bread was handed round, and cold water was available. Dinner was good solid meat and pudding in a regular succession. It was allowable to have two helpings of meat but rarely possible, owing to the shortness of the time the meal was supposed to last. Tea was a repetition of breakfast with an occasional treat of bread and treacle. . . . Supper was also two slices of bread each, with a little cheese occasionally for the elder girls.
>
> The worst part of the school was the lack of fresh air and exercise. An hour was put aside for a walk, but this included the time for putting on outdoor clothes, and the crocodile walk was very dreary. We walked very slowly, and were not allowed to swing our arms; messages came up from the mistress at the back if any such breach of good manners occurred. . . . There was croquet in summer.[1]

---

[1] E. Lodge, *Terms and Vacations.*

Another cause of ill-health among girls—though this was not so fashionable at the beginning of the century—was tight-lacing. "Girls quite often used to faint in class, because of their tight stays, you know," explained a mistress who had taught in the early days of a big public school, apparently quite unconscious of the shock she was giving to a teacher of the present day who did *not* know and who did not wear the garment herself. And right on into the nineties one heard accounts, perhaps exaggerated, of young women who seriously and permanently injured themselves by attempts to pull in the natural plumpness of sixteen years or so to an eighteen-inch waist. Fashion thus dictated to the girls, but in the end girls dictated to the fashion. When the great god Sport was born his devotees gradually laid before him any garment that was likely to hinder them in their worship. Had Miss Beale encouraged games at the beginning of her long reign perhaps fashion-makers might have turned half a century sooner to the cut of shorts and the set of slacks. Even bicycling must have helped to do away with the bustle, and tennis in time shortened the skirt, while war work produced the 'pull-on' hat—and breeches. Mrs Bloomer, of knickerbocker fame, had not lived in vain.

But though there were exceptions, early nineteenth-century schools of the more fashionable type regarded physical exercise as approaching the indecent. It must be remembered that in this age girls were taught that "horses sweat, gentlemen perspire, but ladies merely glow." (And in their stuffy clothes and hot schoolrooms life must have been one perpetual glow.) Again and again comes the complaint—from Dorothea Beale, from Margaret Jeune, from Mrs Ewing—of the lack of provision for health and freedom. The description of the school in *Six to Sixteen* gives the last-named occasion for a rather remarkable outburst, considering her date.

To growing girls, not too robust, leading sedentary lives, working very hard with our heads, and having wholesome and sufficient meals but . . . not as much animal food as most of us were accustomed to [1] the nag of never being free from supervision was both irritating and depressing. Much worst off were we than boys at school. No playing fields had we; no leave could be obtained for country rambles by ourselves. Our dismal exercise was a promenade in double file under the eye and ear of Madame herself.

Mrs Ewing goes on to stress the necessity for giving girls instruction in hygiene. She complains of most girls' crass ignorance of the laws of health and their reckless imprudence, and ascribes it partly to a general low standard of education and partly to "an unfortunate . . . confusion between ignorance and innocence," to "mistaken notions of delicacy—a kind of delicate-mindedness which is apt to bring delicacy of body in its train." Naturally she censures most strongly such ignorance in those who are in charge of numbers of young people. But knowledge of hygiene was not often required in a schoolmistress of the nineteenth century.

Moreover, such was the ignorance, apparently, of those responsible for the girls' health that the attempts to remedy the lack of exercise sometimes appear worse than the disease. At the school attended by Dorothea Beale, for example, it was necessary for each girl to take a certain number of walks ('turns,' they were called) round the playground during the short interval assigned to them for eating their lunch. This entailed hurrying their meal to an extent that must have meant frequent indigestion if the 'turns' were to be honourably carried out—as we understand was *not* always done by Dorothea's less scrupulous companions.

The iniquities of the private school went farther than mere omission of what was after all not yet recognized as a part of a young girl's life—organized physical activity. If we want an example of its worst effect we must turn to the account of the school from which Arthur Young had

[1] A rather curious complaint, not often so exactly stated.

to take away his fourteen-year-old daughter absolutely broken in health, to die shortly after. He writes:

> I brought my dear, angelic child with me, who went to school in January, in good health but never in good spirits, for she abhorred school. Oh, what infatuation ever to send her to one! In the country she had health, spirits, and strength, as if there were not enough with what she might have learnt at home instead of going to that region of constraint and death, Camden House.
>
> The rules for health are detestable—no air but in a measured, formal walk, and all running and quick motion prohibited. Preposterous! She slept with a girl who could hear only with one ear, and so lay ever on one side; and my dear child could do no otherwise afterwards without pain; because the vile beds are so small that they must both lie the same way. The school discipline of all sorts, the food, etc., etc., all contributed. She never had a bellyful at breakfast. Detestable this at the expense of £80 a year.[1] Oh, how I regret ever putting her there or to any other, for they are all theatres of knavery, illiberality, and infamy!

We turn thankfully to Miss Austen's picture, said to be reminiscent of her own schooldays, of Mrs Goddard's school in *Emma*.

> Mrs Goddard was the mistress of a school—not of a seminary, or an establishment, or anything which professed, in long sentences of refined nonsense, to combine liberal acquirements with elegant morality, upon new principles and new systems— and where young ladies for enormous pay might be screwed out of health and into vanity—but a real, honest, old-fashioned boarding school, where a reasonable quantity of accomplishments were sold at a reasonable price, and where girls might be sent to be out of the way and scramble themselves into a little education without any danger of coming back prodigies. Mrs Goddard's school was in high repute—and very deservedly, for Highbury was reckoned a particularly healthy spot; she had an ample house and garden, gave the children plenty of wholesome food, let them run about a great deal in the summer and in winter dressed their chilblains with her own hands. It was no

---

[1] He was still paying for her in May, though he had taken her away in March.

THE 'CARVED PARLOUR' OF CAMPDEN HOUSE SCHOOL, KENSINGTON

From a rare coloured lithograph in the Kensington Public Library.

By courtesy of the Libraries Committee

wonder that a train of twenty young couple now walked after her to church.

To "let them run about" showed a very liberal spirit on the part of Mrs Goddard, for as a rule girls' exercise was limited to something far more restrained, in preparation for a decorous existence in the future. "The twenty-four Young Ladies of Miss Bate" were walked three times a week along the road

> Like coupled hounds, whipped in by two she-dominies,
> With faces rather graver than Melpomene's.

Similar walks were enforced at Mrs Latom's school in *The Newcomes* and at Mrs Ballard's school in *Middlemarch*.

Yet certain types of activity were considered suitable for women by even so stern a critic as Miss Yonge. She approves of walking—which was more than Miss Bingley had done thirty years before; witness her consternation at Elizabeth Bennet's three-mile tramp to see her sister—of skating, and even of waltzing. This last shows considerable emancipation, for waltzing at its first introduction was somewhat fast in every sense. She dislikes seeing a woman take part in sports connected with the destruction of life, so disapproves of fishing and of hunting, but riding she will permit and even encourage. And her disapproval of hunting certainly did not prevent the existence of the 'horsy' woman who appears occasionally in novels throughout the century.

In spite of occasional disastrous results, the habit of sending girls to a boarding school was on the increase among the class just below the richest and most aristocratic. It is possible that the improvement of travelling facilities, and in particular the increase in the railway system, had something to do with this, as it undoubtedly helped in the redevelopment of the boys' public schools during the nineteenth century. Miss Yonge recognizes the fact, though she disapproves, that a girl often will not be brought up at home, and she proceeds to discuss the size that a school should be. The kind of school that found favour in her eyes—and in those of many other Victorians—was often so small as to be no larger than a good-sized family, as families were then reckoned. She approved of a school of ten to twenty girls, and we frequently hear of such—*e.g.*, in Mary de Morgan's *The French Girl at our School* or *Mrs Leicester's School*, by Mary Lamb.

The smallness of the numbers meets the important charge that Miss Yonge makes against schools in general —that if the semblance of family life is lost confidence between the head and the members is lost. Hence grows up a tendency to feel that all those in authority are the child's natural enemies, and to acquiesce in small deceptions for the sake of "sticking together." (Did this never happen in a family where "the Olympians" were out of touch with the younger generation? one may ask.) The other objections she makes to large schools are similarly of a moral nature: the girls lose, through lack of privacy, a certain sense of security and decency; they find it difficult to continue habits of prayer and meditation. This question still arises in schools where there are no partitioned cubicles. Finally, she says that there is no scope for motherliness in a school, as the little ones, whom she pictures as being from eight to ten, are not small enough to rouse this sentiment in the girls of sixteen or so, who are apt even in large families to be unkind to the "middle-sized" children, and only pet and look after those who are real babies. A Victorian family, one must remember, might produce a difference in age of anything up to twenty years.

Miss Yonge points out that "if the tuition is to be of a superior order" a small school cannot be remunerative without very heavy charges, for in the country these high-class teachers must be resident, and therefore expensive, while in towns the rent is too high for any but

the most successful schools. Miss Yonge is here thinking
of the certificated young woman who was beginning to
appear in the second half of the century, or of the music-
or drawing-master with something of a 'name,' but the
lot of the visiting master or resident mistress at the average
girls' school seems to have been deplorable. The assistant
mistress was the counterpart of the poor usher at a boys'
private or preparatory school—a position which had not
altered materially since George Primrose had been advised
not to undertake it, or since Nicholas Nickleby did. It is
little wonder that such a post was a matter of necessity
among young women, seldom of free choice. Nor was
the situation much better when regarded from the point
of view of the employer. Doubtless there was plenty of
material, for even in the Victorian era of trade expansion
there were always bound to be 'failures' like that of
Mr Sedley, respectable families who lost their livelihood
through the incompetence or gambling propensities of
the father. In such cases teaching was often the sole way
for the girls to make a living; but that was not to say
that it was a profession for which they were qualified. It
was to teaching that poor Miss Matty's thoughts first
turned before Mary's brilliant idea that she should sell
tea. But as for her 'accomplishments,' they were as
follows:

> Once upon a time I had heard her say she could play *Ah!
> vous dirai-je maman?* on the piano, but that was long, long
> ago; that faint shadow of musical acquirement had died out
> years before. She had also once been able to trace out patterns
> very nicely for muslin embroidery, by dint of placing a piece of
> silver paper over the design to be copied, and holding both
> against the window-pane while she marked the scollop and
> eyelet-holes. But that was her nearest approach to the accom-
> plishment of drawing, and I did not think it would go very far.
> Then again, as to the branches of a solid English education—
> fancy-work and the use of the globes—such as the mistress of
> the Ladies' Seminary, to which all the tradespeople in Cranford
> sent their daughters, professed to teach. Miss Matty's eyes were
> failing her, and I doubted if she could discover the number of

threads in a worsted-work pattern, or rightly appreciate the different shades required for Queen Adelaide's face in the loyal wool-work now fashionable in Cranford. As for the use of the globes I had never been able to find it out myself, so perhaps I was not a good judge of Miss Matty's capability of instructing in this branch of education; but it struck me that equators and tropics, and such mystical circles were very imaginary lines indeed to her, and that she looked upon the signs of the Zodiac as so many remnants of the Black Art.

Even reading and spelling presented considerable difficulties to dear Miss Matty, and her chief accomplishment was "making candle-lighters or 'spills' (as she preferred calling them) of coloured paper cut so as to resemble feathers, and knitting garters in a variety of dainty stitches." Yet in the days when teaching was the only way of earning a livelihood there must have been other elderly ladies not much better qualified who took it upon themselves to instruct children in subjects of which they were themselves singularly ignorant.

Moreover, if the headmistress did engage a competent instructress of respectable parentage she was often a young woman seeking by this apprenticeship to qualify herself as a governess in a good family or for a school of her own, and left as soon as she could. Such was Charlotte Brontë at Roe Head, and this course presented itself in a moment of despondency to Miss Weeton. Or the assistant teacher might really be an articled pupil, like Emma's Harriet, or like Becky Sharp, who taught music and French—but seldom so clever.

The difficulty of obtaining teachers was often met by the principal's employing her younger sisters, as Miss Pinkerton did Miss Jemima. It was the obvious plan for sisters to set up a school together: Hannah More and her sisters did so for a time; the Brontës aimed at it; the Misses Edmunds of St Margaret Hall, Bournemouth, did so for the last forty years of the nineteenth century; and there are dozens more examples. The most famous of such 'firms' were, of course, the Misses Lawrence, founders of Roedean. Often one sister would do the housekeeping, and in any case the 'technical' subjects—music, drawing, perhaps Italian, which was more widely learnt at the beginning of the last century than German—these would be left to the visiting masters. In one such school that I have heard of, kept by three sisters, a 'governess' was employed to teach 'grammar,' which, considering there were only about a dozen girls, seems extravagant. Perhaps she was not 'full time.' But most private schools must have found themselves in the dilemma of either having to employ a great number of expensive specialists or of making the existing staff teach subjects for which they were very little qualified. As a rule a member on the staff of a private school had to be prepared to teach almost anything, and the further the century progressed the more difficult might be the problems presented. Mrs M. Vivian Hughes, describing a school of the eighties in West Kensington, explains that there were three mistresses, who divided the work between them, and she describes her horror when quite suddenly she was required to teach mechanics to matriculation standard. In addition, she was persuaded, when boarders were acquired, to 'live in,' in order to help make ends meet.

For the financial shadow has never ceased to hover over the private school. Boys' public or endowed schools, though not entirely freed from the threat of bankruptcy by reason of disordered currencies and national upheavals, are on the whole secured; high schools may have to be closed occasionally, but some provision or transfer for their occupants can often be made. The headmistress of the small private school for girls, however, if she has no other means of subsistence, is seldom free from anxiety. It takes so very little to break a school like this that a run of bad illness, a national calamity, or local changes, even involved family affairs, may easily cause it to fail. Neglect of minor ailments which become serious, bad feeding or

teaching, even apparent unkindness to the children—
these things can more often than not be traced to money
difficulties and to the nervous tension created in a single
woman trying to cope with them. Often she has been
entirely unfitted by temperament or training to deal with
this side of affairs. It is no wonder that the private school
was as a rule in no position to set the pace for girls' education during the last century, harassed as it so often was
by poverty and debt. As the first qualification for a headmistress of a private school—always granted that she was
undertaking the job through fondness for children and not
merely to keep herself—I should put a good financial brain.

The fees charged for a girl's education might vary in
an amazing way—the Schools Inquiry Commission could
arrive at no closer limits than from £3 to £22 a year for
a day school and from £25 to £100 for boarders as an
average. Mr Squeers went lower with £20, and as his
pupils were boys there were probably schools as cheap
and even cheaper and less educative for girls. At Kate
Nickleby's school £50 was paid for what was regarded as
a sufficiently fashionable education. Miss Frances Cobbe,
however, states that her father paid ten times this amount.
In her school the higher figure was arrived at by the
addition of 'extras.' 'Extras' were included in the fees at
Cheltenham when Miss Beale went there; two years later,
however, by a new and satisfactory financial reorganization, such accomplishments as music were separated from
the main curriculum.

Besides the difficulty of attracting pupils and of finding
teachers there were other difficulties in running a school
that should provide a good education. (When parents
did require some solid achievements in their daughters it
was quite difficult to obtain competent mistresses for
arithmetic.) The actual provision of text-books from
which they could learn anything seems to have been
almost impossible. The famous Mangnall's *Questions*,
standby, as we shall see, of the home governess, were

found in the sixties to be in use in about half the schools. Other 'arid manuals' of the same type existed—little books that would tell one, for instance, that gunpowder was first used at Cressy, but not who fought at that battle or won it, nor when it was fought, nor why. We find constant references in stories, reports, and memoirs to Lindley Murray's *Grammar*, an improvement in itself, perhaps, on previous attempts to synthesize grammatical rules, but misused when it was set to be learnt off by heart in chunks. And although *Little Arthur's History* came out in the thirties, children were kept chiefly to Mrs Markham, for what reason I have been unable to discover. As to arithmetic, it appears that the books were sometimes as uninstructive as the teachers. For instance: "If 15 clerks can do a piece of work in 52 days, in how many *weeks* will 6 clerks do the same?" is answered as "15 : 52 :: 6 :   ?" Another example of confusion between work and days is given in the Schools Inquiry Commissioners' Report. It is not surprising that they condemn the schools as being furnished with "an inferior set of text-books." All that can be said is that few good text-books appear to have been obtainable.

Another difficulty for private schools was the competition. There were so many of them. A small town like Burford, in Oxfordshire, of about 1500 inhabitants at the beginning of the century, is said to have contained three schools for girls. And Mr G. M. Young in *Victorian England* describes London as "ringed with such institutions, through which the drawing-master and the music-master wearily circulated on foot."

No account of the young lady's education would be complete without reference to the foreign finishing school, most vividly described, of course, by Charlotte Brontë. The author herself says:

> All that relates to Brussels, the Belgian school, etc., is as good as I can write; it contains more pith, more substance, more reality . . . than *Jane Eyre*.

She wrote its description twice—first in *The Professor*, which was not published till after her death, and then, supremely, in *Villette*, and in both she shows up, as Professor Oliver Elton puts it, "the sham-romantic conception of the *jeune fille* and the orderly, cheery surface of the school covering its real vulgarity and corruption." She does, as a matter of fact, exempt the English girls from the general charge of being "mentally depraved." Their characteristics she gives as

> clean but careless dress, ill-arranged hair (compared with the tight and trim foreigners), erect carriage, flexible figures . . . grave, modest countenances, a general air of native propriety and decency.

Charlotte Brontë is probably prejudiced in favour of her Protestant countrywomen, but the account she gives of the "miscellaneous assortment"—there were no less than a hundred, of different nationalities and classes, in one division for "the Professor's" English lesson—would be enough to account for the British father's contempt and dislike of the foreign school. (And, in fact, most of the English girls who were given six months in France and Germany went to families—if possible to some kind of connexion—not to a *pension*.) The tone was

> rough, boisterous, marked by a point-blank disregard of all forbearance towards each other or their teachers; an eager pursuit by each individual of her own interest and convenience; and a coarse indifference to the interest and convenience of every one else. Most of them could lie with audacity when it appeared advantageous to do so. All understood the art of speaking fair when a point was to be gained, and could with consummate skill and at a moment's notice turn the cold shoulder the instant civility ceased to be profitable. Very little open quarrelling ever took place amongst them; but backbiting and talebearing were universal. . . . Scarcely one of those girls having attained the age of fourteen could look a man in the face with modesty and propriety. An air of bold impudent flirtation or a loose, silly leer was sure to answer the most ordinary glance from a masculine eye.

94

Yet even this scathing denunciation by the ex-teacher in M. Héger's *pension* at Brussels is less convincing than the details with which she fills in the picture—the prying of the principal into a teacher's drawer, the appearance of the girls, their hair "glossy with gum and grease," and the petty persecutions. And she is at pains to show that such a school had a reputation for the *convenable*, and that the girls were supposed to be reared "in utter un-consciousness of vice."

It would be as unfair to imagine that all finishing schools abroad were as bad as the *Villette* pension as it would be to condemn all early Trust schools on the score that they resembled Jane Eyre's Lowood. From the educational point of view they were probably better than finishing schools in England, which were later condemned by a wrathful Commissioner as "simply schools that were more expensive than others and in no way better." The same complaint of hollowness, of exalted ideas of conduct and religious principles which led in practice to petty deceits and a great deal of silliness, is made against the English school. But an interesting light is thrown on the foreign finishing school by an English girl who, going abroad in the early years of this century, found that she had walked (as she expresses it in *Four Miss Pinkertons*) "into another fold of time"—the period of her own mother or even grandmother.

The female was in most respects a different and differently treated being from her English counterpart. No sincere attempt was as yet being made to train her in mind or body to be a responsible creature; it was thought only natural for her to be deceitful and furtive, demure and coquettish. . . . Every one of these girls would marry; some were already affianced. They would have husbands to look after them; therefore it was quite unnecessary for them to know how to look after themselves, and I think in some respects they were purposely kept childish. . . . Foreign languages were an asset, and that was why they had been sent to a place where they would meet foreigners. . . . It was their *rôle* to giggle and smirk, to make eyes at the young man who passed the window, to dress in fluffy clothes that would catch his eye.

The product of a bracing English public school naturally regarded this attitude and the treatment it involved with complete stupefaction, the more so as she did not then realize the "adventure in period," and was not unnaturally a fish out of water in such surroundings.

The tendency to send girls to boarding schools seems to have grown up chiefly in the middle classes, and to have been less pronounced at the upper and lower ends of the scale, though there certainly are girls' schools of all classes in Dickens. But Paul Dombey is sent to Dr Blimber's, while Florence remains at home. Similarly, in *The Mill on the Floss*, Tom Tulliver is given a school education, the best that his father can procure, but Maggie has to pick up what she can from old books—with the help, later, of Philip Wakem. Mr Young in *Victorian England* thus summarizes the Schools Inquiry Commissioners' Report of 1869, which shows that:

(*a*) In the upper classes education was a domestic industry, carried on by the mother, who sometimes delegated the routine work to a governess, and by visiting masters. If the family made an annual stay in London further intensive teaching was added in music, drawing, and languages, and for an intelligent girl in a sympathetic home there was a most stimulating provision of books, travel, and conversation.

(*b*) Next ranked the boarding schools—of all degrees, many of them, of "silliness and shallowness," and yet . . . of such variety that it was hard to generalize.

(One should remember that two years after this was written girls were going up from schools like Miss Octavia Hill's and Miss Kyberd's for the Cambridge Local examinations, and George Eliot's excellent boarding school at Coventry must be weighed against Miss Cobbe's fashionable institution where the latter learnt nothing.)

(*c*) Below the boarding-school class was that unfortunate situation just too high to make use of the Charity and the National School. For them there was rarely anything better

than a superior dame school in a parlour or a very inferior
visiting governess.

Perhaps it was with an eye to this third class, but more
likely for families who would have preferred (*a*) but for
financial reasons were destined to (*b*), that Miss Yonge
wrote:

> Would it not be possible to establish good day schools con-
> ducted by really superior teachers to whom the girls in each
> town might resort from their houses, establishing in combina-
> tion with them small boarding houses under ladies of such
> qualifications as would make really motherly homes of their
> houses and under whose charge girls could be put to form little
> families? . . . Different grades in social rank might probably
> meet at the school, but as it would only be in class, it could
> hardly lead to inconvenient intercourse. However, this is a
> thing of speculation.

It was not. Miss Yonge wrote in 1876. In 1873 had
been founded the Girls' Public Day School Trust.

CHAPTER IV

THE GOVERNESS

PERHAPS the first public appeal on behalf of the governess—made at Manchester Town Hall in 1864—comes in the middle of a period when such a character was a byword both in fiction and in fact:

> And give your girls not only noble teachings, but noble teachers. You consider somewhat, before you send your boy to school, what kind of a man the master is;—whatsoever kind of man he is, you at least give him full authority over your son, and show some respect to him yourself; if he comes to dine with you, you do not put him at a side table; you know also that, at his college, your child's immediate tutor will be under the direction of some still higher tutor, for whom you have absolute reverence. You do not treat the Dean of Christ Church or the Master of Trinity as your inferiors.
>
> But what teachers do you give your girls, and what reverence do you show to the teachers you have chosen? Is a girl likely to think her own conduct, or her own intellect, of much importance, when you trust the entire formation of her character, moral and intellectual, to a person whom you let your servants treat with less respect than they do your housekeeper (as if the soul of your child were a less charge than jams and groceries), and whom you yourself think you confer an honour upon by letting her sometimes sit in the drawing-room in the evening? [1]

Yet, in spite of her having become a stock character, the status of the governess varied enormously. She can no more be said to have enjoyed (or suffered) a particular position than to have been invariably of a particular type; and it was no more accurate, though doubtless as common, to describe the "brown, dull, and resigned" Miss Morgan of *Middlemarch* as "just the sort of person for a governess" than it is to generalize to-day about schoolmistresses.

[1] John Ruskin, *Sesame and Lilies.*

98

Victorian fiction produces such varying characters as
Charlotte Yonge's iron-willed Miss Fennimore, and the
heroines of Rosa Nouchette Carey's *Only the Governess*,
and Lanoe Falconer's Mademoiselle Ixe, of the nineties,
who turned out to be an anarchist spy. Her position in
real life varied no less—the classic examples of odious
and uncivil treatment are, of course, the Brontës, with
their "oceans of sewing." But when Miss Weeton went
to Dove's Nest she undertook, "as well as literary studies,
the proper direction of servants and household," down to
such details as carving, and clinched the justification of
her claim to be regarded as a companion rather than as
a ladies' maid by stating proudly, "I *visit* with Mrs
Pedder." Moreover, in the most exalted circle of all,
the influence of Baroness Lehzen on Queen Victoria,
stronger, as we have seen, than even her mother's, was
overcome only after the Queen's marriage, and then not
without a bitter struggle.

From what class and homes came the 21,000 women
who in 1850 were registered as governesses? *The
Quarterly Review* [1] describes a governess as "a being who
is our equal in birth, manners, and education, but our
inferior in worldly wealth." Her social position, therefore, would vary according to that of her employer. Often
these "martyrs of wrecked fortune" came from families
of the clergy, but they might be the victims of a father's
unfortunate speculation, or even less deserved mis-
fortune, for, as it is hardly necessary to recall, becoming
a governess was the only means of earning her livelihood
open to a woman of gentle birth. Jane Fairfax, in *Emma*,
will, it is feared, be forced into such a position; Maggie
Tulliver tries, unsuccessfully, to earn a living in that way;
and Miss Yonge gives a sketch of an even more pathetic
figure—an elderly widow who comes to take charge of
young Countess Kate in the story of that name. Hers
was "the very saddest face" the little girl had ever seen.

[1] Vol. lxxxiv, p. 186.

The eyes looked soft and gentle, but as if they had wept till they could weep no more. . . . Poor lady, it was only that morning that she had parted with her son, and had gone away from the home where she had lived with her husband and children.

And doubtless Mrs Lacy was fortunate to obtain a post in the severe London household into which the un-disciplined Kate fitted so badly, for the supply of governesses was in excess of the demand.

Miss Eyre (not Jane), who was governess, in Mrs Gaskell's *Wives and Daughters*, to Molly Gibson from the time Molly was eight, was thirty-five and a respectable woman, daughter of a shopkeeper in the town who had left a destitute family. Mr Gibson was a surgeon who took in pupils, and as he was uncertain of being in at meal-times Miss Eyre was engaged partly that she might make tea and conversation for them, but she stayed with Molly from before breakfast till bedtime. The Doctor's advice on the upbringing of his only daughter has frequently been quoted, and probably did not sound so extra-ordinary to his contemporaries as it does to us:

Don't teach Molly too much; she must sew and read and write and do her sums, but I want to keep her a child, and if I find more learning desirable for her I'll see about giving it to her myself. After all, I'm not sure that reading or writing is necessary. Many a good woman gets married with only a cross instead of her name; it's rather a diluting of mother-wit, to my fancy; but, however, we must yield to the prejudices of society, Miss Eyre, so you may teach the child to read.

Molly "by fighting and struggling" later persuaded her father to let her have French and drawing lessons; but these were given by masters, and it is obvious that Miss Eyre's qualifications were not required to be very wide, and were chiefly summed up in the sentence, "She was a lady, in the best sense of the word." After all, that seemed to be the essential, and intellectual distinction was hardly required in a governess. In the same book there is an amusing comment on the governess in a more exalted circle, who ultimately becomes Molly's step-mother. Lady Harriet, the clever, heedless, but good-hearted younger daughter of the noble household, remarks of their former governess, who has lately lost more than one subsequent post:

> She's not very wise, certainly, but she's so useful and agreeable, I should have thought anyone who wasn't particular about education would have been charmed to keep her as a governess.

To the reply that "most people who keep governesses for their children are supposed to be particular" the irrepressible Lady Harriet answers:

> Oh, dear Mamma, you did everything you could think of for us, but you see you'd ever so many other engrossing interests. . . . You gave us the best of masters in every department, and Clare to dragonize and keep us up to our preparation for them as well as ever she could; but then you know, or rather, you didn't know, some of the masters admired our very pretty governess, and there was a kind of respectable veiled flirtation going on, which never came to anything to be sure; and then you were so often overwhelmed with your business as a great lady—fashionable and benevolent and all that sort of thing— that you used to call Clare away from us at the most critical times of our lessons to write your notes or add up your accounts, and the consequence is that I'm about the most ill-informed girl in London. Only Mary [the elder sister] was so capitally trained by good, awkward Miss Benson, that she is always full to overflowing with accurate knowledge, and her glory is reflected on me.

Yet the governess's standard *could* be a very high one, if we are to take Miss Yonge's character in *Hopes and Fears* as anything but a caricature.

Miss Fennimore was

> a finishing governess of the highest order, thinking it an insult to be offered a pupil below her teens or to lose one till nearly above them. . . . A highly able woman and perfectly sincere, she possessed the qualities of a ruler and had long experience in the art. Her discipline was perfect in machinery and her instructions admirably complete . . . and there was principle likewise, though no one ever quite penetrated to the foundation of it.

As a teacher she was excellent, but her own strong conformation prevented her from understanding that young girls were incapable of such tension of intellect as an enthusiastic scholar of forty-two. . . . Her very best pupil she had killed. Finding a very sharp sword in a very frail scabbard, she had whetted the one and worn down the other by every stimulus in her power . . . perfectly unconscious of her own agency in causing the atrophy. . . . She seldom remained more than two years in a family.

Unfortunately (for had she been a more common type she might not have run to such extremes) a woman of Miss Fennimore's distinction was seldom either found or required. In fact, until late in the century some households would have a definite prejudice against a 'certificated' young woman. And earlier (1848) Mrs Jameson, in her *Essays and Memoirs*, explains that "the recommendation of an English governess must rest more upon her moral than her intellectual qualifications." But equally necessary was it that she should be able to teach 'accomplishments,' and in order to acquire these a young woman sometimes trained as an assistant at a school. Such was Miss Weeton's intention at one time, and we shall note later the qualifications of two of Miss Pinkerton's ex-pupils. Indeed, *Fraser's Magazine* (vol. xxx, p. 577) scathingly remarks that mothers commit their girls' training "to a woman whose only qualification is that she has had a twelve months' apprenticeship in an inferior boarding school and that her father failed last week."

There was one other source from which the governess might be drawn besides the impoverished home or the 'select' boarding school. She might be a refugee. The troublous forties of Europe (and other decades as well) flooded the English market with many thousands of poverty-stricken or destitute women, chiefly from France and Italy. Often whole families of the cultivated, intelligent middle class (always the first to suffer in any political trouble) would settle in England, and might become naturalized. Such were the Rossettis. The presence of

the Italian master or governess may account for the spread
of that language along with French among the girls in
upper-class families. Italian was more widely learnt
during the early part of the century than German.

Nevertheless, not every parent was willing to take an
"outsider into his family." There must have been many
Colonel Blimps like Miss Jane Harrison's father, who
asserted roundly that "all foreigners were Papists, all
Papists were liars, and he wouldn't have one in the
house." (In parenthesis, the result in this particular case
was that one of the cleverest women of her generation
was brought up by "grossly ignorant" though "good,
kind women," except one who read with her "German,
Latin, Greek Testament, and a little Hebrew, and was
shortly afterwards removed to a lunatic asylum." So
much for Miss Fennimore in real life!)

What position a woman of striking personality might
attain we can see from Miss Edgeworth's tale of *The Good
French Governess*. The period is early, but the treatment
realistic, save for the romantic ending which such a tale
needed both to expound the Utilitarian principles of the
Edgeworths and to take the place of "the sugar at the
bottom of the cup." Mme de Rosier is a widowed French
émigrée who becomes a governess in the house of a
fashionable lady, mother of four children. The difficulties
she has with the elder girls (one conceited, the other
diffident), with the jealous maid and the frivolous mother,
with the spoilt darling, and with the stubborn schoolboy
are described in detail; so is her successful way of dealing
with them. Mme de Rosier is only working on the
methods put before every conference of teachers at any
meeting—encouragement, interest, patience, and the
stimulation in children of the desire to do or find out
something for themselves. Her pupils grow to love and
depend upon her, and when she has by her presence of
mind saved the youngest from falling off the leads of the
house, whither the child had disobediently wandered, it

is no wonder that the mother puts absolute trust in her, and even seeks to be herself instructed in the history, literature, political economy, and general knowledge in which Mme de Rosier is educating the daughters. The happy conclusion is appropriately reached through a piece of scientific instruction given to young Herbert. His thirst for knowledge leads him to experiment somewhat destructively on a tortoiseshell box of his sister's.

> I thought you would be pleased that I remembered how to distinguish animal from vegetable substances. You know, the day that my hair was on fire, you told me how to do that; and Matilda wanted to know what the box was made of; so I tried.

Inside the lid are found the words "Henri-Montmorenci de . . .," and the missing ending is, of course, "Rosier," so Madame is able to trace her long-lost son. In this story the relations of governess, children, and parent are extremely cleverly drawn, and, considering the need of conforming to the title of *Moral Tales*, the victory of the paragon governess's good influence is not unconvincing.

How disastrous might be the result if the governess was the very reverse of a paragon is shown in the story of *Mlle Panache, or the Bad French Governess*. This Frenchwoman, maid and governess to Lady Augusta S., was rightly judged by the sage Helen Temple to have been formerly a milliner's assistant—the deduction being made from the number of pins which she was able to carry in her mouth, till, unfortunately, she was overtaken with a fit of coughing. She it was who taught her charge to tell fibs, to be flighty and cruel ("Augusta's image, her gesture stamping upon the caterpillar, recurred to her lover's mind many times in the course of the evening and in the silence of the night," and finally dissuaded him from pressing his suit any farther), and to carry on an intrigue. Poetic justice is satisfied when Lady Augusta elopes with the tutor, designed by Mlle Panache for herself, and we leave the governess in hysterics.

Another deplorable figure, though of a very different type, is the heroine's first governess in *Six to Sixteen*:

> She is so good-natured, Margery, you can't think. When lessons are over she takes me walks on the Esplanade, and she calls me her dear Matilda, and I take her arm and she tells me all about herself. She says she knows she's very romantic.

Later her pupil explains:

> She was a great novel-reader, and I think a good many of the things she told us of as having happened to herself had their real origin in the Riflebury Circulating Library. For she was one of those strange characters who indulge in egotism and exaggeration, till they seem positively to lose the sense of what is fact and what is fiction.

Modern psychology might add that it was very far from strange for a young woman in a subordinate and slightly degrading position to indulge in and expound these daydreams by way of compensation.

But the 'folly' with which Miss Perry filled the heads of her charges was not the only harm they acquired from her. She "was much attached to the schoolroom fire," and therefore "sensitive to the smallest inlet of air."

> How we contrived to distinguish a verb from a noun or committed anything whatever to memory in the fever heat and stuffy atmosphere of the little room which was sacred to our studies I do not know. . . . This was no doubt one cause of the very severe headaches to which Matilda became subject about this time. . . . They were apt to end in a fainting condition, from which she recovered by lying on the floor. Then, if Miss Perry happened to be in a good humour, she would excuse Matilda from further lessons, invariably adding in her 'mystery' voice, "But not a word to your mamma!"

The lack of straightforwardness with which governesses, in fiction at least, were frequently credited was naturally a trait of Miss Perry's character.

> The sleight of hand with which she threw needlework over a novel when Aunt Theresa came into the schoolroom was not more skilful than the way in which she turned the tail of a bit of scandal into a remark upon the weather as Uncle Buller opened the drawing-room door.

It is interesting to note how this young woman got her place. She was a *protégée* of Mrs Minchin's (one of the "regimental ladies"), who had persuaded "Aunt Theresa" to take her.

> I do not think that our interests had entered in the least into Mrs Minchin's calculations in the matter. She had "taken Miss Perry up," and to get Miss Perry a comfortable home was her sole object.

One is reminded of Lady Catherine de Bourgh.

Mrs Ewing adds:

> To do our new governess justice, she did her best to impart her own superficial acquirements to us. We plodded regularly through French exercises, which she corrected by a key, and she kept us at work for a given number of hours during the day; tatting by our sides as we practised our scales, or roasting her petticoats over the fire whilst Matilda and I read Mrs Markham's *England* or Mrs Trimmer's *Bible Lessons* aloud by turns to full stops.

This leads one to consider exactly what the schoolroom young ladies were supposed to learn, and how far their instructress was capable of teaching them.

The governess has long been ridiculed for her reliance on those books of 'Questions' which dominated the schoolroom from the publication in 1800 of Miss Mangnall's famous volume to the *Child's Guide to Knowledge* in 1861, which within living memory was in regular use for instruction. No doubt some startlingly irrelevant and useless pieces of information were thus crammed down a girl's throat. There could be little reason, except perhaps the desire that she should "know what people are talking about,"[1] to store her memory with such items of information as the following:

> *Q.* What is the common maple?
> *A.* A low tree, common in woods and hedges, so much valued by the Romans that they gave an extravagant price for it for their tables.

---

[1] C. M. Yonge, *Womankind.*

Q. If the Romans reproached their wives for extravagance in jewels, etc., what used the latter to do?

A. To *turn the tables* upon their husbands—that is, to put them in mind of what they spent upon their tables of this wood.

Or

Q. What did Queen Elizabeth think of silk stockings?

A. In the third year of her reign she was furnished by her silk-woman with a pair, which she admired "as marvellous delicate wear," and she would never afterwards use cloth ones.

Q. Was not this queen very fond of dress?

A. Yes; it is said that after her death three thousand different habits were found in her wardrobe.

Q. Were not some of her robes emblematical?

A. Yes; the lining of one of them was worked with eyes and ears, and on her arm a serpent was embroidered with pearls and rubies, holding a great ruby in its mouth.

Q. What were all these symbols to denote?

A. *Vigilance* and *Wisdom.*

Or even

Q. Did not the Queen recently present a beautiful jewel to Miss Florence Nightingale?

A. Yes, as a token of Her Majesty's gratitude to this most excellent lady for her patriotic exertions in alleviating the sufferings of our brave soldiers during the late war.

Q. Can you describe this jewel?

A. Yes, it is oval, the groundwork being white enamel, with a crimson cross, on which the royal initials and crown are set in diamonds.

Q. What appropriate inscription does it bear?

A. The words "Blessed are the merciful" are inscribed upon its black oval band.

National pride and a healthy scepticism for legends were fostered by such portions of the catechism as:

Q. Was it not commonly thought that Whittington made his immense fortune by the sale of his cat?

A. Yes, but it was not the *whiskered, mouse-killing cat,* but the coasting, coal-carrying cat that realized his fortune.

Q. How?

A. It is said that this worthy merchant constructed a vessel, which from its swiftness and lightness he aptly named "a cat," which traded between Newcastle and London with coals, and laid the foundation of great wealth.

And the concluding passage:

Q. What was the origin of the figure of Britannia?
A. The Romans, who recorded all events on medals, cast it to signalize their conquests over our island.
Q. Has it not been preserved as testifying their high opinion of us?
A. Yes; the warlike nation of Britain is shown by the female's accoutrements; she sits upon a rock, or a globe, and the waves of her island home beat upon her feet.
Q. . . . Was the lion assigned her by the Romans?
A. No; it was added afterwards, probably to denote the magnanimous character of her hardy sons.

But that which in our eyes damns completely the "noxious brood of catechisms" and general-knowledge questions (save as a distraction for families at Christmas-time or an 'unofficial' examination paper at the end of term) is the lack of any scheme or systematic thought in presenting its (somewhat dubious) information. Taught, as the questions generally were, in 'blocks' of about a dozen, they produce such transitions as:

Q. What is whalebone?
A. A sort of gristle found inside the whale in long, flat pieces, three or four yards long; it supplies the place of teeth.
Q. Are there not four hundred or five hundred of them in one whale?
A. Yes; they stick to the upper jaw and form a kind of strainer to keep in the sea-snails and other small creatures upon which whales live.
Q. What is whalebone used for?
A. To stiffen stays, umbrellas, and whips.
Q. Are not umbrellas of great antiquity?
A. Yes; the Greeks, Romans, and all Eastern nations used them to keep off the sun; *ombrello*, in Italian, signifies "a little shade."
Q. Did not the use of this article travel from Italy into the other countries of Europe?
A. Yes; but very slowly, for they have scarcely been used in England above eighty years.

The nature of stays is not further inquired into, but the next question proceeds with the manufacture of whips, leading to cables, which in their turn are followed by telescopes. A somewhat longer extract takes one from "Of what country is the leopard native?" (followed by "Is it not a mark of the kindness of the Creator that these savage beasts go in search of prey during the night?" "Yes, for in the day when man is abroad they usually

QUARRELSOME CHILDREN
From "The Cowslip," by Elizabeth Turner (1811)

sleep in their dens"), by way of the seal and its habits, the wolf and Edward I, the lion whose skin was used as the tunic of heroes, to

Q. What do you mean by a tunic?
A. A sleeveless coat or vest.

And so on. No wonder Ethel May protested.

Evidently from the days of Jane Austen it was considered necessary for a young lady to know these things. Fanny Price could read, work, and write, but she had been taught nothing more.

"Dear Mamma" [remarks one of her cousins], "only think, my cousin cannot put the map of Europe together . . . or tell the principal rivers in Russia, and she never heard of Asia

Minor . . . and she does not know the difference between
water-colours and crayons. . . . We asked her last night what
way she would go to get to Ireland, and she said she should
cross to the Isle of Wight. . . . How long ago it is, Aunt,
since we used to repeat the chronological order of the kings of
England with the dates of their accession and most of the
principal events of their reigns!

"Yes" [added the other], "and of the Roman emperors
as low as Severus besides a great deal of heathen mythology
and all the metals, semi-metals, planets and distinguished
philosophers."

Their mamma's reply is very soothing: "It is not
necessary that she should be so accomplished as you are."

Similarly, though for a different reason, Ethel Newcome at thirteen "had none of the accomplishments of
her age." Her mother, Lady Ann, was constantly falling
in love with her new acquaintances, and all the governesses
were darlings during the first week and monsters ever
after. As a result:

She could not play on the piano; she could not speak French
well; she could not tell you when gunpowder was invented;
she had not the faintest idea of the date of the Norman Conquest
or whether the earth went round the sun or *vice versa*. She did
not know the number of counties in England, Scotland, and
Wales, let alone Ireland; she did not know the difference
between latitude and longitude. She had had so many governesses; their accounts differed. Poor Ethel was bewildered by
a multiplicity of teachers.

The governesses may have been many and ignorant,
but it is difficult to understand how they managed to
disagree about "1066 and All That."

It is only fair, however, to the much-abused governess
to remember what—and whom—she had to teach.
C. M. Yonge's Miss Fosbrook (*The Stokesley Secret*) was
in charge of a whole family, ranging from a baby to a
thirteen-year-old boy, and had all subjects to teach. It is
enough to make many a young woman of twenty quail.
This variety of ages, stages, and sexes had to be tackled
singlehanded (save when the elder boys went off to a

'tutor'; but even then Miss Fosbrook had to explain the homework to the stupid ones), unless, as frequently happened, the elder sister was employed in teaching the younger children or "hearing their lessons"—doubtless questions of the above type. True enough, classes of larger size and equal variety have been handled for years by single elementary-school teachers in small villages, but when one remembers that the governess took the children for walks, superintended their meals and manners, and often was required in addition to sew or make herself useful in the house, it is not surprising that she had little time in which to prepare lessons.

The variety of subjects in which it was necessary that the governess should claim to be proficient must have thrown many an honest young woman into despair. Anne Brontë doubtless professed, like her own Agnes Grey, to be able to teach music, singing, and drawing, French, Latin, and German. Higher pretensions were often made, and Thackeray is only exaggerating a real situation when he causes Miss Pinkerton to write, in recommending a governess:

> I have the honour (epistolarily) to introduce to her ladyship my two friends, Miss Tuffin and Miss Hawky.
> Either of these young ladies is *perfectly qualified* to instruct in Greek, Latin, and the rudiments of Hebrew; in mathematics and history; in Spanish, French, Italian, and geography; in music, vocal and instrumental; in dancing, without the aid of a master; and in the elements of natural sciences. In the use of the globes both are proficients. In addition to these, Miss Tuffin, who is daughter of the late Reverend Thomas Tuffin (Fellow of Corpus College, Cambridge), can instruct in the Syriac language, and the elements of Constitutional law. . . . She is eighteen years of age. . . . Both ladies are endowed with *every moral and religious virtue*. Their terms, of course, are such as their accomplishments merit.

Naturally enough, few parents, let alone their daughters, desired such prodigies of learning. What the governess whom Miss Pinkerton had previously recommended into a situation actually *did* teach, this governess being Becky Sharp, was very different.

> She did not pester their young brains with too much learning, but, on the contrary, let them have their own way in regard to educating themselves; for what instruction is more effectual than self-instruction? The eldest was rather fond of books, and as there was in the old library at Queen's Crawley a considerable provision of works of light literature of the last century, both in the French and English languages . . . she and Miss Rose thus read together many delightful . . . works, among which may be mentioned those of the learned Dr Smollet, of the ingenious Mr Henry Fielding, of the graceful and fantastic Monsieur Crébillon the younger, . . . and of the universal Monsieur de Voltaire. Once . . . Mr Crawley . . . was rather scandalised at finding his sister with a book of French plays; but as the governess remarked that it was for the purpose of acquiring the French idiom in conversation, he was fain to be content.

Not all families were so blind as to the upbringing of their girls, nor were all girls of the same stuff as Miss Rose Crawley. In the second half of the century the teaching may have been bad, but there was some comprehension in the girls' own minds of *how* bad it was. Miss Grant, one of the earliest pupils at St Andrew's School for Girls (as St Leonard's was called in 1877), writes:

> Hitherto I had been taught by a beloved but entirely unmathematical governess, who decreed that certain sums must be worked by certain rules, but was quite unable to explain why, and if my answer did not correspond with the answer in the key it was simply marked "Wrong" and we went on to another.

She joyfully contrasts with this method the excellent teaching of Miss Lumsden and Miss Dove. Miss Harrison expresses similar rapture at understanding at last, when she goes to Cheltenham, "why you turned the fractions upside down in division."

The difficulty of the inadequate governess had been

felt thirty years before by some of the more enlightened parents. Mr and Mrs Beale, though not pioneers in education as their daughter was to become, were thoughtful and intellectual people. They anticipated, for example, a fashion in sending their daughters to a school in Paris— rather disastrously, it turned out, for the school was broken up at the time of the Barricades. According to Dorothea Beale, they at least took some care about the person to whom they were to entrust their children's education. She says:

> My mother advertised, and hundreds of answers were sent. She began by eliminating all those in which bad spelling occurred. . . . next, the wording and composition were criticised, and lastly a few of the writers were interviewed and a selection was made. But, alas! an inspection of our exercise-books revealed so many uncorrected faults that a dismissal followed and another search resulted in the same way.

Many other examples of fact and fiction could be added, but one need not labour the point, that governesses were commonly bad. Yet it is equally true, and not only of the outstanding teachers both to-day and in the last century, that their pupils, both girls and boys, have sometimes gone through public schools and universities to a distinguished career relying largely on the good grounding in Latin that they received in the schoolroom from the governess.

As her capacities varied so did her treatment, though less with her own merit than with her employer's disposition. Miss Yonge, indeed, says, "Insolence to a governess is a stock complaint. In real life I never heard it from anyone by birth and breeding a lady," except for two instances which she proceeds to quote. In the same chapter of *Womankind*, however, she comments on the harm done by the "pathetic and ridiculous" figure of the governess in books. She might have added "in pictures," the illustration in *The Cowslip* being an example.

In her own books she has numerous descriptions of

governesses, many placed in responsible positions and having considerable authority. Miss Fosbrook, mentioned above, is in her employer's absence in sole charge of the household, including servants, and being only seven years older than her eldest pupil needs all her force of character and some rather unfair argument to exert discipline. She is lucky in what is shown as her first attempt. The boys had grown rowdy at tea, and were beginning to throw their remaining crusts at their sister's cup, when Miss Fosbrook, who had been joining in the general laughter, recovered herself and said gravely:

"This must not be, Sam; I shall send you away from the table if you do."

Sam wanted to see whether she would, and threw the crust.

"Sam," she said, very decidedly, though there was a quiver in her voice, as if she were frightened.

Sam looked up and did not move.

"Oh, Miss Fosbrook!" cried Susan; "we were all just as bad. Don't punish Sam!"

"It is time that Sam should show that he has the feelings of a manly boy," said Miss Fosbrook, looking full at him. "He knows that I must keep my word and that I have no strength to fight with him. Sam, go and finish your tea on the window-seat."

All the young population watched to see what he would do, and when he obeyed her Miss Fosbrook breathed freely and almost said, "Thank you, Sam," but collected herself sufficiently to make a few remarks on the impropriety of complaining of the food provided.

Miss Yonge gives advice on the governess's position and the disposal of her evenings when the family is at home. If the family is a large one or there is much coming and going of strangers she should be one of the circle; if it is small "she should perceive it to be as intrusive to come constantly among them as if she lived in another house." But she should not feel cut off from all that is bright and pleasant and "set aside from all that occupies young people of her own age."

Alas! only too few took this well-meaning and kindly, if slightly patronizing attitude. On the whole governesses were treated as a race apart. In the second decade of the century Becky Sharp was only brought into dinner at the rich aunt's special desire. And in the nineties the heroine of *The Man from Blankley's*, being a governess, is sent in with the 'paid guest' to avoid a dinner table of thirteen. So embarrassing might her situation become that a strong-minded young woman like Mrs Ewing's Miss Blomfield would take the bull by the horns and make a point of announcing her dependent position to strangers. "It is best to avoid any awkwardness," she was wont to say.

It is one of the most pleasing traits of Colonel Newcome's character that he behaves with delightful courtesy to Miss Quidgley, the governess. He "takes wine with her," with a profound bow, and she thinks his late Majesty must have bowed in just that way. This makes one of her few pleasures as "she sits alone in the schoolroom high up in that lone house before her dismal tea-tray and her little desk containing her mother's letters and her momentos of home."

Besides her social difficulties the governess had a very delicate situation to handle in regard to her pupils. It was not only that she might have difficulty in managing them, and often had not the authority to punish. But again and again it happened that she had to succeed to—or, in the eyes of children and servants, to usurp—the place of a dear nannie or old servant. One example of this situation is enough. Molly Gibson's Miss Eyre, already referred to, had trouble from the first with Betty, the nurse. Betty,

who was vehemently opposed to any division of her authority and influence . . . took up her position as censor of all Miss Eyre's sayings and doings, though she could not help respecting the patience and painstaking of the good lady. Molly early perceived the injustice of the nurse's attacks, avowedly in her own defence as an oppressed little personage, and began to respect Miss Eyre for her silent endurance of what gave her far more pain than Betty imagined.

Mr Gibson had been a friend in need to her family, so Miss Eyre restrained her complaints sooner than annoy him. And she had her reward in Molly's passionate defence on more than one occasion of "her silent, trembling governess" and in her charge's appreciation of "a very happy childhood."

"Countess Kate," on the other hand, did not behave well to Mrs Lacy, and preferred the unscrupulous French maid. And, indeed, it must have been dreary for the eleven-year-old girl to look up and discourse to nothing but the black *crêpe* veil which the widow lady always kept down. The worst struggle was over music lessons. "This was a grievous work, for the question was not *how* the learning should be managed, but whether the thing should be learnt at all." For, though she had "no more ear than an old pea-hen," Kate was told that it would be highly improper that she should not learn "the accomplishments of her station," and became "a grievous torment to poor Mrs Lacy and her patient—'One, two, three—now, my dear.'"

It is probable that the pupils were not always to blame; at least one governess of the last century used, when she had neuralgia, to throw things at her pupils. "I grew quite expert at dodging books," is a personal reminiscence. But, all things considered, is it to be wondered at that Harriet Martineau in an article on the industrial and social position of women speaks of the nervous attacks and "insanity" that was too often the fate of a governess, and deplores the fact that she was frequently cast off at sixty, broken-down and pensionless? No wonder either that Mrs Jameson writes, "I never in my life heard of a governess who was such by choice."

Charlotte Brontë's experiences, as we see them in her letters, were enough to embitter her for many years, and the outrageous conversation from *Jane Eyre*, exaggerated as it sounds, is only an echo of real and wounding words.

" You should hear Mamma on the chapter of governesses. Mary and I have had, I should think, a dozen at least in our day; half of them detestable and the rest ridiculous, and all incubi—were they not, Mamma?"

" My dearest, don't mention governesses; the word makes me nervous. I have suffered a martyrdom from their incompetency and caprice. I thank Heaven I have now done with them!"

Mrs Dent here bent over to the pious lady and whispered . . . a reminder that one of the anathematized race was present.

" *Tant pis!* " said her ladyship. " I hope it may do her good!" Then, in a lower tone, but still loud enough for me to hear, "I noticed her; I am a judge of physiognomy, and in hers I see all the faults of her class. . . ."

"I have just one word to say of the whole tribe," went on Miss Blanche Ingram; "they are a nuisance. Not that I ever suffered much from them; I took care to turn the tables. What tricks Theodore and I used to play on our Miss Wilsons, and Mrs Greys, and Madame Jouberts. Miss Wilson was a poor, sickly thing, lachrymose and low-spirited, not worth the trouble of vanquishing, in short; and Mrs Grey was coarse and insensible; no blow took effect on her. But poor Madame Joubert! I see her yet in her raging passions when we had driven her to extremities. . . .

Amy Eshton joined in. . . . "Louisa and I used to quiz our governess too; but she was such a good creature, she would bear anything; nothing put her out; we might do what we pleased—ransack her desk and her workbox and turn her drawers inside out; and she was so good-natured, she would give us anything we asked for."

"I suppose, now," said Miss Ingram, curling her lips sarcastically, "we shall have an abstract of the memoirs of all the governesses extant."

Even allowing for the natural tendency to disparage the authority of one's tutors and to exalt one's own misdeeds, the whole conversation sounds like a caricature, till we put it beside her letters:

The children are constantly with me. . . . As for correcting them, I quickly found out that was out of the question; they are to do as they like. A complaint to the mother only brings black looks on myself and unjust, partial excuses to screen the children. . . . I said in my last letter that Mrs Sidgwick did not know me. I now begin to find that she does not intend to know me; that she cares nothing about me except to contrive how the greatest possible quantity of labour may be got out of me; and to that end she overwhelms me with oceans of needlework, yards of cambric to hem, muslin nightcaps to make, and, above all things, dolls to dress. . . . I can see more clearly than I have ever done before that a private governess has no existence, is not considered as a living rational being, except as connected with the wearisome duties she has to fulfil.

And, a month later:

If you were near me, perhaps I might be tempted to tell you all . . . a private governess's trials and crosses in her first situation. As it is, I will only ask you to imagine the miseries of a reserved wretch like me, thrown at once into the midst of a large family at a time when the house was filled with company . . . people whose faces I had never seen before. In this state I had charge given me of a set of pampered, spoilt, turbulent children whom I was expected constantly to amuse as well as to instruct. I soon found that the constant demand on my stock of animal spirits reduced them to the lowest state of exhaustion; at times I felt and, I suppose, seemed—depressed. To my astonishment I was taken to task on the subject by Mrs — with a sternness of manner and a harshness of language scarcely credible; like a fool, I cried most bitterly. . . . I thought I had done my best—strained every nerve to please her; and to be treated in that way, merely because I was shy and sometimes melancholy, was too bad. . . . I have never had five minutes' conversation with her since I came, except while she was scolding me.

Even if the children were 'possible' there was all the snobbery of the parents' attitude to contend with. Mrs Gaskell, having given a small incident to show that the children "honoured her for not 'telling tales,'" goes on to quote:

One day, at the children's dinner, the small truant, in a little demonstrative gush, said, putting his hand in hers, "I love 'ou, Miss Brontë"; whereupon the mother exclaimed, before all the children, "Love the *governess*, my dear!"

THE GOVERNESS

In 1840 "a Lady" wrote to *The Young Ladies' Friend*:

> Nothing can be meaner than the false pride exhibited by some girls towards the ladies who give them lessons in music, drawing, and languages. Some have even been known to pass their instructress in the street without acknowledging the acquaintance.

It was no doubt a tradition, and of such long continuance as to make it possible for a delightful elderly lady of to-day to observe, "I never routed our governesses as my sister E. did; she was much cleverer and more high-spirited," and to end the conversation with "But, after all, one never likes one's governess."

But the governess's chief complaint was lack of time. Miss Weeton writes that she has

> little time for reading, little time for writing, less for music, and none at all for drawing. The principal care and direction of the house have devolved to me, and a part of the sewing.

Her employer, however (unlike Mrs Sidgwick), was only too much with her, for after her pupil's instruction came a walk, tea, and in the evening sewing or cards, which latter she considered a great waste of time. She also complains of incivility from the master of the house, but adds that "in the presence of guests Mr Pedder treats me with respect and even good humour."

Charlotte Brontë found, even in her second and more agreeable post:

> Mrs White expected a good deal of sewing from me. I cannot sew much during the day, on account of the children, who require the utmost attention. I am obliged therefore to devote the evening to this business.

We hear fewer complaints than we might of the salary —or lack of it. Charlotte Brontë writes in 1841:

> My salary is not really more than £16 per annum, though it is nominally £20, but the expense of washing will be deducted therefrom.

119

Miss Weeton, on the other hand, tells us (1809):

> He enquired what salary I should expect. I answered, thirty
> guineas.[1] He engaged me, and—I am going.

The comparison of dates shows that there is no steady
development in the influence and status of the governess
as there was later for the secondary-school teacher.
Everything fluctuated, and it is difficult to gauge what
was really demanded of the average governess in a middle-
class family and how she might be expected to respond
to these demands. It is interesting to note that by 1876
Miss Yonge was recommending that no professional
teacher under twenty-five who could not produce a
certificate from a university ought to be engaged for
girls over fourteen. (She excuses the elder generation,
but explains that the younger governesses ought to offer
proof of their capacity—thus showing how much had
already been achieved in the way of setting a standard by
those whose work is described in the next chapter.) Miss
Yonge further explains that it is the "truest economy"
to give a good salary, and suggests that two or three
families might unite to share the instruction, or an extra
scholar be brought in. She says that when schoolroom
life ends (at about fifteen) a girl should be "well grounded
in an English education; should know French almost as
well as her own language" (but Miss Yonge prefers that
she should not be taught by a foreigner). She should
have the elements of Latin grammar and be able, possibly,
to construe "an easy classic." German and Italian ought
to have been begun and brought to a state in which she
can keep them up by reading if no master be available.
To "go into algebra" is "a very beneficial study and full
of new interests, but impossible to some intellects"—
as later education authorities have found to their cost.
She should have a knowledge of English history and of
French history "as a key to that of other European

---

[1] Yet one of Miss Yonge's heroines, a striking young woman but
inexperienced, received £70 a year.

states" (Miss Yonge had written a text-book to help younger pupils in this). Finally,

> When the educators resign their charge the pupil should be turned out with all her faculties of mind and body in the best working order possible, with the groundwork laid and an intelligent power of attention capable of being used in whatever direction circumstances may lead.

That the work of the governess might be no less successful thirty years later is shown by Lady Wilson's tribute to her own governess, "Zellie" of *Dear Youth*.

> Measuring myself—a very average person with only average ability—at the age of eighteen with girls who have had all the advantages of a first-rate school, I submit that I had more general culture when I emerged from Zellie's schoolroom than they have at school-leaving age to-day. Not that Zellie was a person of remarkable attainments—quite the contrary. But I was for twelve years—and these the most impressionable ones— in contact with some one from whom I was learning subconsciously both in and out of lesson-time.
>
> She attempted to give me a sensitiveness to the lovely things in learning and literature, an awareness of their beauties, and a desire for them. . . . To transform the raw material of a child's mind into what will stand it in good stead in the future, to teach it to sit under the shade of the tree of knowledge, to direct a child's vision to the true and fair perspective of life and appreciate its true values, in other words "To plant the great Hereafter in the Now," is a fine task, and a very enviable one.

With such an ideal it is no wonder that Miss Yonge says:

> The governess is a lady with a profession; to teach and be with her pupils at such times as their mother cannot attend to them. . . . Fortunately there is much less nonsense now than formerly about losing caste; and if she cannot be a governess she can perhaps be a certificated schoolmistress, a nurse, or enter on some of the occupations that are becoming more and more open to educated women.

There is a modern ring about the last phrase.

121

CHAPTER V

THE LADYLIKE ATTEMPT

QUEEN'S COLLEGE in Harley Street, "the first college for women," sprang from the same root—the theory of equal opportunity for all—as the contemporary developments, the People's College at Sheffield and, in 1854, the Working Men's College in Great Ormond Street. But its immediate cause of existence was an immediate need, for, as so often in the story of women's education, the practical outstripped the theoretical. In this case the need was twofold. The chief problems connected with the bringing up of girls were: how to produce a supply of educated women to train the girls either at home or in schools, and, such women having been found, how to differentiate between these and the incompetent gentlewomen who had taken to teaching because it was in effect the only profession open to them. As the experience of Mrs Beale and others proved, it was almost impossible for ladies to know how much their governesses knew. The woman to whom an inexperienced parent entrusted her child might turn out to be a trained and cultured teacher or a girl who considered herself competent if armed with Mangnall and the *Child's Guide*; she might be a Charlotte Brontë or a Miss Perry.

This difficulty was also felt by the better class of governesses themselves, and in 1846 a registry of teachers was established by Mr Laing, Vicar of Holy Trinity, Kentish Town, the Honorary Secretary of the Governesses' Benevolent Institution. A scheme was also started for the granting of diplomas to the competent, and this led to a series of examinations for teachers, which disclosed such a woeful lack of knowledge on the part of those who were to be considered capable of instructing the young that it was evident some means must be found to instruct the teachers themselves. It is worth noticing that owing to the efforts of Kay-Shuttleworth a training college for elementary teachers had been established some time before any such training was considered necessary for the governess or teacher of the upper-class girl. Ruskin's plea quoted above ("Give your girls . . . noble teachers") was not the obvious statement of fact that it appears to us now.

> The Governesses' Benevolent Institution, beginning as it did with a provision for distress among governesses, also came to associate distress with incompetency, which it so often is, and saw the immediate necessity of providing better instruction for the governesses themselves. Classes were arranged for them to attend in the evenings, to which professors of King's College came, voluntarily, to instruct. These classes grew quickly, taking in other pupils as well, and out of this educational nucleus was formed that remarkable centre designated as Queen's College. . . . It was not till 1852 that it was incorporated as a separate identity.[1]

This new college, then, gave an opportunity both to the would-be teachers and to girls who were eager to continue their education beyond the point to which a governess or the desultory efforts of a busy parent could lead them. Courses could be taken in theology, English, Latin (Greek was added later), French, German, Italian, history (which was *par excellence* the subject of the college), mathematics, "Natural Philosophy," fine arts, music, and methods of teaching. Those who took a number of courses became 'compounders' at lower fees. At the end of such courses the students could present themselves for an examination, and a certificate might be granted. The recipient—for instance, Dorothea Beale— might be described by the examiner (Professor Maurice) as having "shown much intelligence and a very satis-factory acquaintance with those subjects" (English

[1] *G.B.I. Notes*, November 1937.

literature and grammar), or as "well qualified to teach the language [French] theoretically and by practice."

One remarkable thing about Queen's College was the fact of its great importance. For it was not, as has sometimes been implied, the first college *open* to women. Education of a considerably higher standard than that given there was available to those able to profit by it both at University College and at King's.

Yet for various causes the pioneer women were not going to University College, and rejoiced exceedingly at the foundation of this new educational centre. For one thing, the very standard of the London University colleges made then inaccessible to all but exceptionally placed or exceptionally gifted women. Queen's College really provided not much more than a good secondary education—and even this often proved too much for those who wished to join, so that a section soon had to be organized for the less advanced students.

But even more important were the non-academic arguments. The fact that University College was undenominational, and for that reason morally suspect, would rule it out in the eyes of Miss Beale, a clergyman's daughter, and many more. Moreover, to share lectures with the men students was too 'advanced'; it was not ladylike—and in this word lay the test for the pioneers of the new female education.

How strongly this idea underlies all the work of this period! We find it in Miss Beale's answer to the critics of Cheltenham Ladies' College, who were afraid of the effect that the publicity of examination might have on girls' "natural reserve and modesty." She replied that "unless girls can respond to a general testing of the work in a quiet, ladylike manner it does not speak well for the moral training of the school." Again, the highest compliment that can be paid even by the militant Miss Davies is that a certain girl is so ladylike; and the same Miss Davies, wishing to collect signatures for a memorandum, is careful to include the names of ladylike supporters. And when a few women are giving evidence before a Royal Commission,[1] on the inadequacy of female education, the Assistant Commissioner, Mr Fearon, writes: "We were all so much struck by their perfect womanliness. Why, there were tears in Miss Buss's eyes!"

The college was a practical venture; its very name shows the realism and common sense of its founders. They were fortunate in receiving this (together with the disposal of some funds which had been collected for the benefit of women's education) through the interest and support of Miss Murray, one of Queen Victoria's maids of honour. She succeeded in interesting the Queen sufficiently to allow the new college to be given a name that should testify to the approval of the highest lady of the land. This move was not due to snobbery, nor even solely to the realization that the cause of women's education would be immensely strengthened by a queen's support, but to the feeling that a movement which met with the approval of the sternest of women's critics might indeed be considered 'ladylike'; and certainly, hard as was the criticism it had to meet, this branch of the woman's movement did save itself a vast amount of misunderstanding and ridicule by the adoption of such a standard, though no one can fail to realize that it was the approval of their own consciences rather than of outside critics which the earliest students of Queen's College so earnestly desired.

The committee and lecturers of the new venture included persons well known and respected in their various capacities. Its first Principal was Frederick Denison Maurice, one of the leaders of the Christian Social movement, outstanding among a group who accepted a principle to-day widely acknowledged—that the profession of Christianity in a country must bear a close relation to the standards of that country's social life.

[1] See p. 157.

Another supporter, and later professor, was Charles Kingsley, who as "Parson Lot" had written scathing denouncements of social and political evils, and who in *Hypatia* was to draw the character and fate of one of the world's first woman lecturers, but who is most familiar as the author of *Westward Ho!*, *The Heroes*, and *The Water Babies*. There was Dean Trench, later Archbishop of Dublin, whose lectures on "Words" were to popularize the study of language, and who was to originate the suggestion of the Oxford Dictionary; while among the musical directors of the college were persons so well approved in their own time as John Hullah and Sterndale Bennett. Other and later well-known professors included Stopford Brooke and Canon Ainger, E. C. Marchant (of Greek), Sir Henry Craik, and Dean Stanley.

The students probably proved even more varied than had been expected. Not by any means all were governesses seeking to qualify themselves for immediate work. They included besides the two pioneer schoolmistresses, Miss Beale and Miss Buss, such women as Miss Adelaide Procter, Miss Jex-Blake, Miss Wardell, Miss Julia Wedgwood, and Jean Ingelow the poetess.

One of the first acts of the Committee had been to secure "the supervision of ladies of rank and talent (the Lady Visitors)," for naturally all lectures had to be attended by chaperons. Miss Beale later acknowledged her gratitude to those ladies who had made possible these early studies "by undertaking, of course gratuitously, the often burdensome duties of chaperoning." Among these gracious figures Lady Stanley of Alderley is conspicuous. Her long life (1807–95) almost covered the century, and her friends included men so far apart as Carlyle, F. D. Maurice, and Jowett. She was a woman of remarkable force of character and, at times, sharpness of tongue, which earned her the memory of "a terribly fierce old grandmother," while even a Girton scholar found the ordeal of being presented to her at a tea-party rather overwhelming. But she was a *grande dame* of the Victorians, and Miss Beale writes of the early days: "Stately and beautiful all her life, but especially then, she could not fail to win the admiration of the girls." Through her husband, the second Lord Stanley of Alderley, who held office at several times during the supremacy of the Whigs, she had much to do with politics (a sphere in which women had long been allowed, and, indeed, assumed, to have an indirect 'interest'), and she was known, in Palmerston's phrase, as "joint Whip with her husband of the Whig party." She strove to extend this interest to other women by her work for the Women's Liberal Unionist Association. During her long widowhood (her husband died in 1869) she did much for the education of girls and women. Her signature was on the appeal (drawn up by Miss Davies) to the Taunton Commission that female schools as well as boys' schools of the middle class might be included in the investigation, on the grounds that "so long as they [the Commission] thrust aside female education it will not come before the nation as worthy of serious thought." She was one of those who supported Mrs Grey at the Albert Hall meeting at which the founding of the Girls' Public Day School Trust was put forward, and she is remembered along with Maria Georgina Grey, Emily Shirreff, and Mary Gurney in the Trust's bidding prayer. She took an active part in founding Girton College and visited it frequently, joining the College and Building Committees—though she refused in 1872 to become Mistress of the college—and she was a liberal benefactress. Her personality and ability were of tremendous value to the women's cause, as well as— later on—her age, rank, and experience. Miss Davies longed for "a few more old ladies like Lady Stanley of Alderley, who has six grown-up daughters and a multitude of grandchildren."

Of the company of earnest and vital young women who took advantage of the opportunities for learning and training at the new college several in their different spheres were notable pioneers, but they are overshadowed by Miss Buss and Miss Beale—the latter especially. Perhaps no single woman, except Florence Nightingale, has so much altered the outlook of a whole profession, and, through it, of countless lives, as the Principal of Cheltenham Ladies' College. It is true that Miss Beale was fortunate in appearing just at the moment when the education of girls was becoming a serious problem and when possibilities for it were opening out, but the genius of any character often seems to consist in being *en rapport* with the spirit of the age—just sufficiently in advance to lead, without snapping the cords which enable public opinion to follow.

Dorothea Beale was fortunate also in possessing educationally distinguished relatives [1] (Mrs Cornwallis was her aunt, and Mrs Sarah Trimmer a distant connexion) and a wise and sympathetic father, but otherwise hers was the lot of many upper-class girls of the period. She had a succession of governesses, a private school, and a brief sojourn at a *pension* in Paris. She was not even instructed by her father, but read independently, and supervised the lessons of her younger brothers. She refers

[1] Miss Beale's connexions:

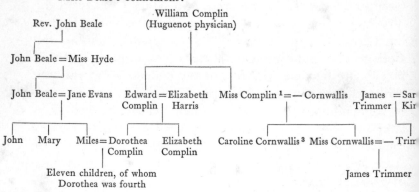

[1] Wrote devotional books. [2] Wrote several books for the young.
[3] Wrote *Small Books on Great Subjects* and articles for *The Westminster Review*.

DOROTHEA BEALE
From the painting by J. J. Shannon.
Photo Martyn Bros., Cheltenham
By kind permission of the Principal, Cheltenham College

later to the "miserable teaching" of her first school, at which she remained only to the age of thirteen, where they were instructed in arithmetic and languages without understanding principles (the same process to which Ethel May so strongly objected), and were even given lists of prepositions for learning by heart "to save them the trouble of thinking." She long retained a horror of the school-girl's "French conversation." Perhaps her greatest loss, though she did not recognize it, was that she never learnt to play, and therefore never really understood the desire of other girls for free movement and organized games. Yet Miss Beale was too wise and sympathetic to be cramped by this lack of comprehension, and in due course Cheltenham gave opportunities for the games which were to become such an important part of public-school life. Miss Beale had a dislike of uniform, especially of the then fashionable 'boater' hat. "Why wear those hard things instead of pretty ones?" she once asked a Cheltenham mistress. Nevertheless she could yield gracefully, acknowledging, "They do look better in uniform." Similarly she had a prejudice against having bicycles brought to the college, yet when it became obvious that the bicycle had come to stay she saw to it that bicycle-sheds were made out of the old narrow 'labs.'

These are illustrations of the remarkable judgment and sympathy with coming movements which stand out among Miss Beale's characteristics. Nevertheless, to balance this tact and delicate feeling she possessed a remarkable eagerness and tenacity of purpose, which was called into play particularly during her early life. Miss Beale, after attaining to the standard of proficiency required in mathematics at Queen's College, became "Lady Tutor" in that subject. The rest of her certificates were gained while she held this post. But though she was successful and happy there, she resigned in 1856, because she had differences with the authorities on two points of principle.

One was her view that the standard of the college should not be lowered to admit those who through lack of previous training were as yet unable to profit by the education there; for these, she maintained, the separate provision made in the "College School" should be sufficient; otherwise the better students would suffer. The second difference was concerned with the limited authority allowed to the women tutors. It was perhaps at this time that she first formulated (in a letter to the Principal of the college, Dr Plumptre) the idea that girls can be thoroughly educated only by women: "though some classes may be profitably undertaken by men, the education of girls as a whole must be in the hands of their own sex." The same view she later reiterated before the Schools Inquiry Commission.

Miss Beale's next venture was even more unsuccessful. She became head teacher (but not headmistress) of the Casterton school for the daughters of clergy—the original, it is generally admitted, of Jane Eyre's "Lowood." Since the days of Charlotte Brontë there had been considerable reforms, and the school had been moved, but the principles of rigid discipline and harsh doctrine remained, and Miss Beale found it impossible to work in such an atmosphere, while she was powerless to change it. She was unable, since she was obliged to give lessons in a great number of subjects, to reach the standard of teaching which she set herself; she was depressed by the ugliness of conditions—even of the uniform—and, above all, she was saddened by the low moral tone which resulted from the system under which the girls lived. Miss Beale protested to the Council, endeavouring to introduce some kind of incentive into the girls' lives, some "distinctions and responsibilities," but the Council responded to her criticism by raising the question of her own religious doctrines. Her wise and far-seeing parent had written that if her authority was questioned, or if she found herself unable to work on the lines laid down by the Council, she should send in her resignation; this she was, however, only contemplating, when the Council took action. It may be a comfort to lesser and unsuccessful teachers to remember occasionally that from this job Miss Beale was definitely sacked.

With remarkable strength of mind Miss Beale determined to wait for a position in which she could do the work for which she really felt herself destined. She occupied her time by writing a history text-book, but refused to be drawn into the headship of a penitentiary, as she was conscious of a vocation for teaching—a consciousness which had perhaps been roused by F. D. Maurice's lecture on the opening of Queen's College.

> The vocation of a teacher is an awful one: you cannot do her real good, she will do others unspeakable harm if she is not aware of its awfulness. . . . You may confirm her in the notion that the task of training an immortal spirit may be just as lawfully undertaken in a case of emergency as that of selling ribands. . . . Your business is to make her feel the greatness of her work and yet to show her that it can be honestly performed.

Miss Beale was one of those to whom such a call had come, and she was not to be dissuaded from following it. In 1858 she applied for and was appointed to the headship of the Cheltenham College for Young Ladies. This school had been founded five years before, but was in a somewhat precarious financial state. Neither was the education of a very satisfactory quality. In her struggles for the first two or three years Miss Beale felt the difficulties, as she later put it, of the "want of money and want of ideals."

The first question that arose, however, was one which, Miss Beale being what she was, would have to be settled early, even if it had not been forced upon her. Some query as to her doctrinal views was suggested to the Council by a member of the Casterton Committee. As Miss Beale was to make Scripture-teaching the centre of all her educational work, her position in this matter had to be made clear at once, for in divinity instruction she "could not resort to the least untruthfulness." Her views on these questions having been approved, or at least not disallowed, there was no further trouble of this kind during her rule at the college.

The financial position was greatly improved by the wise reorganization made in the curriculum by Mr Houghton Brancker, the treasurer, who lowered the fees, but put music and drawing on the list of extras. Miss Beale must have appreciated this change. She was inclined to disapprove of the large amount of time devoted to accomplishments—time which, she knew from her own and her contemporaries' experience, was often misused, either because the girl had no taste for them or because of bad methods of teaching. It was not that she wished to ignore 'the arts,' still less that she desired, in the common catchword of the college's critics, to turn girls into boys, but it was her reaction from the old ideals of education by accomplishments only. The protest that girls have not their own living to earn she met with the conviction that many a girl, if she could become independent by her own efforts, might be saved from the temptation to make a mercenary marriage merely for the sake of comfort and security.

The work for these first few years was very hard, and required all the devotion of Dorothea Beale and the others teaching under her. We hear, for example, of the Principal and Vice-Principal's giving up their weekly holiday to chaperon the lessons that were taken by masters. Another difficulty was the distribution of the time-table into morning and afternoon lessons; some parents objected to sending their maids twice a day to bring and fetch the girls. When, however, Miss Beale decided that a longer morning and no regular afternoon lessons would benefit the girls' mental and physical powers there was at once a protest that the teachers were lazy—"demanding a half-holiday every day."

The development of the college belongs to another chapter; it is enough here to quote the ideals of Miss Beale as seen by one who learnt under and worked with her for a period of nearly forty years.

> She set herself to do away with that corruption of the ideal by which girls were taught to use their fingers only, while their mental powers were left untrained and their characters undeveloped, so that, being housekeepers rather than true help-mates, they failed in the very work for which they were supposed to be prepared. The next task was to convince an easy-going generation that, desirable as marriage might be, it was not possible for all women, and that it was becoming increasingly necessary for girls to be so trained that they might themselves support with dignity if unmarried. . . . Undue haste would have defeated its own end, and it was still necessary either to allow the immense number of extras desired by the conservative parent or to see the child sent to a more 'complaisant' school.[1]

(As to the last remark, we find it was not uncommon for a parent to wish a girl to learn eight or nine extras such as the following: piano, solo singing, violin or other instrument, painting, drawing, china-painting, woodwork, crewel-work, embroidery.)

Miss Beale was not without sympathizers, though it is interesting to contrast her aims with those of one who became a friend of hers and of the college, and who must have influenced her considerably. One can compare as well as contrast, however, for though Miss Beale's aims sound to us the more modern, yet in his own way John Ruskin was a great pioneer of women's education, and his lecture *Of Queen's Gardens*[2] shows how far Victorian England was progressing from the days of Jane Austen and Miss Pinkerton.

> All such knowledge should be given her as may enable her to understand, and even to aid, the work of men; and yet it should be given, not as knowledge—not as if it were, or could be for her an object to know; but only to feel and to judge. It is of

---

[1] F. C. Steadman, *In the Days of Miss Beale.*
[2] *Sesame and Lilies.*

no moment, as a matter of pride or perfectness in herself, whether she knows many languages or one; but it is of the utmost, that she should be able to show kindness to a stranger, and to understand the sweetness of a stranger's tongue. It is of no moment to her own worth or dignity that she should be acquainted with this science or that; but it is of the highest that she should understand the meaning, the inevitableness, and the loveliness of natural laws, and follow at least some one path of scientific attainment as far as to the threshold of that bitter Valley of Humiliation, into which only the wisest and bravest of men can descend. . . . It is of little consequence how many positions of cities she knows or how many dates of events, or how many names of celebrated persons—it is not the object of education to turn a woman into a dictionary; but it is deeply necessary that she should be taught to enter with her whole personality into the history she reads; to picture the passages of it vitally in her own bright imagination. . . . But chiefly of all, she is to be taught to extend the limits of her sympathy with respect to that history which is being for ever determined . . . to the contemporary calamity which, were it but rightly mourned by her, would recur no more hereafter. She is to exercise herself in imagining what would be the effects upon her mind and conduct, if she were daily brought into the presence of the suffering which is not the less real because shut from her sight. . . .

I believe that a girl's education should be nearly, in its course and material of study, the same as a boy's, but quite differently directed. A woman, in any rank of life, ought to know whatever her husband is likely to know, but to know it in a different way. His command of it should be foundational and progressive, hers general and accomplished for daily and helpful use. . . . Speaking broadly, a man ought to know any language or science he learns, thoroughly, while a woman ought to know the same language, or science, only so far as may enable her to sympathize in her husband's pleasures, and in those of his best friends.

Yet, observe, with exquisite accuracy as far as she reaches. There is a wide difference between elementary knowledge and superficial knowledge—between a firm beginning and a feeble smattering. A woman may always help her husband by what she knows, however little; by what she half-knows or mis-knows, she will only teaze him. And indeed, if there were to be any difference between a girl's education and a boy's, I should say that of the two the girl should be earlier led, as her intellect ripens faster, into deep and serious subjects.

Ruskin's ideals for the education of girls, as one sees, are limited. The most obvious limitation comes from his belief that woman only finds her full development in one capacity—as a wife. His schooling makes no provision for the unmarried woman—she does not enter into his calculations socially or economically. Even if the great number of spinsters and widows (whom Josephine Butler put as equal to one-third of the married women over twenty) had been mentioned he might with some justification have said that principles were to be laid down for educating those who were to fulfil the destiny of the majority—and that the others would not be worse off than they already were under an upbringing such as he devised, but rather better. Nevertheless, the idea remains that a woman is never to pursue her own bent beyond the point where she may be a support to her husband, and that she should turn aside to follow *his* tastes and *his* interests rather than strike out for herself. So far as its aims are concerned mid-century education has gone some way towards the development of woman's powers, but by no means all the way.

Yet in the account of *how* a girl should be brought up Ruskin has made a magnificent advance. He has recognized those defects of girls' schools which are so markedly brought out in the Report of the Schools Inquiry Commission—restraint and superficiality. In *Sesame and Lilies* he pleads first of all for a girl's physical development, quoting Wordsworth's "Lucy," the child of nature. If Ruskin had been taken at his word, what a revolution that would have meant, for instance, in dress! Where in a bustle or a crinoline were a girl's "steps of virgin liberty"? How could "vital feelings of delight" swell her maiden bosom, when that bosom was firmly enclosed in calico and whalebone? And, to take one of the three great helps in education (literature, nature, and art), how much useless copying of the drawing-master's watercolour sketches would have been saved if parents had followed his advice: "Keep the finest models before her . . . the truest, simplest, usefullest." Moreover, the whole basis of the girls'-public-school system is anticipated in his words:

> Give them the same advantages that you give their brothers— appeal to the same grand instincts of virtue in them; teach *them* also that courage and truth are the pillars of their being; do you think that they would not answer that appeal, brave and true as they are even now, when you know that there is hardly a girls' school in this Christian kingdom where the children's courage or sincerity would be thought of half so much importance as their way of coming in at a door.

Besides, in his exhortation that women should go out of their little rose-walled gardens into the wilderness of poverty, desolation, and war Ruskin is opening the door to the whole field of social service. And, though no one may have pressed the argument to its natural conclusion, if women have a duty to the State, as Ruskin claims, this duty belongs not only to the married, but to all who enjoy the Queenship, as he would put it, of Education. The great thing was by careful and enlightened education to make the most of a girl's faculties of body, mind, and spirit, and this was the work attempted in the new schools and by the women to whom the second half of the nineteenth century was bringing new inspiration, new ideals, and a new hope.

Since the word 'ladylike' summed up so much that was desirable and even necessary in the education for this long period, a study of the quality involved, and its opposite, calls for some attention. There does not appear to be any positive adjective to denote those who slightly offended against the canons of taste or propriety: 'vulgar' would be going too far in condemnation; 'advanced' was too vague. The offenders were 'unladylike' or 'not quite nice.' Perhaps this lack of a word was an attempt to ignore what one did not like. In modern speech we have taken the opposite course. All too frequently words such as 'Victorian' or 'conventional,' 'stuffy' or 'repressed' (according to the range of our vocabulary), are used, and no trouble is taken to find out wherein the Victorianism, conventionality, stuffiness, or repression consists.

In analysing what we may call 'the proprieties' we can divide them into taboos of body, of speech, of action, and, more indefinitely, of attitude. If one needs to assign a cause to the first, or physical, convention it may perhaps be attributed, in so far as it was peculiarly exaggerated in this century, to the possessiveness of the Victorian male— not necessarily husband, for repression is found as surely in Mr Barrett of Wimpole Street as in Soames of *The Forsyte Saga*. Not that the average female seems to have shown any resentment towards it—on the contrary, it is *Mrs* Grundy whose dictum becomes the criterion of what is 'nice.' Ideas inculcated at an early age are most tenacious, and the convention of correct attire, designed to conceal both form and surface, was implanted from the schoolroom, this concealment being definitely connected with the male sex. The incident of the "muslin bodies" in Mrs Ewing's *Six to Sixteen* illustrates the attitude of the mid-century.

"Our toilettes," says the autobiographical heroine, "were of the simplest," and she explains that in "dressing for tea" they wore muslin Garibaldis for coolness in the summer, and their second-best skirts. One evening they are told, "You mustn't put on your muslin bodies to-night. The arithmetic master is coming after tea." Her friend looks up "with a puckered brow and general bewilderment," and asks, "What has the arithmetic to do with our dresses?" "Have you so little of delicacy as to ask, mademoiselle?" is the answer, given in mimicry of "Madame," the headmistress. "Should the young ladies of this establishment expose their shoulders in the transparency of muslin to a professor?"

The convention about shoulders seems to have applied —at any rate by the end of the century—to girls and unmarried women only. Certainly some of the dresses handed down from one's grandmother are low-cut enough to embarrass even a modern young woman accustomed to an entirely backless frock. "It really made me blush to wear it for fancy dress," said one such; "there wasn't any of my top you couldn't see."

The hiding of the form was an even more important convention, adherence to which led to curious results. Helen Faucit, the actress, tells us of the difficulty she had over one of the disguises into which Shakespeare so inconveniently forces his heroines. (Be it noted, incidentally, that of all *his* women there is only one—Jessica, and she a minx—who makes the slightest demur at taking man's garb, if we disregard Julia's very natural resentment at being told that she must cut her hair.) One feels, indeed, that for Miss Faucit the trouble must have been continually arising, but it is in her letter on Imogen that she tells us of her embarrassment. For her page's dress she had ordered (in those days before "Costumes by Motley") "a tunic that descended to the ankles," and was somewhat distressed at finding, when she arrived for rehearsal, that Macready had taken the liberty of having it shortened.

> Although he could understand the reasons which had weighed with me in ordering the dress to be made as I had, he was sure I would forgive him when he explained that . . . all who did not know the play would not discover that it was a disguise, but would suppose Imogen to be still in woman's attire.[1]

(One has only to look at the illustrations of some editions of Shakespeare at this period to realize that this was more than likely!) So Miss Faucit appeared in the abbreviated tunic, but as a compromise was allowed to swathe herself in the cloak of her "franklin's riding-habit."

Illustrations might be multiplied—even as the garments of the Victorian era were multiplied. Lady Acland's *Good-bye for the Present* has a list of the under-

[1] *On Some of Shakespeare's Female Characters.*

clothes normally worn by a little girl of the period, while
in a modern 'period' play depicting an evening chat
between two young women the whole history of the
family is recounted between the taking off of the over-
skirt (and bustle) and the point at which the female
figure begins to be shown. Lady Acland explains:

> We must not assume that the only object of the prevailing
> wealth of personal upholstery was to keep the body warm. . . .
> I remember inquiring of a just grown-up cousin if ladies' skirts
> really had to have such yards and yards of stuff in them. She
> answered with a prim repressiveness that . . . "any nice girl
> is very glad they do, because if they didn't—just think, people
> would see one's shape showing."

It is only fair to add that I personally remember
precisely the same half-dozen words as those of the
cousin's last sentence used as lately as 1925—that year
of cylindrical dresses, so uncomfortable for any girl with
a natural bust. The speaker, an Oxford woman undergraduate, believed herself to be entirely emancipated from
convention, but she considered a tightly braced bodice
as necessary as any Victorian lady did her stays. So
powerful and so subtle are the influences of fashion!

A discussion on propriety of speech would be connected less with Victorian ideals in education than with
a study of language development as a whole. The
practice of calling a spade 'an agricultural implement'
was not confined to women, though perhaps the assump-
tion that they did not—and should not—know what a
spade was like strengthened the convention that certain
words were not suitable for women's lips. There was also
an army of words that, without being actually taboo, were
considered slightly unladylike, and for which synonyms
should be found; such were 'sweat' and 'belly.'

A rather curious convention was attached to the use of
Christian names. To those of us who have grown up in
the age of *Punch's* saying, "You have to know a man so
frightfully well before you get his surname," it comes as

a surprise to remember that wives of two generations back would refer to their husbands as "Mr So-and-so" before quite near relatives. And the use of a girl's Christian name, especially by men, was confined by the strongest code. One of Miss Yonge's heroes is inexpressibly shocked at the misuse, not merely of his beloved's name, but its diminutive. Lucilla and her cousin Horatia are young women whose conduct borders on impropriety, and Robert's feelings may be imagined when he heard "Cilly Sandon and Rache Charteris" referred to "by those names" at her brother's club!

Similarly the stress of the speech code lay in condemnation of free expression between men and women—or even girls and boys. In the following experience of Miss Jane Harrison it is rather difficult to see whether the objection is to (a) the words themselves, (b) the sex of the correspondent, or (c) the use of the postcard—this form of communication having only lately been invented and being still considered rather fast. Jane Harrison was working at Cheltenham for the Matriculation exam—just open to women—and was summoned one day to the headmistress's throne. Miss Beale had before her a postcard written in a schoolboy's scrawl and signed with his name. It was from a young friend who had been helping Jane in her work during the holidays, and was to wish her luck in the ordeal. The unfortunate recipient was greeted with, "This must go to your parents," and a long harangue ending, "You are too young and I hope too innocent to realize the gross vulgarity of such a communication or the terrible results to which it might lead." The offending words were, "P.S. Give my love to the examiners."

Such being the freedom of communication between the sexes at the educational stage, one may inquire how far the chaperonage which is such a feature of this period was a mere matter of convention and how far it was justifiable. The most unexpected reasons are sometimes given! For instance, one can understand well enough the propriety of having a duenna present at the solo lessons given by the music-master or drawing-master, infuriating as this must have been to the teacher (as distinct from the man). Such lessons if unchaperoned might well be, for girls in some circumstances, the only *tête-à-tête* conversations with a male being outside their own family circle, and we may assume that occasionally an elopement did take place, though not nearly as often as fiction would lead us to suppose. But what was the point of having a chaperon for a class taken by a lecturer or a singing-master? "Well, my dear, suppose some one had fainted?" was the answer given me, this possibility being due to the tight stays already mentioned. One would have thought that another girl could have rendered the necessary assistance, but apparently first-aid was not taught in the Victorian schoolroom. Another possibility was that a girl on being sharply criticized might burst into tears, and the chaperon had to be at hand with the smelling-salts. Anyway, such chaperonage was continued, at Cheltenham, for instance, till very late in the century, and was applied also to women 'students' attending lectures given to men undergraduates.

Of course, those who held by the conventions could often, when these were defied, turn round and say, "I told you so." The education of women at the universities was waylaid by all kinds of social pitfalls—rather naturally in a town which could be described in the fifties by Mrs Butler as "a society of celibates with little or no leaven of family life . . . and not much freedom of intercourse between the academic portion of the community and others." (It was not so much the coming of the woman undergraduate, however, as the lifting of the ban against married Fellows that was responsible for "North Oxford.") In 1891 a woman graduate engaged on a difficult piece of work was gently told that while she lived in lodgings the professor by whom she was being directed could not come to coach her; their classes, however, could go on if she was in a married friend's house. (By this time the presence of the friend herself was not necessary—the four walls were evidently considered to do duty.) But Mrs Grundy might have considered herself justified by results, as the young woman did marry her tutor—and, if this was the first union of the kind, it was certainly not the last.

Apart from the attitude and behaviour towards 'those of the opposite sex,' there were other ways of offending against the proprieties—the chief being to make oneself in any way conspicuous by doing that which other women did not do. We cannot sufficiently realize how much women like Florence Nightingale, Josephine Butler, and Mrs Grey, to name a few only, must have felt the pressure of social convention, not only in *doing* their work but in having to appear before the public while doing it. Elizabeth Fry was more fortunate, as it was generally admitted among the Society of Friends that the Word of God might come through female lips, so she had some experience in speaking, but others were told, and often enough by their own sex, that "women have no business on platforms." Such was the opinion of Mrs S. C. Hall. What the ordeal of addressing the public, of appearing before Royal Commissions, of having her name in the papers meant to an ordinary 'nice' woman—this can only be gathered in our days from a perusal of their letters or journals, and by a strong exercise of the imagination. Here is one example—in a letter from Mrs Butler to her husband:

> It is over. It was even a severer ordeal than I expected. . . . To compare a very small person with a great one, I felt rather like Paul before Nero, very weak and lonely.

Miss Buss too was lonely. She writes to a young woman supporter:

> How brave and earnest you are! It is such a comfort to me. You can have no idea of what work and worry I have to face, and almost single-handed too.

Mrs Grey was one of the early women candidates for the London School Board. She said, at a meeting in Chelsea (November 1870), how much she wanted encouragement.

> I feel that I stand here in such a very new position—one that may seem a very bold one, as a woman addressing a great public meeting; but it seems to me that it is not the thing itself but the manner and spirit of doing it which makes it womanly or the reverse. . . . I hope it is possible to do what I am now doing in such a way as to make it perfectly womanly.

A fortnight later she likes public speaking no better.

> The magnitude of the task I have taken grows upon me. It must seem a very daring thing for a woman to come forward and compete for your suffrages.

And when Mr Grove, who is supporting her, says, "She has entered upon an arduous task, for which she will get nothing (except perhaps abuse), from the sole feeling of duty," she stresses the point by saying, "I lose the privacy which is most precious to a woman."

Even, to take a smaller occasion, the early women candidates for examinations had a great deal more to contend with than the mere papers. It was not lack of knowledge in Greek and Latin which made Jane Harrison so "senseless with nervousness" when she entered the university buildings for the Matriculation examination that she forgot her own name. (But their male contemporaries understood the difficulty. How charming is the Registrar's remark on this occasion: "It is of no consequence; later on, perhaps . . .") Those who took the Cambridge Locals—*i.e.*, examinations set by Cambridge University and held at Local centres—took them under conditions less trying to their modesty. Even so stern a critic as Miss Yonge positively advised these as an incentive to study:

> As these are conducted in writing and are not competitive, they do not seem to me to involve anything unfeminine or undesirable.

Such incidents and examples touch merely the fringe of the great evil that overshadowed Victorian womanhood. Taboos of body, speech, and action are only reactions to the great conspiracy of silence, the distorted sense of values, and the confusion that made innocence synonymous only with ignorance. The ideal type of woman, as we see her in books and hear of her in letters and comments, was a repressed personality, in that she was fragile in body (if the manhood of Victorian England was less coarse and less virile than that of the previous reigns the woman had to be refined away almost to nothing) and 'good' in mind. The chief ingredient of 'goodness' was innocence; innocence, as before remarked, meant ignorance; ignorance implied silence of all 'unpleasant' subjects, particularly that which the Bible most distinctly connected with the Fall—namely, sex.

> A pure woman, it was reiterated, should be absolutely ignorant of a certain class of evils in the world, albeit those evils bore with murderous cruelty on other women. . . . Silence was thought to be the great duty of all on such subjects.

Josephine Butler, whose words these are, was not the only woman to judge men's standards and—desperately afraid of her own temerity—to find them wanting.

CHAPTER VI

THE ASSAULT ON THE UNIVERSITIES

It is proposed immediately after Easter to open a college in London for the education of females. The word 'college' in this connexion has to English ears a novel and an ambitious sound. I wish we could have found a simpler which would have described our object as well. . . . It is commonly associated, I think—in England at least—with the notion of a body which is intended first to form the teachers of the land, but which on that very account is suitable for all who seek a general, not a merely professional, culture. It is less vague and high-sounding than the words 'institution' and 'establishment'; for our purpose it is more convenient than the honest monosyllable 'school,' because that would be likely to suggest the notion that we undertake a superintendence which we rejoice to think will be in better hands. The teaching of a college must be in classes; the different studies must be related to each other; but the pupils of it *may* obtain all that is most precious in their experience and discipline, all their highest wisdom, at home. There are a great many parents . . . [who] are not insensible that there are disadvantages in solitary, even in merely family instruction, and in the disjointed feeling which is left on the mind, by a succession of masters who have no mutual understanding and no common object. Without having set before themselves any sublime ideal of female education . . . such persons nevertheless ask again and again why there are no colleges for one sex as well as the other.

THUS, with the wisdom of the serpent, spoke Frederick Denison Maurice on the objects and aims of Queen's College, the first college for women.

In this branch of education London led the way, for Queen's College and Bedford College, which shortly followed it, were for a long time alone of their kind. It is true, as mentioned before, that from 1828 there had been lectures and courses occasionally attended by women at

University College; later there was a course here in animal physiology, for ladies only, followed by others. In the fifties, too, the Mechanics' Institute, now Birkbeck College, opened two of its courses to women. But at University College—as later at the older universities—they were the classes of the professors, not of the college, merely held in the lecture-rooms for the sake of convenience. Indeed, the ladies attending met and dispersed at the *half*-hours, to avoid any possible contact with the men. In 1873 examinations and certificates were arranged for the women's classes, but the lectures were still held separately. This naturally meant considerable duplication, till some stout-hearted professor refused to give his course a second time over, and lectured once for all to a mixed audience. Gradually this became the rule rather than the exception, and by 1878 the women, who numbered 309 (approximately half the number of men), were given full admittance to the college, and in the same year to the London degree.

Though out of place, it is worth noting that a similar development occurred in Cambridge at about the same time (1872). Mr Jebb was to give to the women, by then established at Girton and Newnham, a course of lectures on Macedonian history. This would have been in a room hired by the Lectures Association Committee. Some undergraduates of Christ's College, seeing the announcement of these lectures, asked leave to attend this course. The Master after deliberation proposed that Mr Jebb should lecture in the Hall of Christ's, and that the women should attend his lectures there. Soon after more than half the professors gave formal leave for women students to attend. The incident showed that if the women got hold of a good thing the men had no hesitation about wishing to share it—just as when the Cambridge Higher Local examinations were instituted, originally for women, they were very soon adopted by men and boys as well.

To return to London—the founding of Queen's College was an event of moment. Six months later the work of Mrs Reid and Miss Bostock—the latter a friend and associate of Emily Davies—led to the foundation of Bedford College. This started as a set of classes in Mrs Reid's house in Bedford Square, and supplied education of much the same standard as its Harley Street companion. There was a difference, however, in the management. Queen's College was run by a men's committee, and had a man as Principal—the women concerned, though undoubtedly influential in the organization, were officially only lady visitors. Bedford College had from the start a mixed board, and the headship of the institution might be held by any visitor, man or woman. The Council included Miss Davies and Lady Goldsmid (later much concerned in the founding of Girton), Mrs Wedgwood, and Miss Anna Swanwick, who afterwards became the President. Among the men connected with the college as members of Council, professors, or visitors were Erasmus Darwin, Mark Pattison, F. W. Newman, and R. Holt Hutton, the critic.

Yet the London colleges could not in fact approach the "gorgeous visions" which had been raised in the mind of at least one scholar by the Poet-Laureate-to-be. An early reminiscence of Miss Wedgwood's confesses to a vague disappointment that Queen's College was not more like that associated with *The Princess*. Tennyson's poem has met with a vast amount of ridicule and criticism, chiefly (but not entirely) from those who know little of it except the lyrics and the line about "girl-graduates"— which, as a few of them point out, presumably means undergraduates. It is true that W. S. Gilbert studied it closely enough to write the skit *Princess Ida*, from which a great many people get their knowledge of the story. It is true also that Julia Wedgwood, writing at the jubilee of Queen's College, thought "its chief interest lay in its picture of a contemporary state of mind which apart from such testimony would be almost incredible." But when we look at the poem, even from this latter point of view, we need to remember the context. The remarkable thing is that the idea is in itself a new one, *not* an attack on, or support of, something already established. *The Princess* was written more than twenty years before the existence of Hitchin College, the original of Girton, and thirty years before the foundation of the earliest Oxford women's colleges. It preceded by a couple of years even "the first college for women."

The founders of Queen's College seem to have considered Tennyson's fantastic story as helpful rather than otherwise to their cause. They had read the poem with care. They had, indeed, according to the preface of their *Jubilee Book*, talked over their plan of establishing this college with the poet—the founders themselves being such recognized authorities on education as Kingsley, Hullah, Mrs Marcet, and Mrs S. C. Hall. And in the Principal's lecture, quoted above, reference is made to "the deep wisdom which the author of *The Princess* has concealed under a veil of exquisite grace and lightness." Tennyson is in sympathy with the most progressive minds of his time on this matter of female education. It is as uncalled for to make fun of his conception as it is to believe that he was making fun of theirs.

In spite of this Miss Wedgwood's main criticism may have been justified. But whose state of mind is the "incredible" one? Granted that the Prologue is wholly of its period, "Sir Walter Vivian," encouraging "the village" to make themselves merry in his grounds on the equivalent of a Bank Holiday, while "the patient leaders of their Institute" explain to them all the newest tricks of science, is a magnificent study of the liberally-minded squire; the maiden Aunt, who flushed because she thought they were laughing at her heroic ideas, belongs, no less than the pettish, "rosebud" Lilia, who wants to found the college, to the past of a hundred years ago. But in the poem itself there is not one "state of mind," but many. It is true we find the familiar

> Man for the field and woman for the hearth:
> Man for the sword and for the needle she:
> Man with the head and woman with the heart:
> Man to command and woman to obey;
> All else confusion.

But this (which continues with reference to "the grey mare" and "a lusty brace of twins") is the speech of the rough, dictatorial monarch, who obviously stands as a caricature of conservatism and suppression. And it is an attitude which, to say the least, is not incredible in any dictator.[1] Here it is as much 'in character' as the boisterous answer of Prince Arac, Ida's brother:

> There's a downright honest meaning in her;
> She flies too high, she flies too high! and yet
> She ask'd but space and fairplay for her scheme;
> She prest and prest it on me—I myself,
> What know I of these things? but, life and soul!
> I thought her half-right talking of her wrongs.

The "lecturer," Lady Psyche, talks with the same tongue as her Head, though, like her royal mistress, she is least attractive when she "fulmined out her scorn" of the wrongs laid by men on women. But she is not being held up to ridicule when she prophesies:

> Everywhere
> Two heads in council, two beside the hearth,
> Two in the tangled business of the world,
> Two in the liberal offices of life,
> Two plummets dropt for one to sound the abyss
> Of science, and the secrets of the mind:
> Musician, painter, sculptor, critic. . . .

And the Prince, who as hero may be presumed to represent Tennyson's view of the matter, ends with a long discourse, of which perhaps the most notable lines are:

---

[1] Dr Hodgson, quoting Napoleon's dictum "Women should be brought up to believe and not to reason," adds, "Why not men also? They would so be the fitter tools of tyrants."

The woman's cause is man's: they rise or sink
Together, dwarf'd or godlike, bond or free: . . .
If she be small, slight-natured, miserable,
How shall men grow? . . .
We . . .
Will clear away the parasitic forms
That seem to keep her up but drag her down—
Will leave her space to burgeon out of all
Within her—let her make herself her own
To give or keep, to live and learn and be
All that not harms distinctive womanhood.
For woman is not undevelopt man,
But diverse: . . .
Yet in the long years liker must they grow;
The man be more of woman, she of man;
He gain in sweetness and in moral height,
Nor lose the wrestling thews that throw the world;
She mental breadth, nor fail in childward care,
Nor lose the childlike in the larger mind.

And so they reach the Happy Marriage. But, be it noted, Tennyson does not imply that Ida has to unlearn anything, in an intellectual sense, before this can be achieved.

What had been taught in her college? A wide course for those days:

On the lecture slate
The circle rounded under female hands
With flawless demonstration; follow'd then
A classic lecture, rich in sentiment,
With scraps of thundrous Epic lilted out
By violet-hooded Doctors, elegies
And quoted odes, and jewels five-words-long
That on the stretch'd forefinger of all Time
Sparkle for ever: then we dipt in all
That treats of whatsoever is, the state,
The total chronicles of man, the mind,
The morals, something of the frame, the rock,
The star, the bird, the fish, the shell, the flower,
Electric, chemic laws, and all the rest.

All, in fact, that "can be taught and known"—except medicine, apparently because that involved dissecting, which "pleased us not"—though the Princess had studied it herself in case of emergencies. With six hundred students, not to mention professors, maids, and "daughters of the plough," one would have expected her to be kept busy, but apparently the "ministering hand" of nurses (before the days of Miss Nightingale), the "tender face" of the beloved, and the "sweet order" of the college sufficed of themselves to heal the sick, even after a battle.

In spite of Ida's great appeal, from which later the Girls' Public Day School Trust were to take their motto—"Knowledge is now no more a fountain seal'd"—there was no immediate striking development of higher education. Yet from about the mid-century the advance of the women on the ancient strongholds of learning was like that of an army with banners. The banners were many and differentiated, the most conspicuous being perhaps that of Emily Davies, founder of Girton College. Miss Davies would have approved the metaphor: her chief biographer says of her, "It is constantly noticeable that she thought of life as a battle, and of herself as leading an attack upon hostile forces."

The story of the campaign, a campaign extensive and somewhat confusing, has been told before. There is something to be said for pursuing separately each line of Miss Davies's attack: middle, low, and higher education —i.e., the opening of the Local examinations, work on school boards, and the founding of Girton College, with its footing in Cambridge and its eventual place as part of the university. But, since on the academic side as a whole the attempts are so closely linked, it will be best to follow in chronological order of events and successes.

In 1856 London University had received an inquiry from a Miss Jessie Meriton White, who asked whether a woman could become a candidate for a diploma in medicine "if on presenting herself for examination she shall produce all the requisite certificates of character, capacity, and study from one of the institutions recognized by the London University." Miss White had also made application to all the London hospitals, fourteen in number, for permission to enter as a medical student.

This leave was refused, and the reply from London was

> That Miss J. M. White be informed that the Senate, acting upon the opinion of its legal adviser, does not consider itself empowered to admit females as candidates for degrees.

We hear no more in this connexion of Miss White, who afterwards married an Italian officer and wrote a life of Garibaldi, but the next applicant was more persistent. In 1859 Elizabeth Garrett, Emily Davies's great friend, met Dr Elizabeth Blackwell, the only qualified English medical woman, who had received her training and degree abroad, chiefly in America, but was looking for recruits for her profession. Almost before she knew where she was Miss Garrett found herself trying to engage in medical studies, and the next year she went to the Middlesex Hospital, where she held an unofficial position between that of a nurse and a medical student. She must have been both exceptionally brilliant and exceptionally persistent, for, meeting with all kinds of difficulties from both professors and students (though she speaks with great gratitude of those who were unprejudiced), she continued by picking up what scraps of training she could in the various hospitals where she could obtain a footing. In 1862 she applied, with a view to gaining a degree, for permission to take the London Matriculation examination, but the university continued to deny "the admissibility of females to examinations." It so happened that at this date the university was applying for a new charter, and Miss Garrett's father wrote to the Senate and presented a memorial bearing a considerable number of signatures, suggesting that in the new charter "the technical legal objection" might be removed. The Vice-Chancellor moved "that the Senate endeavour to obtain modification of the Charter," but after discussion the motion was lost by the Chancellor's casting vote. Whereupon Miss Davies and her friends formed a committee for obtaining the admission of women to university examinations.

Sensibly enough, they began at the bottom, where there was an opening. The University of Cambridge had lately instituted the Cambridge Local examinations, which could be taken at various centres, and, of course, involved no more than the writing—nothing in the way of *viva voce* or residence. These seemed, therefore, eminently suitable for girls' schools, and application was made to Cambridge for permission to make an experiment on them which would at least show whether girls were constitutionally unfit to take any kind of examination—as was not infrequently declared. The advice of her friend Mr (Sir Thomas) Dyke Acland, who had lately managed to get a centre in Exeter, was of the greatest value to Miss Davies, and she remembered it for ever:

> The way to get an old institution to take up a matter is to prove its feasibility without committing the institution. . . . We showed them at Exeter that our ideas could march.

(The last sentence she quoted later, in her evidence before the Schools Inquiry Commission, when she mentioned the results of the "trial trip" of 1863.) The answer from Cambridge was satisfactory. The Local Examinations Committee agreed to print extra copies of the papers, to be given to "some responsible person," for the girls to do simultaneously, and leave was given to make private arrangements with the boys' examiners (and to pay them) for looking over the answers of the girls. A list of the examiners was supplied, and Miss Davies's committee were distinctly pleased at the friendliness of the reply. Time was very short; it was only six weeks before the appointed day, and there was considerable flutter lest there should now not be enough candidates to enter at such short notice. However, the schoolmistresses, especially Miss Buss, played up nobly, and eighty-three candidates were finally entered. They did not all come from London, and Miss Davies and friends had to put up and chaperon those from the country. The whole business, extraordinarily nerve-racking for one who had staked so much on proving the groundlessness of the objection that "the examinations were not fitted for the girls, nor girls for examination," was carried out successfully. The Honorary Secretary of the London Committee, Mr Tomkinson (presumably the "responsible person" referred to in the Cambridge letter), said afterwards that "nothing could have been more becoming and creditable than their conduct on that occasion," and that, owing to their sterling work and readiness to follow the rules, he had far less trouble with them in details than with the boys. The next year a memorial to Cambridge requested the extension to girls of the University Local examinations, and was agreed to, for three years. The examinations were to be held at the Local centres under committees composed of ladies, "care being taken to prevent undue publicity or intrusion." No names nor class-lists in order of merit were to be published, but—and this had been Miss Davies's chief point—the syllabus and subjects for boys and girls was to be the same.

Application was made for similar permission to enter for the Oxford Locals, but "no steps were taken" by this university. In 1866 Durham opened its University Locals. Scotland is quoted as holding examinations open to boys and girls alike "as a matter of course, and not of favour"; and when the three years' probation period for the Cambridge exams came to an end the admission of girls was made permanent and regular.

The report of the examiners on the first "unofficial" attempt, in 1863, was extremely illuminating. It was made and accepted in all seriousness, which was in itself a great advance in the treatment of the question of girls' education. At a meeting held by the Association of Social Science to discuss it F. D. Maurice said:

> I trust there will be no affectation of politeness in passing over mistakes because they are female mistakes. . . . All such civilities would be disdained and regarded as an insult by those who are most interested in this movement.

EMILY DAVIES
Photo Press Photographic Agency

154

The examiners were very frank about the faults and failures of the girls, especially the low standard of arithmetic. This they considered to be due to bad teaching, for the majority of girls did not appear to have had any explanation or understanding of the rules by which they did their sums. (And we have ample testimony in memoirs and autobiographies that this was the case.) Out of forty senior girls thirty-four failed in arithmetic, and even out of Miss Buss's twenty-five candidates ten failed, which caused her to take strong measures about the teaching of the subject in her own school. Other criticism was made—of their writing (but not spelling), of their diffuseness, and of the fact that (in Scripture) they answered, and quite well, not the question that was set, but some other (a trait of examinees which experience seems to indicate is not confined to women). Latin had not been taken, but the German and French were creditable, the latter showing, however, the same weakness as arithmetic—a lack of understanding principles.

On the whole Miss Davies and her backing of schoolmistresses were immensely pleased with the recognition accorded by the report and the meeting which followed to the educability of girls. True, there was the usual cry, raised by the Reverend Charles Lee:

> Let the girls take their music and needlework and the boys mathematics and so forth. . . . If these important subjects are neglected [and with some truth he points out that, not being examination subjects, the accomplishments may receive less attention] we shall have the ladies made strong-minded women, instead of good sisters, good wives, and in time good mothers.

"What a bugbear is this phrase 'strong-minded'!" comments Dr Hodgson later. There was even the voicing, in a singularly selfish and offensive fashion, of the idea that always roused Miss Davies to fury:

> Let them understand all domestic questions and so much of the accomplishments of life as will tend to make the evening delightful, and then we shall secure all that is necessary.

But at least the ability of girls to take examinations was established, if not the desirability; and, besides, another stock argument had been met by the declaration of Professor Solly, F.R.S., who as "an old physiologist" gave his opinion that there would be less illness among the upper classes if their brains were more regularly and systematically worked.

The attack had been diverted from the London Matriculation to Cambridge Locals, because the former university, it was hinted to Miss Davies, did not like to be considered a *corpus vile* for women's experiments. Now London itself made an offer, but not at all what Miss Davies wanted; indeed, she felt, as later at Cambridge (and as Miss Rogers did at Oxford in 1896), that there was a danger that the women's cause was being side-tracked. For the offer was of special examinations for women, "not on the whole less difficult than the Matriculation," and after this certificates of higher proficiency in one or more of fourteen subjects. The compromise did not appeal, for the examination would in the eyes of the world have had no status. "Starting with small repute," says Miss Davies,

> it would have to justify its character, and the most highly cultivated women would not care to submit themselves to an ordeal in which to fail might be a disgrace, but to pass would be no distinction. The mere fact of its special character would in itself repel them. . . . That the greatest of female novelists should have taken the precaution to assume a masculine *nom-de-plume* for the express purpose of securing their work against being measured by a class standard is significant of the feeling entertained by women.

There must be equality or nothing, and she does not consider the offer is "any boon at all." This is how she expresses herself in a letter to R. Holt Hutton, a friend of women's education, though not of her 'section,' but she asks him not to refer publicly to the correspondence lest they (her committee) appear thankless. "I think you are thankless," is his reply, and he calls her "equality" scheme premature. The special examinations were established by an amendment to the Charter in 1868, but were dropped in 1878, when the degrees were themselves granted.

Apart from the promotion of the Cambridge Local examination one of Miss Davies's most effective pieces of work had been to bring pressure on the Schools Inquiry Commission of 1864 (the Taunton Commission) to investigate the education of middle-class girls as well as boys. It has been said that the investigation of girls crept in because the framers of the terms of the Commission had been too oblivious of them to exclude them. It certainly was hardly in their intention that there should be one,[1] but the occasion was an admirable one for Miss Davies's cause, the cause of schools in general. A number of teachers, professors of Queen's and Bedford Colleges, and sympathizers with "middle-class female education" petitioned that girls should be included in the survey, and finally Miss Davies was not only informed that girls would be dealt with (though within narrower limits, as *home* education did not come under the terms of reference), but also asked to suggest witnesses, which she did. A pleasing comment on two names ("I don't think they know anything, but they might be primed") was *not* forwarded to the Commissioners.

Miss Davies was herself called as a witness, and drove with great pertinacity at two objects—the application of endowments to girls' schools and colleges and the opening of examinations to them in order that an outside standard might be available for testing their work. She considered, too, that the common examination would bring schoolmistresses into touch with one another, of which there was very great need, as their isolation at that time seems inconceivable. Her 'creed' was summed up in the

---

[1] "I can hardly think that the new Commission, with all it will have on its hands, will be willing to undertake the inquiry into girls' schools as well as that into boys'!" wrote Matthew Arnold.

question put by one Commissioner and her somewhat ingenuous reply:

"In fact, you wish very much to assimilate the general mental training of boys and girls?"

"I think so. If we could find out what is the best mental training it would be the best for both, but I suppose nobody has found that out yet."

Important as was her work in organizing the plea for the inquiry and for the Local examinations, Miss Davies is yet better known for her success in a different branch of women's education. She had recognized that there was, broadly speaking, no provision for the 'higher' education of women at all, using the word in the sense of 'post-school,' as compared with that for men. The two London colleges were not much more, judged by modern or by men's standards, than places of good secondary education, and, as was seen by Miss Beale's protest, had some difficulty in keeping up even to that standard, because of the infirm foundations on which they had to build in the minds of many of their pupils.[1] Emily Davies's dream was of a college "designed to hold in relation to girls' schools and home teaching a position analogous to that occupied by the universities towards the public schools for boys." It seems obvious enough now that such colleges should exist, and one can hardly realize the total lack of them, just as "in these days of over-examination and of university extension it is difficult for people to realize how great a boon was the opening of examinations for women" (as Miss Beale said in 1898). At any rate, in 1867 Miss Davies, with the help of Mme Bodichon, Lady Goldsmid, Mrs Russell Gurney, Mr Bryce, Professor Seeley, and others, began to put forward a programme and to collect funds for such an enterprise. A General Committee (including three bishops and two

[1] Miss Davies's brother later tried to organize the teaching with a view to preparing the students for Matriculation and the B.A. degrees of London University, but so few girls attempted the degree course that the plan had to be given up.

deans, "to give an air of solidarity and dignity") was formed, with an executive of which Miss Davies herself was the moving spirit. The object was definitely to provide education to the standard of the Cambridge examinations (gradually it became evident that it was the Tripos that was meant) by teachers and professors of university standing. Miss Davies was anxious for all connexion with Cambridge except the actual condition of residence; she wanted the college to be in touch with the university, but the students not to live in Cambridge. By hard work her vision was brought down from the clouds into a house at Hitchin, to which a few devoted dons would go out twice a week by train, and where half a dozen students could reside. A women's college could hardly have had a smaller beginning—one more remote from *The Princess*. Yet from the first there was a real dignity about the attempt and an acceptance of college conditions, and a liberal spirit among both the organizers and those who were being educated. Miss Davies says they "aimed at throwing upon the students much of the responsibility of self-guidance" in the management of health, the apportionment of time, the choice of subjects and of friends. At college they would be free from disturbance; able not only to read in peace, but to think things out,

> to carry on sustained thought without liability to interruption. . . . This great boon—the power of being alone—is perhaps the most precious distinctive feature of a college.

To look ahead for a few years to the time when Hitchin had become Girton College, one can see how the early students responded. As Dr Sara Burstall afterwards wrote:

> We were conscious of our privileges as members, however young and obscure, in a great forward movement. Two things mattered intensely: first, that we should do well in our work and justify the hopes of our founders; second, that we should avoid giving offence or injuring the cause by any breach of conventional behaviour.[1]

---

[1] *Retrospect and Prospect.*

(For, in the words of Miss Jane Harrison, "Women's colleges were a novelty, and distinguished men were brought to see us as one of the sights"—Ruskin, Gladstone, and Turgenev are mentioned among the visitors!) It was not that the first days were entirely easy. Miss Lumsden (Dame Louisa), one of the original inhabitants of Hitchin, explains how a real difficulty arose over their insistence, backed by Miss Davies, to study for the Tripos (Classical or Mathematical), and therefore to stick to the prescribed course, when their teachers evidently regarded them as happy material for trying out new, and doubtless excellent, theories. The mathematics lecturer, for instance, gave a delightful first lecture on conic sections, of which they did not know the elements, instead of helping them on their way for the Little-go, which was the first obstacle to be overcome. Their protests rather shocked the Committee, who deplored their being mere imitators of men and thought them ungrateful and "careless of culture," and there was even a resignation of some tutors. However, they stuck to their point, and in 1870 a private arrangement, similar to that for the Local examinations, was made by which they had the use of the Previous papers, and the services of university examiners, including vivas. Two years later came the Finals, and Miss Davies and her band had their reward: two of the first students passed the Classical and one the Mathematical Tripos.

Emily Davies's character is so clearly shown from her life and her writings that comment is hardly called for. One is struck by the succinctness, directness, and applicability—one might almost say the topicality—of all that Miss Davies has to say. Sir Arnold Wilson tells us how once, being congratulated on the aptness and modernity of his speech at a girls' prize-giving, he confessed that it was an address given by his grandfather on a similar occasion fifty years before. I read that tale (in *Walks and Talks*) as I was about to listen to Sir Arnold on the speech-day of one of our most modern schools, where we heard,

THE HITCHIN STUDENTS
By permission of Mrs Webber

I have not the slightest doubt, the same address excellently delivered, and with a fine Miltonic peroration. It was much appreciated. Should I ever by an unhappy miracle be turned into a prize-giving lion the first thing I should do would be to buy a book of Emily Davies's words of wisdom. They would fit me up for life.

Miss Davies's timelessness is remarkable because she is of the first group of pioneers—one of a type apparently new in England at the time. There is, for all their variety, more than a touch of similarity between her and Miss Nightingale or Miss Beale. Her judgment as a pioneer kept her from running to what she considered extremes: she extracted herself as neatly as she could from connexion with the agitation for women's franchise, lest it should harm her own cause of higher education. In this connexion Miss Davies is distinctly critical of Miss Isa Craig, who "goes in for hard hitting," and she even reproves Elizabeth Garrett, who had headed the poll at the Marylebone election for the London School Board, and reported half in fun that she might be expected to take the chair. "Your jokes are many and reckless," wrote Miss Davies, dismayed at such levity; "they do more harm than you know." She was too much in earnest to court unnecessary opposition.

The keynotes of her character, as an early Girtonian saw it, were pertinacity and self-suppression. Of the former characteristic her succession of interests, all leaning to the same end, is evidence. No sooner, for instance, was the principle of Local examinations granted to girls than she concentrated on the need of obtaining "the Girton College Degree-certificate," which was to be conferred only on precisely similar conditions to the B.A. As to the latter, Miss Davies herself, like Miss Clough and others, but unlike Miss Garrett, was never able to take advantage of the examinations which her efforts opened to others. She experienced the years of famine and of labour, but never reaped a harvest for herself.

Another striking characteristic is illuminated by her own comment on a former student: "She does not know which things are important and which are not; that's a bad fault." Miss Davies knew precisely what she thought important, and was quite capable of ignoring the rest. For example, Miss Davies wanted students for her first venture at Hitchin, and had obtained from Edinburgh the name of Miss Louisa Lumsden, who with true Scots caution wrote to ask what rules were to be laid down for students. Miss Davies replied that the Committee were anxious to find out what rules would be acceptable to grown-up women—Miss Lumsden being at the time twenty-nine years old. When the student arrived she found some of these rules very galling—including that which insisted on the students' going to church every Sunday, unless they asked permission of the Mistress to stay away. Miss Lumsden's comment on the whole affair is:

> Miss Davies could at times have recourse to—one can hardly call it craft—but certainly to a divergence from the truth, never indeed for her own sake, but to forward her darling scheme.

It was merely another expression of the ruthlessness that caused Miss Beale to overwork her staff or Miss Nightingale to break Sidney Herbert. A new ideal had come into the life of women—that of putting a cause before all personal concerns, of giving loyalty not where it was most naturally expected, but where they judged it most important. The comment of "A London Girl of the Eighties" sums up this spirit:

> Our leaders were then of necessity pioneers. There could be no doubt at all of the term 'vocation' as applied to them. They bore cheerfully the petty and galling persecution of public ridicule and possibly of social ostracism. They were touched with prophetic fire and also prophetic austerity. . . . In spite of their dusty warfare, there seems to us something cloistral in their exaltation, their aloofness. Their example shames us, inspires us.

Or, as Emily Davies herself put it more prosaically, about the Suffrage movement:

All this means, it may be objected, that we are to make ourselves dreadful bores. I am afraid we must sorrowfully admit that this is at least partially true. To be a bore is one of the sacrifices that must be made if we are to take part in carrying a great reform.

Which candid statement leads one to believe that, as with lunatics, only those are bores who do not know it.

CHAPTER VII

UNDERGRADUATES BY COURTESY

Miss Davies's concentration on her object had made her suspicious of a parallel development in the same sphere as Girton—that of higher education. Some years before a series of lectures had been organized in four towns in the North—Liverpool, Manchester, Sheffield, and Leeds—which were not only open to, but actually designed for women. Originally it had been suggested that the first course should be for teachers and on teaching, but the Lecturer, Mr James Stuart, of Trinity College, Cambridge, suggested that they would learn more about methods of teaching by being well taught, and proceeded to lecture on astronomy instead. The courses proved extremely popular, and at length a North of England Council for the Higher Education of Women arose, and the organization of the lectures was taken very seriously, as an attempt to bring culture within reach of women in those towns. In connexion with this plan, and with a similar series of lectures begun at Cambridge, examinations for women above the age of eighteen were instituted by Cambridge University. The courses and the examinations were intended to work in with one another, and the syllabus might be assumed to be a specially suitable one for women. This, of course, was anathema to Miss Davies, who protested that "the distinctive advantage of the Cambridge University Local examinations consists in their offering a common standard to boys and girls," whereas "the institution of independent schemes of examination for women exclusively tends to keep down the level of female education." Even when it was put to her that such an examination would merely be taken in Cambridge until the genuine article could be obtained she considered it a hindrance, and doubted the good faith of those bringing such gifts. "The idea of the new scheme is not that it is easy and stopgap, but that it is womanly!"

But Miss Davies was a little unfair, for the advance of women on the universities was to come from another quarter besides her own—Cambridge was to contain Newnham as well as Girton by 1880. Indeed, the history of the former college is perhaps more typical than that of its sister of the movement for women's education. It shows the genius of these early workers for taking advantage of all that might benefit them, never permitting *le mieux* to become the enemy of *le bien*, and welding into a beneficent whole the several favouring elements.

The idea of organizing lectures for women at Cambridge, following on the success of the courses arranged by the Northern Council for the Higher Education of Women, was brought forward by Henry Sidgwick. It was backed by such supporters as Professor and Mrs Fawcett, F. D. Maurice, and W. W. Skeat in 1869, and in the following year a number of courses were attended by ladies. The scheme, organized by a Committee of Management, did not appear to differ from various series of lectures in London, Edinburgh, and the North of England, except that the presence of "trained and practised teachers" in the town gave exceptional facilities. As the university had recently instituted the Examination for Women, which eventually became the Higher Local, in various subjects, the courses were to offer instruction in those subjects, which included English literature and language, history, political economy, and the principles of arithmetic and algebra.

The next step followed quite naturally. Other women wished to share the advantages of the Cambridge lectures, and asked leave to come from a distance to attend them. This attendance was not merely permitted but encouraged, to the extent of the founding of an exhibition for such students, and, shortly afterwards, to taking a house for their reception. This undertaking was also a venture of the Sidgwicks, but the house was presided over by Miss Clough, formerly Secretary of the Northern Council, and a committee, separate from the Lectures Association Committee, was formed to help her. By Easter 1872 there were eight students in residence, and though the actual house had to be changed more than once, the progress of the undertaking was so rapid that by 1874 it was determined that a hall should be built. This was Newnham Hall, and remained as such for the next few years. It was not till 1879 that the Newnham Hall Company and the old Lectures Association were dissolved and the Newnham College Association founded. In 1880 Newnham was incorporated as a college, was doubled in size owing to the building of a new hall, and, being recognized by the university, was established on its present footing.

"Miss Clough's institution," as Professor Seeley said, "created itself." The principles behind it were never the same as those of the Hitchin College, and the attitude of the founders towards degrees was quite different. This was partly due to the outlook of Miss Clough herself. She was, and remained, intensely interested in individuals, and was inclined to place the good of the particular student, certainly at this stage, before the community or the sex as a whole. Her biographer says:

> She wished every student to learn what was good for her, whether her studies led to a university examination or not. . . . The great point was to show that young women could and would work steadily at the subjects of academic study till they had mastered them.

Out of the 215 young women who attended the lectures during the first ten years only twenty entered for the Tripos examinations, though the proportion after this increased tremendously, and by 1885 four-fifths were working for a Tripos and most of the rest for the Higher

Local. Yet the teaching and the study remained the important things rather than the examination, and the promoters or the Association never pursued the subject of degrees, but rather avoided it.

There was another point, also connected with Miss Clough's care for the individual, which prevented the Newnham authorities from asking the university to admit women to degrees on equal terms with men. If a Tripos examination were aimed at it would often be clearly beyond the powers of a girl coming up as ill-prepared as many of the early students naturally were to take it in the stated time. Miss Clough would allow the period of study to be prolonged; Miss Davies insisted that her students should keep the same terms as the men. Some of the Newnham women had not begun Greek or even Latin before coming up to Cambridge for the Tripos; Miss Gray, afterwards Classical Lecturer at Westfield and High Mistress of St Paul's Girls' School, tells us that she barely knew the Greek alphabet. It was obviously necessary for them to take a different course from the male undergraduate.

Moreover, the necessary qualification for entering for the Tripos was to have passed the Previous examination (Little-go), in which Greek was compulsory. Mr Sidgwick and the Association as a whole disapproved of making the classics compulsory even for men, and would certainly not countenance forcing all women students into the same mould. So for some years it was the Higher Local, not the Previous, that was regarded by Newnham as the necessary qualification for a woman attempting a degree course, but this qualification was not recognized by the university.

This attitude towards the degree may have made a difference in the ideals of scholarship held in the two colleges. It is true that the early successes belong to Girton; but if Charlotte Angas Scott, equal to the Eighth Wrangler in 1880, and Agnata Ramsay, head of the

Classical Tripos in 1887, were both Girtonians, Newnham could answer in 1890 with Philippa Fawcett, who came out above the Senior Wrangler. And it shows remarkable patience and forbearance that the two colleges, in spite of their different aims, worked together with singularly little friction.

Perhaps a short sketch of Miss Clough's character will be the best way of illustrating the principles of what may be called the Newnham attitude. The *Memoir of Anne Jemima Clough*, by her niece B. A. Clough, ends with the following quotations, the first from Anne Clough's diary when she was twenty-one, and the second from her last address to those who were leaving college.

> I care not for honour or praise, if I could only really do something to benefit my fellow-creatures. If I were a man I would not work for riches or to leave a wealthy family behind me; I would work for my country and make its people my heirs.

> Take the little pleasures of life, watch the sunsets and the clouds, the shadows in the streets and the misty light over our great cities. These bring joy by the way and thankfulness to our Heavenly Father.

These quotations illustrate two sides of her personality, the gift of looking to the future and the power of enjoying the present. To these must be added what has already been mentioned—her intense appreciation of and care for the individual. Mrs James Ward tells a story which is typical of many anecdotes of Miss Clough. A student of eleven years back was on a visit to the college. Coming down in the morning at the usual time for breakfast, she was met by Miss Clough, with a surprised and disappointed face, and "Why, my dear, you *always* used to be late for breakfast, so I told them to keep so-and-so [which the girl particularly liked] hot for you till nine o'clock." (Let us hope that this shows something more than the early riser's inevitable feeling of superiority!)

Her enjoyment in the personalities of the girls was one form of the readiness to find pleasure in all that was beautiful or interesting. She encouraged dancing, tennis, and in 1891 even gave her approval to a hockey match (against Roedean), and she was particularly keen on the

HONOUR TO AGNATA FRANCES RAMSAY!
CAMBRIDGE, JUNE 1887
Drawn by George du Maurier
By permission of the Proprietors of "Punch"

social side of college life, the debating and other small societies which one now takes so much for granted in such an institution. She liked her girls to be drawn from different classes and circumstances, delighting particularly in any foreign students, and she approved of their going out to further the cause of women's education in such distant lands as Australia and Siam. She liked variety even in colleges; when Miss Le Fevre, first head of Somerville, came to consult her before taking office she appreciated Miss Clough's counsel, and particularly her advice not to follow the example of Newnham in everything! And in the difficult cases where the claims of the college seemed to press hard on the individual, though she did expect discipline—and, indeed, her early students used to think her fussy over details such as changing shoes and wearing gloves—she was always influenced by the feeling "It can never be right to be unkind."

Perhaps this attitude of mind, which certainly prevented her at first from being the ideal organizer of a community, was due to the lack of training and intellectual discipline in her own early life. This she never ceased to regret, and she recommended her students to study logic, in order that they might arrange their ideas better than she did. She even approved of examinations on the ground that they made people learn to express themselves clearly and concisely. (Do they?) In her early days she had recorded, "I always feel the defects of my education most painfully when I go out." Miss Clough had spent most of her youth in Charleston, South Carolina, where her father had business as a cotton merchant, and though her brothers went to school in England, she was taught only by her mother till she was sixteen. After this she continued to work by herself with the encouragement of her brother Arthur (the brilliant friend of Matthew Arnold and subject of the elegy *Thyrsis*), then at Oxford. Like Emma, she had admirable plans.

> I must be very industrious this week; I should like to get up at five, prayers and reading till six, then Euclid and Greek till half-past seven. From nine till eleven at German [this she did sometimes with Arthur], then reading the Bible, French, the history of the Jews with mother till going-out time. In the evening Hallam and poetry.

But, of course, the inevitable:

> I have got a great many invitations for this summer. I shall be away more than I like, but at any rate I shall see something new. . . . I certainly want greater diligence and steadiness in everything.

Her brother's advice—though this is some years later, but she is still living with her mother, after the father's death—is shrewd rather than deep.

> On the whole, I should incline to study arithmetic and grammar perhaps; but you must remember that a great advantage is given by any sort of cultivation (music, drawing, dancing, German, French, etc.) for intercourse with the poor. They . . . carry their liking for a lady almost to the vice of a *fine* lady.

The last reference was to the teaching work she had undertaken. She had begun in 1836 to take classes at the Welsh National School in Liverpool two or three times a week and various other classes. She planned her own scheme of work entirely, and it included visiting the parents of her scholars—a job which she found difficult and distasteful, though apparently *they* liked it, and she thought it important. When her brother was in London she worked for some months as a pupil-teacher at the Boro' Road Training School and the Home and Colonial School. She could not get a school in London, as she would have liked, because "Mother would be quite lost without her usual employments and friends." However, when they moved to Ambleside she was able to collect some pupils (among whom was Mary Arnold, later Mrs Humphry Ward) and to establish a day school, chiefly for the daughters of the tradespeople. The numbers in the school did not rise above thirty, and she did a good deal of the teaching herself, though later she had other women teachers and occasional masters. By nature and training (or lack of this) she was unsystematic, though her intense interest in the pupils and in whatever she taught must have made up in part for her lack of method. In any case her school became well known for the teaching. After the loss of her mother and the shock of her brother Arthur's early death, however, she gave it up, and for quite a long time did practically no teaching. It was not until 1867 that she came into touch with the association which was to lead to her really important work—the North of England Council for Promoting the Higher Education of Women. Of this council she became secretary, and thus was acquainted with those who wished to start similar schemes in other parts. Thus in an almost haphazard way she began her work of presiding over a students' hall of residence at the age of fifty-one.

In spite of the obvious disadvantages of being un-methodical and "no schollard," Miss Clough seems to have been the right person. She could be firm enough when she had made up her mind that any course was for the good of either the individual or the college. The charming comment of an old servant was, "Miss Anne must always have her way, but it was a good way." She acted as a good foil to Miss Davies; she had a timid manner, and her appearance was "unimpeachably feminine." And perhaps one of her most valuable qualities was—she was able to keep quiet. In her own words,

> Many difficulties were constantly arising about Society matters and the conduct of the students, but I was for the most part silent, and did not either speak or write about those matters, so they passed over.

Perhaps because she had so little of it herself Miss Clough looked upon education chiefly as a training for life. Even at her little school she criticized herself for not preparing girls better for the future. She said later of her Newnham girls:

> Some may wish for a quiet life, some for a life of study, some for occupation . . . but to all of us it is most important that we should know how to use our faculties . . . to be exact, to observe, to be able to give out our knowledge accurately, distinctly, clearly . . . to bear defeat and to be willing to try again and again.

172

Above all she pressed the lesson that college education was to help girls to make their homes happy—as present daughters no less than as future wives. She dreaded lest the independent life at Newnham should unfit them for the restraint of the family circle. "My dear, you will be able to amuse them better when you go home," was a comment which precisely agreed with the view of the particular student who recorded it.

It is worth anticipating the account of the women's movement in Oxford to show how exactly this view tallies with the attitude of its promoters there. Miss Wordsworth (Dame Elizabeth) uses almost precisely the same words: "We want to turn out girls so that they will be capable of making homes happy." Hence, too, comes her insistence on the minor graces of life such as neat handwriting, skilful needlework, even the folding of a letter or the way of shutting a door, "all the indescribable things, the neglect of which often makes a really clever woman intolerable." Mrs Johnson, for many years Honorary Secretary of Lady Margaret Hall, never forgot the advice of Dr Mark Pattison, who was so anxious that women students should dress carefully and have gentle manners and not incur the reproach: "In a large party I could detect a Newnham or Girton girl at once." Mrs Johnson thought of this when a deputation of students asked for a long glass to be placed in a convenient and conspicuous place in the Hall, in the interest of tidiness as to skirts and shoes. She wrote in 1932: "The long glass may still be seen, perhaps a little forlorn at the short amount of skirt it now has to reflect."

Of course, that particular criticism of the "learned woman," that she neglects her appearance, is a stock gibe. To note only a few examples, Miss Yonge's Ethel May is continually in trouble with a dragging skirt, and the Clever Woman of the Family—one of the most subtle and devastatingly critical portraits of the strong-minded woman—is negligent and impatient of dress. There is

the rather crude undergraduate wit, from the early days
of "Shabby-hag the Newnhamite" (a nickname which
must have distressed Miss Clough considerably) down to
our own. There is even Taine's illuminating contrast
between what he expected of Oxford women in general
(before the days of 'students,' however) and Mrs
Humphry Ward, whom, as Mary Arnold, he met in 1867.

> She is about twenty, very nice-looking, and dressed with
> taste (rather a rare thing here; I saw one lady enclosed in a
> most curious sort of pink silk sheath). . . . She knows French,
> German, and Italian, and during this last year has been studying
> old Spanish of the time of the Cid; also Latin in order to be
> able to understand the medieval chronicles. All her mornings
> she spends at the Bodleian Library—a most intellectual lady,
> but yet a simple, charming girl . . . not in the least pedantic.

It is to Oxford now that the chief interest shifts, and
the advance of women in this university makes a good
complement and contrast to that at Cambridge. It was
later, slower, may be considered more complete, and was
certainly accompanied by less violent feeling. That is not
to say that there were not fighters, and stout ones, in the
long effort to obtain admission for women to the university. For there had to be in Oxford too a struggle for
that coveted prize the degree, or, rather, for the membership by which the privileges of the university came to
belong to women by right and not by courtesy. If anyone
here represents Miss Davies as organizer of the campaign
it must be the late Miss Rogers, whose connexion may
be said to have begun in 1873, when she took the top
place for classics in the Higher Local examination,
thereby bringing up the question of whether she was
eligible for the exhibition offered to the top candidate
in this examination by Balliol College and Worcester.
It is pleasant to imagine what would have been the reactions of the Balliol undergraduates of 1873 had they
been confronted on their return with Miss A. M. A. H.
Rogers, aged sixteen, among the Freshers. But, of

course, the question was not seriously considered, and Miss Rogers had to be content with a set of classical books as prizes, which no doubt she turned to good account. For in 1886 Miss Rogers became the first Classical Tutor to the women students, in the days when all women's colleges shared tutors, and for a long period she sustained, with Mr Arthur Sidgwick, almost all the lecturing and teaching of classics. She continued to be the backbone of the attempt to gain admission to degrees; when the application of 1896 failed she only set to, and rallied her forces again. Her power of sheer hard work in organizing and study (including accurate study of that complicated volume the *University Statutes*), her clearness of thought and far-sighted planning, her persistency and indomitable spirit, were recorded in her obituary notices by those who knew her well, as was her devotion to the Association for the Higher Education of Women, and to the college of St Hugh's, for which she did so much.

Yet to those who can look back only, as it were, at second-hand on the "advancement of learning" among women in Oxford it is not the refusal of university membership, but the acceptance of scholars' work that stands out during the last eighty years. The colleges of to-day seem to owe so much to the great men of the middle nineteenth century—Dr Mark Pattison, Rector of Lincoln, Walter Pater, Dr Creighton, later Bishop of London, Bishop Talbot, T. H. Green, and others—not only for their efforts (seconding in many cases those of their wives) in founding associations or colleges, but for their attitude that work was work and study study, no matter who did it. The comment, for instance, on Mrs Humphry Ward's first piece of "sheer hard, brain-stretching work" (lives of the early Spanish kings and ecclesiastics, written for *The Dictionary of Christian Biography*)—"You have gone over the ground so thoroughly that there is no gleaning left"—this is from one scholar to another, not from man to woman. We realize the difference at once when we switch back to poor Elizabeth Barrett's protest against her efforts being judged "not as mere work, but as mere woman's work." Similarly, in reading Bishop Creighton's life one finds his attitude towards women attending lectures (and he might indeed feel well disposed towards this habit, for it was at a lecture that he first saw his future wife) so sane and, to us, ordinary. There is no churlish questioning, "Why should women want to do so-and-so?" but an acceptance of their desire for learning as a natural development. It seems in accordance with this tradition, too, that from the first university men and women have sat in concord on such bodies as the councils for the A.E.W. (the Association for the Higher Education of Women) or the various colleges, held joint tutors' meetings in the early days, and that to this day men and women dons seem to take each other for granted in all friendliness. Whatever the trials of the first women undergraduates (as to excessive chaperonage or the occasionally pointed aloofness of the male undergraduate), I do not think that at any time a woman don in an Oxford college can have felt so isolated as did an early Girton tutor who complained that the distance from Cambridge and the difference of opinion between Miss Davies and the other section separated her from the social life of the university.

Not that men supporters have been lacking on the active as well as the accepting side. Professor Thorold Rogers's sympathy (he proposed in 1874 that women should be admitted to examinations in a separate room from men, but with their names published in the same class lists) one can understand when one remembers the intellectual powers of his own daughter. On the technical side, however, Oxford has yielded only very gradually, and nearly two generations passed before full university rights were accorded, the successful effort in 1920 being led by Professor Geldart and A. J. Stocks. While on the subject of degrees one may return for a moment to Cambridge to note that after an outstanding Tripos success of a woman in 1880 a memorial was drawn up, praying

> That the Senate would grant to properly qualified women the right of admission to the examinations for university degrees and to the degrees conferred according to the results of such examinations.

The reply was that the Senate was not prepared to give degrees, but that under the same conditions of residence and Previous examinations as men women would be granted formal admission to the Honours examinations, and that an authoritative record of results would be published in the University Class Lists. And there, with some few alterations, the matter rests to this day.

The details of the Oxford story are of more interest esoterically than exoterically. It was in 1873 that a committee was formed to arrange a system of lectures and classes for women in Oxford, with examinations (corresponding to Collections) at the end of the courses. Ruskin was already lecturing on Art; the courses were held in classics, modern languages, and mathematics. The committee included Mrs Creighton, Mrs Arthur Johnson, afterwards secretaries of the Association for the Higher Education of Women, into which the committee was eventually merged, Mrs Humphry Ward, and Miss Pater. It is worth noting that they organized the financial side well enough to be able to reduce the fees and to admit free a number of elementary-school teachers. Classes were also held, for which papers were written; one lecturer, however, complained that there was at first a feminine character and originality about the women's writing, but that after lectures and examinations they tried to be manly, and were only like the ordinary man. Two years later a delegacy was established to supervise women's examinations which corresponded to, or in some subjects were identical with, the Honours Schools, but could be taken without residence, regardless of the time limit imposed by the university on undergraduates, and with certain optional subjects. In 1884 the examinations for Honour Moderations and the Final Honour Schools of Mathematics, Natural Sciences, and Modern History were opened, and within ten years the remaining B.A. examinations. (Some of the present Honours Schools, notably English Language and Literature, were, however, not recognized by the university till later, and were therefore only taken by women, but were made valid for a retrospective degree.) There was, as in Cambridge, some division of opinion over the preliminary examinations, for the full Oxford course involved a good deal, especially in classics, that was considered the natural conclusion for a boy's education, but was not at all easy for girls, considering their background. Moreover, there was another reason why women wished to proceed to their Finals as soon as possible. The era of the great high schools and public schools was beginning; specialist teachers were badly wanted, and women were encouraged by the prospect of immediate posts to take their Honours without troubling about the intermediate examinations necessary for the degree.

There were then in Oxford already lectures, classes, and a scheme for university examinations in 1878, by which date also the idea of a hall of residence for the women students was beginning to appear. Bishop Talbot tells how he and his wife, on a visit to Cambridge, were much impressed by Girton College, an establishment founded on Church of England principles, and said, "Why should not the Church be for once at the front instead of behind in this development?" But when the proposal of such a residentiary hall was brought forward it was found that the adoption of Church principles was going to prevent some would-be supporters from co-operating, even when the foundation was widened and the Principal was to be given the liberty to admit other students, the reception of Church of England members still being the chief object of the hall. The main object, however, met with considerable support, so much that it was determined to found *two* halls, afterwards known as Lady Margaret Hall and Somerville College, the second being undenominational. The two sets of founders agreed to differ over their principles, and to form what Canon Scott Holland referred to as an "Unholy Alliance" to promote their objects.

An announcement of the advantages expected from the new hall was circulated, explaining that students would find "a common life with the ways and tone of a Christian family; the protection of certain rules as to hours, society, etc., general supervision of studies; definite religious instruction and the advice and assistance of a lady of experience and other high qualifications"—which makes an interesting comparison with Miss Davies's proposal of ten years previously. The Principal was Miss Wordsworth, who, though she started under what some might call the disadvantage of having it continually said that one of her chief merits was her family name, with its guarantee of respectability, ruled the hall successfully for thirty years. The task of governing a college in its early days must have called for very different qualities from the same task to-day, but on any showing those early Principals must have been extraordinarily fine and sympathetic women. An old student of St Hugh's, which began later as a hall of residence, writes of the eighties:

> We were an intimate little party in those days. When one breakfasts, lunches, dines, and often has tea in the same company of ten or twelve people for the seven days of twenty-four weeks in the year, one gets to know and understand those companions rather well, especially one of such outstanding personality as the Principal.

The almost conventual character of the halls in those days does not appear to have been oppressively felt, but was there none the less. One former member said quite casually that she did not remember speaking to a male undergraduate during the three years she was 'up,' and though the rule against going into the town without a companion may, by the nineties, have been frequently transgressed, at least in theory solitary walking was forbidden. In such an atmosphere it was particularly necessary that the Principal should be a woman of some social status if the position of her students was to be assured, that she should understand both the importance of their work and the undesirability of allowing that work to become unduly absorbing. Of one to whom belongs the credit of having "created a college out of a little group of students" it was said that probably her particular work was done when, as the numbers increased, her method of government, so successful in the early years, had become outgrown, and she committed the charge of the community to other hands. But these early days had opened the eyes of the women who came up to the two real joys of learning and of living together:

> It was simply a revelation of what life might be. . . .
> I can never think of a university education as just a means to an end, as a useful way of continuing education and perhaps preparing for useful work. I feel it is an opportunity and an inspiration which is of incalculable value. Above all, it seems to teach appreciation, and the more I loved my life in the hall, the more I also realized the happiness of being with my relations and getting to know them better, as well as the delight of gaining other friends.[1]

Reluctantly we must leave Oxford and see how the rest of the world was getting on. It was in 1878 that London University, considering that the Women's Certificates of General or even Higher Proficiency were not highly valued, and that women would prefer to have access to the ordinary degrees and honours and to be subject to the same tests and qualifications which were imposed on men students, resolved that every degree, honour, and prize

---

[1] E. Lodge, *Terms and Vacations.*

should be accessible to students of both sexes on perfectly equal terms. At the time of this generous admittance there were, of course, no 'colleges' involving residence for either men or women, but four years later a hall of residence for ten women was founded in connexion with University College. The nearest approach to the vision of *The Princess*, however, was perhaps the foundation of Holloway College, which, being situated at Egham and yet affiliated to London University, might seem to combine seclusion with a high standard of learning. Thomas Holloway, its originator, stated his aim in a most interesting charter:

> The founder believes that the education of women should not be exclusively regulated by the traditions and methods of former ages, but that it should be founded on those studies and sciences which the experience of modern times has shown to be the most valuable and the best adapted to meet the intellectual and social requirements of the students. . . . It is the founder's desire that the domestic life of the college shall be that of an orderly Christian household. . . . It is the express and earnest desire of the founder that the college shall neither be considered nor conducted as a mere training college for teachers and governesses.

The founder further showed his judgment in laying down that after twenty years any regulation might be changed by a competent authority (the governing body). One of the first changes was due to his having constituted this governing body exclusively of men. At the end of the twenty years application was made for an alteration in this matter, and was accepted.

In the meantime other universities were being opened to women. Edinburgh had been one of the first places to inaugurate lectures for the higher education of women: it was through the association which managed these that one of the Girton pioneers, Miss Lumsden, came into touch with Miss Davies. In due course the Scottish universities were thrown open; at St Andrews a hall of residence came into existence, with the same Miss Lumsden as Warden. The Victoria University (1880) made no distinction of persons (though the arrangements were not quite similar in the various Northern colleges of which it was composed), nor from their inception did the Welsh colleges. (The University of Wales received its Charter in 1893, but there were women at Aberystwyth ten years before this.) Durham admitted women in 1895, except to degrees in divinity. Dublin made its degree accessible to those who had taken the degree examinations at the older universities—on payment. This was said to be a money-making expedient, but it did provide women with the outward and visible sign of something which they had undoubtedly earned, and many of them took advantage of it.

The development of university education for women is, if not the most important, at least the most spectacular of the many advances of women's education in the last century. It may perhaps have attracted an undue proportion of interest, but the new standards it set up are of inestimable importance in the formation of modern ideals in the upbringing of girls. Another development, of course, was the admission of women to the study of medicine; this, though in itself of immense importance, does not specially affect the principles of education, so has here been omitted. But if we are to understand anything of the early struggles it is worth looking at some of the abuse, the ridicule, or even the well-meant criticism that the first promoters of higher education had to face.

Throughout the middle of the century their chief opponent in the Press was *The Saturday Review.* "No one—except perhaps a Saturday Reviewer—will deny that women have intelligence, affections, conscience, will," says Mrs Gurney. Its attitude towards an early pamphlet of Mme Bodichon's (then Miss Leigh Smith) on women's work is:

As a piece of 'pretty Fanny's talk' it would be charming, but we should be sorry to trust 'pretty Fanny' with any business more important and intricate than the payment of a milk bill.

In 1864—at the opening of the Local examinations—came a peculiarly offensive anonymous article containing all the stock jokes, fearing that the examiners, if men, would be biased in favour of a pretty candidate ("It would be next to impossible to persuade the world that a good-looking first-class woman came by her honours fairly"), whereas should "learned ladies . . . if any such were to be found" be appointed as examiners, the difficulty would be inverted. (All this apparently in ignorance of the fact that the examiners would see not the faces of the candidates, but their scripts.) The article goes on to be similarly amusing at the idea of choosing wives by competitive examination in geography or Latin prose, and at the expense of "the classical or mathematical heroine of actual life . . . never happy unless she is flirting with a professor or putting on her bonnet to go and hear a lecture." More generally, "an accomplished young lady is a terror to young men as things are; if erudition be added to the accomplishments the terror will become a simple panic." The article is headed "Feminine Wranglers."

Opposition to the proposed women's college might be less cheaply expressed, but was very general. Sometimes it was based on ignorance like that of the clergyman in the railway carriage who on passing Hitchin remarked, "There go the infidel ladies"—to be answered by the retort, "Indeed we are not; we have prayers morning and evening." Dr Pusey, however, at the first mention was "violently opposed"; Miss Rossetti declined joining anything that did not belong to the Catholic Church ("Anglo-Catholic, I suppose," adds Miss Davies); and Mrs Gatty, with a dig at the effects of publicity on the ladies, however excellent, who are prominent in the Social Science Association, remarked: "*Frivolity* is sooner cured than *conceit*, and I think your experiment dangerous."

Miss Yonge, alas! disapproved of girls being brought together in large numbers; she must have looked forward to the Girton *de nos jours*, and could not have realized that Hitchin would start with six. "Superior women," she said, "will teach themselves, and inferior women will never learn more than enough for home life," but, judging by references to Oxford and Cambridge in her later works, she afterwards allowed some good in them.

The Times granted that for exceptional cases this proposed college might be serviceable, but insisted that anything would be mischievous which tended to place the standard of female education in intellectual excellence and in a kind of public life. It might be desirable to educate those "who have only themselves to think of," but, as Miss Davies remarked in another connexion, "for mothers there is nothing like good, sound ignorance!"

Any reference to 'public life' roused a feeling in one type of Victorian male that was akin to hysteria. He talked of the "abominable publicity which threatens to displace women from their legitimate spheres of work and duty," inquired, "Who are these women who find time and energy for business, the platform, the hunting-field?" and, as if the last word had then been said, announced, "I prefer not to hear women speak in public." The last quotations are from Sir Dyce Duckworth, Physician to the then Prince of Wales. Duckworth appears to have been a veritable Colonel Blimp, and even in 1891 could not give more than the grudging concession:

> We have learnt that such a career [a university training] is not necessarily unfitting for an after life which comprehends the gracious fulfilment of matrimony, maternity, and many social duties. . . . The truth is, I suppose, that we have not yet sufficient experience to warrant any strong opinions upon the question.

But his abuse and *The Saturday Review* Miss Davies soon learnt to put up with.

> I do not wonder at — being against the scheme. . . . The only thing that ever surprises me is to find anybody *for* it. As

Lady Augusta [Stanley] said, "Of course it is received with shouts." I got used to working almost singlehanded through the Local examinations, and winning at last.

It was more difficult to meet the criticism of friends. R. H. Hutton, Professor of Mathematics at Bedford College, at the close of what is on the whole a sympathetic address, pronounced that the suggestion which had recently been made—to put before women the same intellectual standard which is now put before young men—would be at once unpractical and unwise—premature by generations.

> I do not wish to exaggerate the difference between ordinary men and women, but I do say it requires investigation before proceeding to set up a standard for ordinary women. . . . No blunder could be greater than hastening to model the standard of women's education on the received standard for men . . . [entailing] so much spade-husbandry for delicate hands [!].

Emily Davies must watch her step. Does she know "what is actually required by the London University for ordinary degrees?"

She does, and answers that they already do a good proportion of this at Queen's College,

> and who shall say at what point they are to stop? Why should simple equations brighten their intellects and quadratic equations drive them into a lunatic asylum? Why should they be the better for the three books of Euclid which they are required to master at Queen's College and 'stupefied' by conic sections? Would a knowledge of physiology make them worse mothers, and an acquaintance with chemistry of food less fit to superintend the processes of food?

The arguments on both sides now seem threadbare; it is only worth quoting one more—her answer to the objection (in 1896) that if the women's colleges became part of the university they would have to come under university discipline:

> There is no reason to suppose that either Girton or Newnham would object to their students being subjected to proctorial supervision, but experience gives good grounds for supposing that it would be superfluous.

Until a few years ago there was at every Exhibition of the R.A. one kind of portrait that we could reckon on seeing. Portraits of this type had one thing in common. They might be by different artists and of different subjects, and it probably occurred to few people that they held this common factor. Yet their presence at the Exhibition had a deep significance, for the cessation of the series marked the close of an age. The face they represented was the Face of the Pioneer Woman, typical of her epoch and, in this country, not to be repeated. The face is one that many of us remember and respect: a broad forehead and well-set brows, a mouth expressing determination, yet not tight-lipped but generous, a countenance often deeply lined, but not with lines of temper, a well-set figure, erect rather than stiff, and above all remarkable eyes, whether clear blue, piercing black, or kindly brown—the eyes of one accustomed to sum up character, to listen intelligently to argument—and then to go on her own deliberate way. There is always humour in such a face, whether in a trick of the eyebrow, a twist at the corner of the mouth, or a sparkle in the wide-open eye—there would have to be, in order to keep sanity and good temper in a world that was making few allowances for a pioneer—but above all there is determination. The expression of many of these women must have been caught from their predecessors, for, of course, these are not of the first generation of pioneer women, but they followed on; I remember it in a great-aunt of my own who was Matron at Westminster Hospital in the days of Miss Nightingale's activity, and in a headmistress who reflected the influence of Miss Beale. But it has not passed down for a third generation. We have noble and gracious headmistresses in plenty; they are well dressed, cultured, and affectionate—but they have not the Face of the Pioneer Woman.

PENELOPE LAWRENCE
From the painting by Sir John Orpen, R.A.
By permission of the Principal, Roedean School, Brighton　　186

CHAPTER VIII

THE HIGH SCHOOL

In the last quarter of the nineteenth century the higher education of women rose very high indeed. But it is not only by its peak that a pyramid must be judged. To be perfect it must be solid and regular. It was not the successes of Miss Ramsay and Miss Fawcett that marked the greatest change in women's education, brilliant as these successes were, and great as was the glory they added to the cause. The most remarkable achievement of the last three decades was the foundation and growth of a system which aimed at putting a good secondary education within the reach of any girl whose father was willing and able to pay about £16 a year for it. It is true that the secondary schools were not the base of the educational system, and that this base also was being laid during the latter part of the century, from the time of the 1870 Act which began the process of making elementary education compulsory and free. But this great primary movement had to pass a hard test, and the era of overcrowded schools, of hard-worked pupil-teachers, and of payment by results, inevitable as these things may have been, can hardly be considered a time of educational success. It is the second course of the pyramid, to return to our metaphor, that was so well and truly laid at this period— those great high schools, founded up and down the country from Newcastle to Exeter, and from Ipswich to Swansea, where an ever-growing number of pupils was being given an education at the same time liberal and practical.

One needs to realize something of the state of schools in the sixties to grasp the magnitude of the change, and, of course, the best hunting-ground (one can scarcely call it a happy one) for this information is the Report of the Schools Inquiry Commission (the Taunton Commission), issued in 1868. That section which related to girls was so outspoken, so condemnatory, and so exactly suited to the opinions of the pioneers that Miss Beale got permission to republish it separately with a foreword of her own, and with the evidence given by herself, Miss Buss, another headmistress, Miss Wolstenholme, and Miss Emily Davies. The Commissioners, one can see, had been considerably influenced by the statements of the women whom they had examined—eight in all, out of a large number of witnesses—extraordinary as it was for women to come before such a commission in person at all. The witnesses did not spare their words about the defects of girls' education. Indeed, their great object had been, in Miss Beale's words, "to bring the work to light." Miss Beale herself said that the education of girls entering Cheltenham—apparently right up to the age of eighteen —was "defective to an extraordinary degree in the rudimentary parts," and, to judge by a comparison of papers, they were worse educated than the children in the national schools. She had come up fortified with forms of admission, lists of results, and bundles of examination papers. Miss Davies, of course, had less direct evidence, but showed how the standard at the London 'colleges' was kept down by the ignorance of girls entering unprepared, and how "education of girls after leaving school" (a suggested heading in a memorandum) meant "absence of it." Afterwards she was asked back, as she was refreshing herself with claret and biscuits in the secretary's room, to support Miss Buss—a Commissioner remarking, "This witness is not so self-possessed as the other." Miss Buss, however, recovered from her womanly nervousness, to reply, in answer to a suggestion that she found girls ignorant when they came to her, "Extremely ignorant," and to add that whether they came from schools or from home "they could hardly be worse prepared."

But the Commission did not depend only on the evidence of witnesses called, complete as this was—Miss Beale, for instance, going into all details of what class of children exactly could be admitted to Cheltenham, of extra subjects and the amount of time spent on them, and of how carefully a French exercise should be corrected. Half a dozen Assistant Commissioners were appointed to investigate schools in different areas. Some met with considerable opposition (as at Clifton, where Mr Stanton suspected the headmistresses of having banded together to resist what they considered an invasion of privacy and an inquisitorial investigation) or with difficulty, as in Yorkshire, where of 156 schools approached fifty-six made no answer, sixteen were too new or too small to give the information required, and nine had been given up. But often the head was only too willing to co-operate, and received all the Commissioner's sympathy and support against what was described in the report as "the general indifference of parents to girls' education both in itself and as compared to that of boys." One "governess," it is said, "expresses herself most anxious to introduce other teaching, but complains bitterly of the apathy of parents, and of the way in which they discourage all efforts to do so." Here it was the fathers, prosperous manufacturers, who seemed the difficulty, but the mothers would similarly remark, "Now, Miss —, you must not turn Augusta into a 'blue,'" with other discouraging sentiments. The Assistant Commissioners did their work very thoroughly, examined the girls, talked to the teachers, looked at the salary lists, heard lessons, went over the buildings (one was even so advanced as to criticize in his report the position of the lavatories in a boarding school), and then filled volumes with their complaints.

These complaints might come under several headings.

The first and most deplorable, as hinted above, was the complete lack of any high ideals, moral, intellectual, or physical, set before the girls by parents or, consequently, by teachers.

> There is a long-established and inveterate prejudice, though it may not often be distinctly expressed, that girls are less capable of mental cultivation and less in need of it than boys; that accomplishments and what is showy and superficially attractive are what is really essential for them; and, in particular, that as regards their relations to the other sex and the probabilities of marriage more solid attainments are actually disadvantageous rather than the reverse.

Even in the more cultured schools there was "no adequate motive for exertion" of the intellect; the girls were put into the way of such reading as they might have been doing at home, but there was no system, and instead "a total absence of life and interest in school work." How could it be otherwise when one of the "governesses" turned to the Commissioner and said, "You gentlemen do not like learned ladies; our great aim is to make the young people attractive in society." That she said it "archly" did not endear her to the "gentleman" addressed.

Complaint of the teaching itself was very general, though the Assistant Commissioners saw enough to find exceptions to this. The habit of employing visiting masters was still very widespread: in fact, the names of well-known masters were definitely an advertisement to the school. But there was no co-operation between these, or between them and the female superintendents, and on the whole the Commissioners did not consider men teachers a great advantage—except that the girls were inclined to regard their advent as an *occasion*, and to prepare more conscientiously for them. Moreover, as a rule they had to be employed because women had only "inadequate knowledge" of the subjects, but "where there was a lady teacher who understood her business" the results were as good as with a man. Unfortunately, however, the teachers had no standard of comparison, and did not realize how bad they were. There was, indeed, a common tendency to attempt "the higher ranges of learning" without supplying adequate foundations. For instance, astronomy as a subject meant little more than a few calculations and "the use of the globes," bearing little enough relation to the understanding of the heavenly bodies. The Commissioner grew quite heated at the "vulgarization of the sublime science." Or, again, even a series of quite good lectures from a visiting professor might be utterly unintelligible to little girls, because it presupposed knowledge they did not possess. "And," added the Commissioner, "I cannot express my sense of the meretricious character of a course of instruction which professes to explain heraldry, architecture, or botany in six lectures." He had found it difficult in some schools to persuade the headmistress that where such courses existed science as a school subject was not "being taught." The classics were dismissed briefly: Greek was practically unknown, and the Latin learnt in ladies' schools as a rule was "worthless."

The lower branches of learning fared little better. Arithmetic, on which a girl spent on an average one hour in thirteen of her educational life, as compared to one in three on music, was taught in a manner "merely empirical"; so was grammar. In the one subject, as a rule, the girls (and probably their teachers) juggled with the figures till they came to the right answer; in the other they "committed to memory" some pages of a well-recognized book such as Lindley Murray's. There was no attempt to explain principles. "The noxious brood of catechisms" ("Mangnall and All That") came in for a good deal of criticism. Perhaps the severest condemnation was of French, for (as it almost amounted to an 'accomplishment') "it is supposed that girls at least learn *French*."

> I never expected to find young ladies of sixteen and eighteen whose parents were paying £100 to £150 a year for their education ignorant of the most common irregular verbs . . . and unable to turn simple sentences into French without blunders.

But they *were* ignorant, and the Commissioner gives quotations and a list of their worst howlers.[1] French conversation is described not only as "a practice very wearisome to the pupils," but as begetting slovenliness and inaccuracy and a ready habit of slipping into mere jargon.

To leave the academic side (though it is tempting to linger over Miss Beale's account of the girl who said, "I think Chaucer lived in the reign of George III, but it may have been any other reign"), the teaching of needlework is examined, but the time found to be spent mostly on tatting, crochet, or some other form of "fancy-work." One teacher complains that the girls "prefer fancy needlework to books, partly because it gives them something to show at home, and partly because it wants no mental effort." (Should we in these days regard that as a just condemnation of handicraft?) Of the inevitable

---

[1] Examples of these are that *L'hôtesse dormait dans un coin de la cuisine* is translated by a girl of sixteen as, "The hostess slept in a [blank] with the cook," and by a girl of twenty-two as "The hostess slept in a [blank] with her cousin." There are the following renderings into French: "Hampden's regiment was described by Cromwell as a mere rabble of tapsters and serving-men out of place" as *Ce regiment fut ecrit par Cromwell comme une collection d'hommes brusques et domestiques mal-apropos,* and . . . *fut descrit par Cromwell comme une mère . . . des . . .* And "in spite of his mismanagement" is, pleasantly, *malgré son deshabille.* On learning this language the girls spent roughly one-eighth of their school lesson-time.

Of the teaching and learning of other subjects here are two examples. In grammar one answer to the question "How do nouns substantive form their plural number?" was "Sometimes by changing a voewl, as Ox, Oxen." In geography the misspelling of certain common names was quoted; as to rivers, of which they were often made to learn long strings of names, one girl wrote the Oder and the Elbe together as "Orderandable."

music there is a good deal to say, as well there might be, considering that on one calculation it took up nearly twice as much time as even the "miscellaneous knowledge"—*i.e.*, 'Questions'—or as French, and six times as many hours as German or grammar. It is common knowledge that every girl, taste or no taste, was supposed to learn 'the instrument.' It is only a further condemnation of the lack of reality and enthusiasm about the whole process to realize that often enough one of the governesses had to spend her time "superintending that torturing of the piano which goes on unremittingly all day long." Yet except for music, fancy-work, and callisthenics there was nothing distinctively appropriate even to a girl's destiny as a wife and mother, for 'domestic science' was not taught, nor even recommended.

> Everywhere the fact that the pupil is to become a woman and not a man operates upon her course of study negatively, not positively. It deprives her of the kind of teaching which boys have, but gives her little or nothing in exchange. It certainly does not give to her any exceptional teaching adapted to her career as a woman.

This is the Commissioners' verdict.

Not only the teaching but the conditions came in for a good deal of criticism. The 'private adventure' schools, in which almost all middle-class girls were taught, were held in dwelling-houses more or less adapted for the purpose. A 'school' of twenty-five might have only two sitting-rooms to use. There would probably be no proper apparatus, not even a blackboard or ink-wells. The common tables and chairs of household use might be the school furniture, at which, or on which, the pupils sat 'in disorderly array.' Or they might sit on benches round the walls, with scraps of writing material in their hands, the teacher on a chair in the middle—knitting she was found on one occasion, and the Commissioner remarked that the children might as well have said their lessons to the old armchair, for all the help they got. He

N   193

felt that the absence of desks, and even of a definit•
place for the class to assemble, helped to produce "tha
irregularity and slovenliness which is so frequent a faul
in girls' schools." Another defect was the close atmo•
sphere and the unreasonable dread of fresh air, and thi
was connected with another serious criticism. There wa
a total neglect in nearly all schools of any kind of physica
exercise or real recreation. The only outdoor exercis•
besides walking was croquet, which is said to be conduciv•
to "a good deal of idling" and lounging about. Girl
seem never to let themselves go—and, indeed, a wal)
with a book or conversation in French is not an in•
vigorating form of recreation. They need, says on•
Commissioner, to play with more "abandon" and self
forgetfulness.

There is plenty more in the report: criticism of th•
small schools which parents prefer because they ar•
"more like home," but which mean over-staffing anc
therefore under-paying if they are to be run with anythinɡ
like efficiency. (Twenty-five is the average number o
pupils in Yorkshire, twenty in Lancashire, but sometime
there are as few as six or eight children only.) There i
the suggestion that good and well-regulated day school
should be opened in the principal towns—a seed to bea
much fruit—though it is agreed that boarders are mor•
profitable. There is comment on the fact that the pupil
must always come from one narrow grade of society: th•
mistress having taken girls of one class cannot get girl
from a class above, and frequently has to promise that sh•
will not accept them from a class below. There is a gooc
deal about the teachers, hardly any of whom take uɲ
teaching as a profession meaning to stick to it (presum
ably 'teaching' here does not mean founding one's owr
school), and as they have not themselves been well taugh
they do not know how to teach. For them a libera
education, rather than what is technically called 'training,ᵧ
is recommended, with, if necessary, an additional siⅹ

months' course to qualify them as teachers. But the report puts in the forefront:

> Want of thoroughness and foundation; want of system; slovenliness and showy superficiality; inattention to rudiments; undue time given to accomplishments, and these not taught intelligently or in any scientific manner; want of organization —these may sufficiently indicate the character of the complaints in their general aspect.

In other words, schools had altered very little since the days of Miss Pinkerton.

There was a further complaint, of great importance, which served to show how very little the education of girls was regarded at that time. Miss Davies had been asked, "I believe there are very few endowments which are applicable for the education of young women in this country?" She answered significantly, "Very few, I believe, are so applied." Her contention was that in a very large number of cases money had been left or schools founded to educate "the children of the parish," and that on these foundations the girls were almost universally ignored. Even in cases where there was a girls' school under the same management, as at Christ's Hospital (where eighteen girls were found under the charge of one mistress, as compared with the flourishing school for boys), a very little of the funds was being spent on them, while one Commissioner says that in the West of England there was an almost unbroken custom of excluding girls of the upper and middle classes from endowed schools. In general

> the endowments for secondary education of girls bear but an infinitesimal proportion to the similar endowments for boys; nor has more been devoted for long time past. . . . This appropriation of almost all the educational endowments in the country for boys is felt by a large and increasing number both of men and women to be a cruel injustice.

Without allowing to Miss Davies that "children" was intended to include girls, or even that it had been the original intention of the founders of schools to provide for both sexes, the Commissioners did recommend not only that girls' schools should share such funds in some measure, but that they should be considered in the distribution of further endowments or grants.[1] Miss Davies had suggested that the best Government help to girls' education would be by endowments for buildings and by scholarships, also by assistance where necessary in providing inspection and examination. The Commissioners did not want, however, to make many detailed recommendations (though they did mention Christ's Hospital), saying, "Generally we prefer to leave such appropriation to the administration of the new authorities." This refers to the Statutory Commission set up in 1869 to deal with the endowments for boys. The disparity between the amount accorded to girls and that accorded to boys continued for some time to cause a good deal of heart-burning, though this was not always the fault of the Commissioners. The most notorious case is perhaps that of Miss Buss, who, with her North London Collegiate School full to overflowing and a second school growing up, agitated again and again for a grant for building and furnishing. After a meeting at which a paper of Mrs Grey's had been read describing the need of schools for girls in the London 'suburbs,' and dwelling at some length on the good work that was being done by the Camden schools, £5000 was collected—though it was decided that it should be used not for Miss Buss, but for a girls' school in the City, to correspond with the City of London Boys' School. But six months later it was found that some City endowments were available for this City Girls' School, and the original £5000, collected specially for the use of girls, was calmly appropriated for the boys' school (already endowed with £60,000), being

1 " The education of girls is as much a matter of public concern as that of boys, and one to which charitable funds may properly be applied even when girls are not expressly mentioned in the instrument of foundation.'

the sum needed to make up £11,000 for their new hall. And generally where pounds were obtainable for boys it was difficult to collect shillings for girls.

Yet the recommendations on this head did a very great deal of good. One of the main pleas of those who had implored the Commission to look into the education of girls as well as of boys was the psychological one: if only some attention could be paid to this subject the self-respect of teachers and taught, and the whole attitude of those concerned, would be immensely improved. "Let female education be encouraged; let it be understood that somebody cares!" was the cry. Obviously the Commission *did* care, and the more detailed its recommendations the more likelihood of their being fulfilled. T. H. Green, Assistant Commissioner for Birmingham, had a most specific proposal in connexion with the endowments of King Edward's foundation:

> What is wanted is the establishment on the outskirts of every considerable town of a school which should do for girls what a well-organized grammar school does for boys; that is, one which should take day pupils at about £4 a year, and should be able in virtue of endowment, subscription, or Government grant to give them a sound training in English and arithmetic, in at least one modern language and either music or drawing, at the same terms for which a nominal training in English and arithmetic, with a power of fingering a piano, is now imparted. Such a school would . . . attract the best of those who now go to the cheap private schools as well as the daughters of the poorer professional men, who now have often much difficulty in obtaining education. It would not do its work fully unless it took a certain number of girls free.

It would be a real pleasure to the great philosopher to know how his words are being fulfilled in secondary schools up and down the country. He did have the satisfaction of seeing a local beginning made, and no less than three King Edward VI Grammar Schools for Girls founded in the then outlying districts of Birmingham. Other Commissioners recommended the same thing.

Mr James (afterwards Viscount) Bryce made three very definite suggestions:

1. The establishment of schools for girls under proper authority and supervision; it would be most desirable to provide in every town large enough a day school for girls under public management.

2. Considerable changes in the course of instruction; it would be proper to lay more stress on arithmetic, introduce mathematics everywhere, and Latin where it was possible to give time enough.

3. The provision of institutions where women could receive the higher education given by the universities to men.

The report seems to have taken a few years to 'get across'; it was helped—'shoved' is almost the word—by constant work on the part of both men and women, but especially women. Mrs Grey, Miss Buss, and Miss Davies, for instance, were all "determined to act." It did not matter that they 'pushed' different points of the report. Miss Beale's attitude was: "It is well in the interests of liberty that each of us should solve the problem in her own way." Similarly Miss Buss wrote: "Miss D. shuts herself into one bit of work, Mrs Grey into another, I into a third." And this was very generous of her, because undoubtedly Mrs Grey's scheme, which offered in addition to a thorough education for girls a dividend of 5 per cent., did not increase her own chances of getting the endowment which she so badly wanted. But suddenly, in the seventies, everything began to happen at once. Miss Buss, who had turned her own school into a public trust, got her money from the Brewers' Company, who owned considerable property in the St Pancras district, from which the North London Collegiate drew many of its pupils. A scheme passed by the Privy Council established it in 1873 as a first-grade public school. The National Union for the Higher Education of Women, chiefly Mrs Grey's formation, had drawn up a scheme for a public day school in West London which should be absolutely self-supporting, the funds for which

FRANCES MARY BUSS

Reproduced by kind permission of the North London Collegiate School   198

were to be raised in shares of £5 each by a limited liability company, "capable of extending its operations hereafter in various directions, wheresoever schools are wanted." Thus, under the patronage of Princess Louise, and organized by a council to take the place of a board of directors, began the Girls' Public Day School Company, responsible for the original 'high schools.' Within the same decade came Manchester High School, shortly afterwards to be established as a first-grade public endowed school under a scheme like that of Miss Buss. Out of the old endowments schools for girls were revived or newly formed, such as the Mary Datchelor, the Haberdashers' Aske's, and the Westminster Grey Coat. Bradford and Leeds founded girls' schools, Birmingham followed up with the King Edward VI Foundations, and Bedford with the Harper Trust. There were the Perse schools at Cambridge, schools at Leamington, Warwick, and dozens more.

Miss Buss's work is perhaps not so widely known and generally appreciated as Miss Beale's, but her importance is best realized from the fact that these high schools from the beginning took her creation of the North London Collegiate as their model. In the constitution of the Manchester High School, for example, it is distinctly stated that:

> The rules and regulations of the Trust for carrying on the North London Collegiate and Camden School for Girls shall be adopted as the basis of the permanent constitution of the Manchester Public Day School for Girls.

(The name "Public Day School," by the way, was changed to "High School," because the first headmistress was a Miss Day, and it was thought that confusion might arise.) But it was in more than trust deeds that the influence of Miss Buss was felt. Hers was the only school of its kind, and had twenty years' experience behind it; details of her organization and her ideals were bound to form the very structure of all later public day schools. It was to be distinguished from Cheltenham chiefly because it gave a *cheaper*, though no less adequate, education, and because the question of caste was not allowed to come into it. At Cheltenham, as Miss Beale had pointed out, the proprietors kept the nominations in their own hands, and a very strict tradition continues as to the status of any parent. At the North London, we are told by a pupil of the eighties, "No one asked where you lived, how much pocket-money you had, or what your father was—he might be a bishop or a rat-catcher." There was no snobbery either as regards poverty: "girls would openly grumble at having to buy a new text-book," and it was an act of merit to make your clothes last a long time. This is mentioned as a contrast to the private school, where there has been a distinct superciliousness at a girl's appearance in a 'turned' dress. Back in the seventies Miss Gurney explained that the newly started Camden or "Middle" school, where girls only stayed as a rule till fifteen, was not intended for a different class, "as class distinctions are happily unknown in Camden schools." This healthy tradition was maintained; for one thing it accorded well with the new spirit of the times, which showed itself also in a greatly increased religious tolerance, making the task of secondary education much simpler than that of the elementary school. The Manchester Trust Deed, for example, contained the following clauses:

> The Trust shall be absolutely free of creed or religious persuasion.
> Every school under the Trust shall be open to all girls of suitable age, character, and ability, without any distinction as to religious profession or social rank. . . .
> No religious instruction shall be given in any school under the Trust except simple Bible teaching . . . for every scholar whose parent or guardian desires she should receive it in the school.

But prayers were held, at which those pupils "shall be required to attend whose parents express a desire to that effect." Distinctive religious teaching—for Jewesses, for example—could be given if the number of those seeking it was not less than twelve.

The G.P.D.S. Trust schools, like Miss Buss's own, were predominantly Church in outlook, and religious instruction is given in all the schools, but denominational teaching is not a part of the ordinary course, and there is no restriction on the religious profession of pupils and their parents.

In thirty years or less the high school was a well-established part of English education, with all its typical organization and characteristics—even to the details of form mistresses, of classrooms, and of the 'bifurcation' of its Middle School classes into A and B parallel forms. Its time-table and arrangement of hours goes back to Miss Buss. She took over the idea of having no afternoon school from Miss Beale, but the reason given for making Saturday a whole holiday was characteristic enough of herself. She wanted the girls, she said, to have time with their families, and Saturday morning was left them that they might help in household tasks, and especially to go marketing with their mothers. (Whether this reason of nearly eighty years ago still holds is another question.) The reasons for some of the early high-school regulations are not always obvious, nor are they meant to be; the necessity which prompted them may have disappeared. For instance, most high schools insist now on a uniform, or at least certain details of uniform. There are obvious points about this—the neat appearance of the school as a whole, the encouragement of feeling for it, and the discouragement of personal sartorial vanity, not to mention the advantage for disciplinary purposes, as in taking out parties of girls, when a mistress can more easily keep an eye on her flock. But in these days of the short, loose frocks, as a rule entirely suitable for children, which are the present alternative to uniform, one forgets the heavy, tight, oppressive clothing of the early high-school days, and how it was most easily discarded when superseded by the gym. tunic or other recognizable uniform dress.

Another tradition of the high schools was that they were healthy. Miss Buss saw to it that the conditions of food, ventilation, and sanitation were as good as could be managed, and then had a very short way with cases of hysterical or fancied illness. She "had remarked, as a fact of her experience, that if girls of great natural vanity could not take the lead in any other way, they developed something sensational in health." (We do not know if, in accordance with modern psychology, which has remarked the same thing, she gave the girls some other opportunity for "taking the lead.") Similarly Dr Sara Burstall, of Manchester (though she herself was distinctly against the introduction, for instance, of compulsory games), quotes, not without approval, a characteristic utterance of some pioneer woman: "It is a sin to be ill." If the laws of health were taught and observed, it was understood, women would have the reward of their obedience in perfect health. At any rate, such an ideal was contemplated. The 'laws' of hygiene were taught. Physical training, generally in the form of Swedish or musical drill rather than the old-fashioned 'callisthenics,' was introduced; medical inspection of each girl by a woman doctor began from the time that these made their first appearance, and real care was spent when new school buildings were put up or old ones adapted that they should be sanitary and as far as possible convenient. Of the introduction of organized games more will be seen in our survey of the public schools, but when energetic young women from Oxford and Cambridge began to staff the high schools they brought with them the games they had enjoyed at college, and these soon became a very distinctive mark of the new institutions.

In the same tradition too is the curriculum, which included the sterner subjects which the Commissioners had found so lacking in the schools of the sixties. And

DR SARA BURSTALL

From a painting by Gretchen Tydeman

perhaps it was the direct result of these Commissioners' very forcible condemnation of "piano-fingering" that instrumental music was invariably an extra, while class singing, and generally drawing, remain as part of the regular curriculum.

This traditional curriculum is another result of Miss Buss's aims and outlook—she was one of the 'equal terms' section. The teaching as a whole led up to some public examination—the Locals or Matriculation. Therefore girls had to work at the same subjects as boys, and to work at them well. As mentioned before, Miss Buss was glad and proud to send up girls to the women's colleges, and it was Girton, with its insistence on the men's degree course, that she must have favoured in her heart. Miss Buss was not to be put off by the 'unladylike' bugbear. Before the Commission she had said that she could see no reason why the names of successful candidates for the Local examinations should not be published. She reiterated Miss Davies's contention that probably no one had yet found the ideal education for boys, but that if they did it would doubtless be fitted for girls too. She stressed in the school sphere what Miss Davies emphasized in higher education—the importance of proving, by work under similar conditions, that girls and women could compete with men and boys on equal terms. At any rate, it was her insistence on the Local or other outside examinations which, for better or for worse, linked the curriculum of girls to that of boys for about sixty years. (The Board of Education, assisted by the Headmistresses' Association, is now beginning to unlink it, endeavouring, for instance, to obtain full recognition of "Group IV" subjects in the School Certificate.) Whether her methods are to be admired or regretted, or both, there is no doubt that she influenced very greatly the ideal for girls' education during her long period of supremacy.

One other point is interesting in connexion with her

encouragement of a college career. After the opening of degrees to women by the London University Miss Buss, perhaps in gratitude, strengthened the connexion of her school with that university. The normal thing became for a North London girl to go on to one of the London colleges. That habit of looking to the local university was adopted, certainly in Manchester, and probably in other university towns, where the school could have the benefit of the university's interest on the council and in inspection or examination. Possibly with many openings that do not involve a university training the connexion is now less emphasized, but it was very important at the time.

Yet, though in so many ways the forerunner of the modern high school, the North London was from the beginning run on a personality, and it had therefore characteristics reflecting its founder and her ideals. Miss Buss was strongly emotional, and belonged to an emotional age, and for that very reason she both played on and at the same time sternly directed the power of emotion. Discipline was kept in two ways—by a multiplicity of laws and regulations and by the personal influence of the headmistress. Reproof with Miss Buss became a fine art; she could reduce a girl to tears, either by personal tenderness or by what we might now consider the unfair method of bringing up home circumstances— with a twist or a pressure to suit her purpose. And for this very reason she had, as a strongly 'charged' head always does, considerable emotional appeal: literally thousands of her girls must have felt for her a quite personal affection—difficult indeed to evoke in a large school.

It has been suggested that in thus maintaining discipline by stringent rules and personal effect Miss Buss had a subconscious fear of inefficiency in her own staff of the early days. These were for the most part, as Miss Gurney said, "clever mistresses whom she has herself trained to teach, and who pursue her system." A staff with little outside experience is apt to reflect, with less power, the spirit and methods of its head—though this is not to say that of the North London Collegiate staff many were not exceedingly able women, afterwards headmistresses themselves. But the tradition of willing obedience and discipline was yet in the making, and since the obvious punishments applied to boys, of caning, and even of detention, were impossible (the latter because many girls came from some distance, and there was no afternoon school), the whole burden of maintaining discipline had to rest on the tongue. There was practically nothing between the 'gentle remonstrance'—of which power the Commissioners had appeared doubtful when it was alluded to by other headmistresses—and expulsion. For similar reasons of discipline, and encouragement, a system of marks and prizes grew up, of great force. (This, for better or worse, was transmitted in varying degrees to the high schools as a whole.) As a means of promoting keenness and a high standard of work there was no doubt about the efficiency of this, though the variety of the subjects which carried prizes—needlework (plain!) was always one—prevented a too narrow line of development. In connexion with marks it is interesting that precautions against cheating were considered necessary—such as screens on desks, so that one girl could not see what her neighbour wrote. The very high standard of honour in this respect (which by public opinion girls supported, even if they did not always attain it) had as yet not fully grown up. It was one complaint of the Commissioners that at some of the private schools copying in most barefaced fashion was found, and without much disapproval from authorities. The difficulties in this respect were among those which the North London Collegiate had to face for being first in the field by twenty years.

Perhaps of all qualities sought in the Frances Mary Buss schools efficiency was the one most desired and most fully attained. Miss Buss's ideal was to give girls of the middle class the thoroughness and accuracy and real intellectual training which would fit them to work like their professional brothers for something like a living wage. Again and again in her *Life* one finds proof that this ideal of self-support for girls was at the back of her thoughts; she was battling against the lack of self-respect occasioned by their enforced dependence on brothers or other male relatives in the event of their not marrying. And besides the economic independence there was another and more personal kind of self-respect that could be inculcated by education. Miss Buss tried to give

> such teaching as shall place the pupil *en rapport* with the world she is about to enter, and shall inculcate and inspire industry, frugality, self-dependence, self-control, a definite plan of life, the preference of the claims of the future to present enjoyment, and a steady self-advancement for the sake of others as well as for one's own.

A *bourgeois*, a slightly utilitarian ideal! Nevertheless it was probably exactly what was wanted to counteract the deficiencies of girls' education at that moment. It became more 'refined' and spiritualized, without losing its solidity, as the century progressed. For instance, the Manchester Association for Promoting the Education of Women, originally founded to arrange courses of lectures for older women, determined that

> the education of girls is as much a matter of public concern as that of boys, [for] education is a good in itself, and a committee proceeded to consider the foundation of a high school for girls, the management of which should be in the hands of a local committee and the progress of which should be presented to the public in open reports.

One motive for this was the interesting theory put forward by Sir Joshua Fitch, one of the original Assistant Commissioners, that, especially in a society where boys left school early to go into business, trade, or a profession, women were the natural guardians of the nation's culture. They had more leisure, and it therefore fell to them to maintain this culture at a high level—which obviously they could not do with the education they were at present receiving. The Manchester Committee therefore stated that:

> No pains will be spared either by the School Committee or by the teachers to impart to the scholars the very best education which can be given, and to fit them for any future which may lie before them, so that they may become intelligent companions and associates for their brothers, meet helps and counsellors for their husbands, and wise guides and trainers for the minds of their children.

The Girls' Public Day School Trust combined in an even more remarkable way the practical and the ideal. Mrs Grey's scheme for a company of shareholders, with limited liability, undertaking the business of building and running self-supporting schools which should return a modest dividend on the capital outlay (though in fact this dividend has ceased of late years), was inspired by a hope

> that their schools would be places not only of instruction, but of education in the true sense of the word, and a training of the individual girl, by the development of her mental and moral faculties, to understand the relation in which she stood to the physical world around her; to her fellow-beings, whether as members of her family, her country, or her race; to her God, the Father and supreme Lord; and to know and perform the duties which arose out of these relations.

These sound like words, not of two generations ago, but of the latest conference of educational authorities, and it is a sign of the Trust's extraordinary vitality that their ideals have become rooted so deeply in English education. Their work was not spectacular; their jubilee record (1923), for instance, is of great interest to those connected with their schools, but far less to those outside. One very remarkable feature of the book is the list attached to every school of staff members who have gone out to be headmistresses themselves, some in new Trust schools, others in different schools or colleges up and down England, or overseas, so far as Valparaiso, Pretoria, or Japan. It is perhaps this permeation of the educational world with teachers who have worked with untiring energy and clear ideals that has brought about the solidity and worth of this section—to return to the opening words—of our pyramid.

One phrase in Mrs Grey's speech needs underlining—"the individual girl." The great temptation, when high schools became so large and so many, must have been to turn out a type. And when we think of the mechanical age into which these schools were born, and even of the ideals of the boys' public schools of the century, it is still more surprising that girls escaped this. But it was perhaps the one good influence of the Ladies' Seminary and the Select Home for Young Girls that the personal touch was never lost and the individual girl always considered. Every attempt was made not to force her into a mould, to encourage by diversity of the curriculum, by division of the staff's responsibility in forms, by providing opportunities and hobbies outside the ordinary range of school life, to develop individuality and personal gifts in every girl. These things are commonplaces now, but that they were thought of during the nineteenth century is proved in almost every memoir or autobiography of women who were of school-girl age in the early days of the high schools. Naturally the force of financial circumstances and the desire for testing the female brain by examination ordeal did at times impede this desire for individual development, but it was always an ideal, and the most successful heads were those who emphasized the relation of the school, the staff, and themselves with each individual girl.

The tradition is still alive. No one who has not attended a staff meeting will believe the amount of care, time, thought, and talk spent on the behaviour of every child whenever any kind of necessity arises. (Some would say too much!) This is not to say that the same care is not to be found in boys' schools, but I believe it to be of more recent growth. Of course, this constant sustaining of the personal touch is not without effort, and it is probably responsible quite as much as the actual intellectual application to class and corrections for the strain in such schools, and, naturally, the larger the school the greater the tension may become. But it is found, and it is required, in the main, of those who take up the teacher's calling. For the ideal that Mary Smith must be allowed to *be* Mary Smith, and must not by lack of this opportunity be turned into a poor imitation of Jane Brown— this ideal is on the whole true of high schools and public schools in this country.

There is another, and less happy, characteristic— probably of all educational institutions, but more especially of girls' schools. Their existence is a continual struggle of income *v.* expenditure. In spite of the Commissioners' recommendations, girls have never quite shaken off the tradition of being less expensively catered for than their brothers—a tradition so neatly expressed in Sir Alfred Dale's quotation of the advertisement he saw on the way to the Manchester High School Speech Day: "Strong Boots for Boys. Cheap Boots for Girls." Even in higher education attempts had to be made to 'do it on the cheap.' In the early days of Newnham it was felt that better teachers in girls' schools were so urgently needed that the best thing was to provide as good an education for the largest possible number at the lowest possible cost. And right on into 1898 Mrs Bryant, Head of the North London Collegiate School, was protesting that "an efficient staff cannot be satisfactorily maintained at the low cost per head sometimes quoted as appropriate," and recommending that the cost per pupil should be reckoned at £20 rather than £10.

Yet though there was a desire that in this matter of expenditure and in curriculum girls should be treated more like boys than before, the educators in the high schools did not lose sight of the domestic ideal that had been so much stressed in the previous generation. Of course, criticism continued. It was reported on in 1923:

> We consider that there is some substance in this criticism [that the curriculum is too academic], especially in its bearing on girls' schools, where one of the most important aims of the training, that of fitting girls for the duties of motherhood and for work in the home, has been unduly obscured by the academic trend given in many instances to the curriculum owing to the necessity of preparing pupils for external examinations. . . . Many girls on leaving school seemed unable to correlate their knowledge of different subjects and to apply it to concrete problems. . . . There is some reason to believe that girls are less interested in abstract argument than boys, and it would therefore appear that it is especially desirable in girls' schools that the practical application of apparently abstract subjects, such as mathematics, should be shown from an early stage, and that, in general, the teaching of the different subjects should, as far as possible, be correlated so as to show their bearing on the facts of everyday life.[1]

Yet this had not been forgotten by the early educators. Mrs Bryant had remarked that it was one of the signs of an intelligent mind to study a railway map, as well as Bradshaw (surely one of the most noteworthy examples of 'correlation'!), and that girls ought to learn "how to deal clearly with all questions involving geography when they arise in later life." Even more domestically she insisted that the application of science to practical life should be taught, and, of course, like all the high schools, the North London Collegiate had needlework in its time-table. (One of its early pupils was surprised at finding that in the entrance examination she was required to make a button-hole.) The importance of the subject was made clear by giving marks and holding examinations for sewing as well as for other things. Another way of impressing the importance of 'domestic subjects' was to insist that teachers of laundry, cookery, and dressmaking, when these came to be established as regular or alternative parts

[1] Report of the Consultative Committee (Board of Education) on the Differentiation in Curricula between the Sexes in Secondary Schools.

THE NORTH LONDON COLLEGIATE SCHOOL

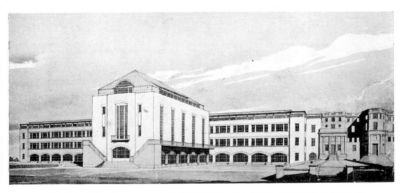

DESIGN FOR THE NEW BUILDINGS OF THE NORTH LONDON
COLLEGIATE SCHOOL AT CANONS PARK: SOUTH-WEST VIEW

By courtesy of the architects, Messrs Richardson and Gill

210

of the curriculum, should be "on a level personally and officially with other assistant mistresses." Still, it cannot be denied that there was in some schools a tendency to relegate the 'domestic arts' to the position of a Cinderella, and even in 1911 we get the unfortunate remark in an inquiry: "A few girls who are backward in intellectual work learn cookery."

Yet the fact that the schools could not afford, and did not want, to ignore either the 'domestic' or the natural sciences, and began introducing the latter, produced its own complication. "Headmistresses were therefore, even in the seventies, compelled to consider the congestion of studies." ("Our time is so short and there is so much to be done that it is hard to find time for everything," is a *cri de cœur* that one does not expect to find in 1878.) Some, such as Miss Day, of Manchester, did protest against the intrusion, for example, of science.

> I believe that for most girls six hours a day is all that can be safely given to headwork, and this leaves only two hours a day for the whole amount of preparation, as in the morning four hours are spent in headwork.[1]

A similar idea of the amount of time profitably spent on 'lessons' is found at the North London Collegiate, where Mrs Bryant insisted that after the four hours' teaching in the morning only one to three, according to age, was to be spent on homework. Miss Dove, of St Andrews, gave a somewhat shorter working day for the boarding-school girl: five hours a day for work, or six at the outside; she insisted also on one and a half hours for exercise. A thirty-three-hour week might therefore be considered the maximum for a public school and a thirty-eight for a high school. Of course, to this total must be added time for going to and fro; besides this a very large proportion of the girls were required to help at home in housework, in looking after the younger children (though not as a rule in teaching them), and, as they grew older, to take their

[1] S. A. Burstall, *The Story of Manchester High School for Girls*.

part in social activities (social in both senses), far more than were their brothers. Nevertheless, though we hear of "overcrowded evenings and oppressive homework" as far back as the eighties, the strain on all those in the schools—girls, staff, and even the headmistress—was probably less than to-day. (One is tempted to think both that it could not in the nature of things be *more*, and also that had it been as bad even those great women would have found themselves, like Prime Ministers, worn out after a limited number of years.) For, strenuous as the life of the high school may have seemed in the last century, when compared with the ladylike languor of the Select Home for Young Ladies, this did not mean that the pace was as severe as it is now. To look at it from the teachers' point of view—before the War it was considered that a form should consist of twenty to twenty-five girls, and that four lessons a morning, or at least an average of twenty per week (for there were no afternoon classes), were sufficient for each teacher, "seeing that time must be allowed for the preparation of lessons and the correction of papers." (Miss Beale, who was very strong on the correcting of work set, did not consider that it should take a teacher more than two hours a day.) A modern secondary-school mistress, who may have a time-table of twenty-five periods and up to four afternoons' work in the week, and be responsible perhaps for a form of thirty or upward, with all the necessary paraphernalia of Board of Education forms, school lists, and what-not, may envy her predecessor. The increased pressure is no one's fault and no single creature's responsibility; it is just the pace of the machine, which runs more quickly for staff and girls alike—and not for them only. One can but hope that mental acclimatization takes place, and that the increased comforts of a labour-saving house, or the distractions of travel, or wider interest may be some compensation for a life which, after all, was perhaps not as leisured as it now seems to us.

CHAPTER IX
THE PUBLIC SCHOOLS

Miss Beale in her evidence had told the Schools Inquiry Commissioners:

> I do not think it would be good to bring a hundred and thirty girls together and give them unlimited leave to talk to one another and play together. . . . We do give them leave to speak sometimes—we do not draw the rein too tight or there would be a tendency to deceit, but they do not hold any long conversations; they are not able to gossip and spend time in that way.

Nevertheless the large public boarding school with its unlimited leave (for conversation at least) was to come into being within a quarter of a century of her evidence. Moreover, Cheltenham was to be a most important influence on many of these new public schools—though they never modelled themselves so closely on the one example as did their 'day' contemporaries on the Frances Mary Buss schools.

A Board of Education report remarks that these new schools "reproduced in almost all respects the arrangements in vogue at boys' public schools," but this would seem an exaggeration—at any rate as regards details. Naturally the pioneers of these new ventures were influenced by the ideas which were inspiring the renaissance of the boys' public schools, and by their great headmasters, Arnold of Rugby and Thring of Uppingham. Miss Beale obviously learnt much from Arnold, and Miss Lumsden, first head of St Leonard's School, St Andrews, mentions his influence; while Thring, who received the Association of Headmistresses—not long formed by Miss Buss—at Uppingham, is often quoted (as well he may be) for sound common sense. Due to Arnold is the tradition

213

of discipline and of vigorous exercise, supported by the
framework of the prefectorial system—the entire lack of
which in the private schools had made the Commissioners
of 1868 regret that such a system of discipline by the
elder pupils was hardly known. Due to him also in part
is the type of Christianity which, if not exactly 'muscular,'
was distinctly 'robust.' Arnold had summed up the
trinity of school life as right principles, gentlemanly
behaviour, and intellectual ability; and this doctrine was
taken over as a whole, some girls' public schools substituting 'ladylike' in the second phrase—others not.
"Your girls play like gentlemen and behave like ladies"
was the curious compliment paid to (and apparently much
appreciated) a headmistress by the mistress in charge of
a visiting cricket team.

From Thring the new headmistresses may have learnt
the value of the 'house' system, by which, in his words,
"the civilization and gentle feelings of the comparative
home" were combined with "the hardy training of a
great school." From him too may have come the tradition
of recreative exercise other than games. At St Leonard's,
which was after Cheltenham the first of the public schools
corresponding to those for boys, it was possible from the
earliest time for a girl to do gardening as an alternative to
games. Thring's insistence also on the need for good and
apt building was not without effect. True, Cheltenham,
Roedean, and others began in ordinary and not too
convenient dwelling-houses, but a real effort was made,
as soon as finances permitted the venture, to house the
girls in buildings generally considered the latest thing in
their day for health and beauty. Here are some words of
Miss Beale's, and if our hearts do not echo them to-day
that proves only that our ideas of the beautiful change,
not that Miss Beale failed to impress her audience:

> The change from the plain bare walls of Cambray to the
> beautiful and stately surroundings of the New College was not
> without its effect upon teacher and taught. Mr Thring of

Uppingham used to insist, by word and deed, that if we would have learning honoured we should build it a fitting habitation. The greater dignity of the surroundings made all feel that the teaching must not be meagre and bare, but as perfect in its form, as accurate in its details, as attractive in its expression, as it was possible to make it, and thus the material reacted upon the intellectual and spiritual; the same music is different in a concert room and in a cathedral, where arches and vaulted roof respond to the pealing organ, and spirit seems answering to spirit in subtones and harmonics.

But, in spite of accepting much that was good from their male contemporaries and predecessors, the heads and organizers of the new schools took full advantage of the fact that they were not bound, like these, by tradition. Theirs was a field for experiment, and they did not fail to make use of their new powers, even if they began rather cautiously. For it was at first a daring thing in a parent to send a daughter to a boarding school of the new type, and many were the prophecies that she would come back spoilt for home life in one way or another. But both the staff and their pupils were exhilarated by the movement of which they found themselves part, and were determined that it should be a success.

They were animated by such a spirit as we see here:

I believe that half subconsciously we felt that we were in the van of a new and great enterprise, and that we were all sailing together into uncharted seas.

Or

We had so much that it was new for girls to have that we pitied those who lived before us. We had freedom, we had trust, we had stimulating teachers, healthy physical exercise, we had sympathy, understanding, and encouragement.

These are the words of an old member of St Leonard's School, St Andrews, which, according to the Board's publication quoted above, served as a model for similar schools in England. It would scarcely be true to say that any one of the great public schools was exactly modelled on another—therein lay their particular strength—but

215

the aim of St Leonard's and the watchwords of the council which founded the school—'development of character' and 'scholarship'—might be taken as the motive for the majority of the other foundations of the next fifty years:

> To give each girl in the school the best chance of self-development, not for selfish ends, but for the good of the community, and to send out capable women, with here and there a true scholar.

The Board of Education's concise account of the "features" of these "newer boarding schools for girls" is found in an admirable summary of the history of curriculum in girls' schools in the somewhat cumbrously entitled Report on the Differentiation in Curricula between the Sexes in Secondary Schools (1923):

> It is not merely a day school with boarding-houses attached; the various houses form an integral part of the school, and each house mistress is one of the staff, her work being divided between the school and her house. The playground for outdoor games, which have been from the first a prominent feature of the curriculum, belongs to all pupils alike, day girls and boarders. Lessons are done in the morning, while the afternoon and evening are devoted to preparation. Afternoon work is compulsory, like morning school, but it devolves on the girls themselves to see that the work of preparation is properly done. Girls of responsible age are placed in charge of their form-rooms, just as they are in charge of the playground. Afternoon preparation takes place in the form-rooms of the school, and evening preparation in the schoolrooms of the houses. Thus St Leonard's and boarding schools of a similar type in England, while retaining the ordinary subjects of study in girls' schools, have also adopted other subjects from the boys' curriculum as well as the whole public-school plan—the house system, the prefects, house games, and colours—and have thus developed a particular kind of tradition and of *esprit de corps*.

Obviously there are divergencies in detail from this in any of the other schools. At Cheltenham, for instance, the position of the house mistresses was not that described above; at Wycombe Abbey and even Sherborne there were practically no day girls; the arrangements about preparation and the amount of responsibility devolving on the girls varies from school to school.

The nineteenth-century girls' schools were linked to the old public schools by other things than the curriculum; in fact, the connexion was considerably closer in other respects than on the work side. In spite of the motive and temptation to imitate them in all things, there was never that stress on classics (with mathematics as a rather slighted alternative) which would have been found in a public school in 1879. The girls at St Leonard's were by then learning Latin, Greek, French, German, mathematics, history, geography, and English literature, with at least one weekly 'gym.' lesson and music and drawing out of school hours. A selection was presumably being made from the four languages; most schools arranged that two should be taken at a time; and science of a kind was generally added as soon as the schools had enough money for laboratories. St Leonard's, not so much from its date as from the temper of its founders, laid rather special stress on classics and mathematics, later on science —and their reward was Miss Agnata Ramsay's sole First Class in the Classical Tripos. But in the early history of Roedean, at Cheltenham, or in the Church Trust foundations (Woodard schools, etc.) there is no evidence of the narrow choice of subjects about which educationists of the next century were going to complain so bitterly in the public schools for boys.

St Leonard's, however, shares with Roedean, and later with Wycombe Abbey, Sherborne, and a dozen others, one characteristic which has attracted a great amount of both praise and blame. Undoubtedly games play, and perhaps up to twenty years ago played more emphatically, a very considerable part in the school life. It had always been expected that there would be far more freedom of physical movement for girls in the schools than had hitherto been the case. From the beginning at St Leonard's the girls possessed tunics and knickers, very different from their ordinary dresses, which were to be worn in the playground. The exercise was originally intended to take the form of gymnastics (late callisthenics), and in the nineties Swedish drill and musical gymnastics became very popular. But even those who most dismally prognosticated that with all this exercise girls would soon be turned into boys did not quite realize either what form this freedom was going to take or what its effect would be. It was true that they ceased to learn 'deportment'—how to come into a room, how to get out of a carriage—but a great deal of attention was still paid to manners. Miss Beale, who never thought that an *intellectual* training based on that given to boys was going to hurt girls, was much more suspicious of 'men's sports.' She set great store by dignity, gentleness, and courtesy of manner, and she did think it possible that these things would be easily lost. It was therefore with some difficulty that Miss Lumsden when on the Cheltenham staff persuaded her to allow tennis, and it was not till 1890 that she sunk her prejudice and submitted to the introduction of hockey. Games did, however, at Cheltenham, as almost everywhere else, become a part of the curriculum.

One of the pioneers in the matter of games was Miss Lawrence, of Roedean. She had been educated partly in Germany, and always had a love of outdoor exercise, particularly swimming, which was unusual at her early date. (This taste she was able, from the position of the school, to gratify and encourage in her pupils.) There is a legend that she herself had taken part in a game of hockey in the early days, though we are told that there is no truth in the legend circulated by a neighbouring seminary, soon after the time of the school's opening in Brighton, that "when one of the Miss Lawrences comes to a gate she does not open it—oh, no! She lays her hand on the top and lightly vaults over it." Miss Lawrence's article included in the Board of Education's Report on Special Subjects II contains an early and admirable statement of the advantages of girls' school games, and particularly of team games; Miss Dove's section on *Work and Play in Girls' Schools* is held as another *locus classicus* of discussion on the subject. One of Miss Dove's chief points is the very practical one that, however admirable it might be to introduce gardening or even farming as part of a regular school course instead of games, the latter "waste the minimum amount of material, and can be played on limited areas," which is all that most schools can afford. (The site of most of the big schools, however, was so well chosen that they were able without great difficulty to buy adequate, and in some cases admirable, playing-fields at an early stage.) She encouraged every game that boys play except football, and would have tournaments and competitions, prizes or cups, and—the St Andrews touch, presumably!—if golf is possible, a spring and autumn medal.

So the public-school girl, like her brother, was to play her part in games and to imbibe the team spirit. And she did, but with a difference. It was true that the school-girl played tennis, hockey (but not always), and even cricket, and that though much attention continued to be paid to her manners, they tended to be less restrained, sometimes less gracious than in the days of croquet and deportment. However, the girls' schools soon evolved their own winter games (there was very little opposition to tennis; for it quickly became a social asset), so danger of competition was excluded even from the comic papers. Both the new typical games came from America. Lacrosse was seen by Miss Lumsden on the prairies of Canada, played by the Indians, and in spite of its comparative difficulty was accepted at once, some schools (notably the Godolphin, Salisbury, and, I believe, Queen Anne's, Caversham) eventually giving up hockey in their preference for lacrosse. The other game was an adaptation of the American basket-ball, known to us as net-ball. It was played under cover in America when the snowy weather prevented outdoor exercise. The first mention of it in England was at Mme Osterberg's Physical Training College in 1895, when for the two goals the students used wastepaper-baskets. In their realist way schools, and especially high schools, took at once to a game which occupied so little space and exercised the players so considerably in such a short time.

The vogue for games rapidly increased; it was not long before even those who had introduced it into schools began to feel a little mistrustful of the fashion they had launched. In 1907 we find the Headmistresses' Association complaining that games were overdone, and a woman doctor reports unfavourably: "There is a danger of making a fetish of exercise, and this is becoming increasingly marked among women." Besides the physical objections to the strain on the growing girl we have the usual complaints of the over-important part taken in the lives of the school by games, and the exaggerated prestige of the athlete—all that was ten years later brought up against the effect of games in boys' schools, *The Loom of Youth* being one of the first protests in fiction. But on the whole those who ran the girls' schools felt there was more to be said for games than against them; Miss B. A. Clough's attitude is probably typical:

> It is undeniable that they frequently occupy a place in girls' thoughts which might be filled by something more fruitful, but one has to take probabilities into account, and consider what would be likely to be in the heads that games fill, and I incline to think that there might easily be less wholesome matters. Games do, I believe, drive out much silliness; they occupy the vacant space, and they also produce an antiseptic atmosphere.

The antiseptic attitude has been often enough found, and in turn decried, in boys' schools; it is unnecessary to dwell further on an aspect of the subject about which there has been so much debate, and in which the girls' problem is not specially different from boys'. But there *is* a difference when we regard games as a part only of something which went much deeper into the life of the public-school girl and into her character. It is worth looking with some care, and in the light of accepted psychology, into the whole-hearted acceptance by girls of the tradition of loyalty, *esprit de corps*, 'the public-school spirit,' or what you will, and what they made of it.

The girl, of any age or race, and particularly the adolescent girl, has a very remarkable capacity for devotion. Sometimes this devotion is expressed (prematurely we should think) in love as related to marriage. Juliet, Perdita, and Miranda are girls of secondary-school age, and what characterizes them, along with Rosalind and Viola and others, is an intense single-hearted and absorbing devotion. The objection that this is Italian precocity is not really valid, for in the *bourgeois* drama of Shakespeare's contemporaries the same type, of the same age, is drawn in a more northerly setting. There is also his own youthful but determined Mistress Anne Page. If, on the other hand, the contrast is made between the Elizabethans and our own school-girls the point is missed when we do not realize that it is the form or object of the devotion, not the intense feeling itself which has altered.

There is, and always has been, another characteristic object of this feeling besides the lover—so characteristic that the word 'devotion' bears a meaning akin to the sense in which *dévote* is still used in French. The religious fervour of the young girl is something which must be reckoned with in every study of her education. In an artistic temperament it often takes the form of a very real appreciation of ritual, or of religious poetry, or of emotional music, or, more vaguely, an identification of religion with the beautiful. In others the motive of service to the suffering, with the almost personal appeal of "Inasmuch as ye did it unto the least of these . . .," will be the dominant one, or even that of self-sacrifice, which, as Ruskin points out to the fifteen-year-old Lucilla in *The Ethics of the Dust*, is too often regarded as an aim in itself.

But a kind of selflessness and a deep emotional fervour, however expressed, is characteristic of the adolescent stage of religion in many women.

It was this deep and widespread feeling in girls that the new schools were bound to tap. But the emotion they set free was conducted down wide but well-defined channels, and became, as a rule, loyalty to a body. The words "not for herself, but for the community" in the aim quoted above were emphasized, and the sentiment was repeated in dozens of mottoes on thousands of school satchels or even pencil-boxes. (It generally took form in Latin, whether for dignity or conciseness is hard to say.) Team spirit, house feeling, and school loyalty—all these things, taken over from their brothers, became the main virtues in the eyes of the public-school girls; they acquired a glow and even a romanticism of which the girl beyond the boy is capable.

Here then the directors of the young were entrusted with a force which might, had they not possessed wisdom and judgment out of the ordinary, have become disastrous. On the one hand, if it were checked it might have frittered itself away, leaving behind the feeling of emptiness and dissatisfaction which an offering rejected always entails— the moral equivalent of that wasted and hopeless feeling of which Miss Davies and the other pioneers complained so bitterly on the intellectual side. On the other hand, the appetite for devotion, if there be such a thing, might have grown with what it fed upon, and the result might have been the extreme of silliness, to which—so it would at once have been said—women are always prone. And certainly the feeling for school ties, team badges, the honour of the house, and the general cult of 'totemism,' both internal and external, was at some stages and in some schools exaggerated among girls—as no doubt among boys. But in both there was something to balance it—though there were people who called the remedy among the boys worse than the disease. The counterblast to devotion was the law of Good Form. You were supposed to feel strongly for your house and school, no doubt, but except on special occasions, notably cup matches, you did not show it. A certain display of superiority was tolerated in the very young, but it was as much part of a house official's business to curb offensive exuberance as to encourage keenness. For good or ill, the public-school girl was to adopt the same reserve as her brother over the things for which she felt most keenly; Stalky's "jelly-bellied flag-flapper" would have received almost as frigid a welcome in a typical girls' public school in this century as he did on that famous earlier occasion.

There was a difficulty inseparable from the crowding together of large numbers of girls at the emotional age which was tackled by experienced women in much the same way. One of the commonest objects of the young thing's devotion is, of course, the older girl or woman of whom she is seeing a good deal. This element could not fail to thrive in such a community as a large school: in fact, a girl of the Middle School age would probably be omitting one of the natural stages of growth if she did not feel a deep affection and a genuine admiration for both contemporary and senior members of her own sex. Those who throw about such 'psychological' terms as 'Lesbianism' need to study both in theory and in practice the development of the growing girl, and to realize how often and how naturally these friendships and enthusiasms pass into the next stage, and only serve to widen and deepen her character. Of course, there *are* unhealthy attachments—the most skilfully drawn is perhaps that in Clemence Dane's *Regiment of Women*—as there will always be human beings whose love of power or emotional gratification urges them to exploit the weakness and affection of others. And there are always people who through inexperience, lack of tact, selfishness, self-distrust, or some other cause, cannot successfully handle any emotional situation. But there is little reason, except the rather vague one that they are unmarried, to expect such folk to be in the majority among schoolmistresses, particularly as their position has improved and they have to attach more respect to their profession and to themselves as members of it. And, to give them a lead, the tone was set of 'common sense' and 'wholesome atmosphere'; 'raves,' *grandes passions, Schwärmerei,* or whatever the term might be were definitely discouraged, and very definitely it was inculcated that if you were 'keen' on a person, staff or prefect, you showed it by devoting yourself to those things which were good in her eyes, not by more personal attentions. Naturally, even this attitude is open to criticism, but it entails a certain self-discipline and outward turning of the emotions which makes for good even if the child does not always attain to it or enjoy it.

No one is contending that all headmistresses, any more than all members of staff, succeeded in introducing the 'healthy' tone they desired. A surprising instance of the way one head dealt with the problem is given in *Four Miss Pinkertons* (Rachel Davis). The games captain, "a very brave girl," was deputed to speak to the school *en masse* on the subject, to bring them to a sense of shame for their stupidity.

> She knew how people talked; she heard them whisper, "*Isn't* she sweet? Look out, *she's* coming!" and fly to open doors for their idols, and fling themselves on the floor, two at a time, to take off their cricket pads in the boot-room. What did we think of ourselves now we had it put straight before us? Wasn't it ludicrous, wasn't it revolting? She had come to tell us it must stop. There must be no more of this—this sickening *nonsense* at Sutton Weald. The school itself was getting a name for it, and had we ever thought how bad it was for the school? (I don't suppose it had ever occurred to her that it was bad for *us* except in so far that we were the school.) But for the sake of the *school* she flayed us alive; for myself I felt raw and bleeding, though I could not be sure of her effect on others, as I could not bring myself to look at any face. . . . There was to be no more of this putrid furtive 'thing,' but real friendship was to

take its place. Idolaters and idols were to be on frank, happy terms together; 'they' would see to that, she knew, and the new order was to begin at once.

"Poor Gertrude, she was an optimist!" is the comment. For
Gertrude's pluck, the commanding little figure she had cut on the platform, only increased the zeal of her worshippers. . . . For the other 'lordly ones,' they never accomplished the task of shedding the glamour with which their adorers had haloed them and putting something sounder in its place.

The showing-up and redirecting of young enthusiasms needed more experience and skill than could be expected of a prefect in a school where the head had proved her own inability to deal with the matter. But the spirit of Gertrude Johnson and the no-nonsense-about-it attitude became part of the tradition in many schools.

In any case the bracing atmosphere was not suitable for every constitution. A proportion of girls, as of boys, must be in every school unsuited through physical or temperamental delicacy to accept the treatment of the majority; they may become definitely unhappy, introspective, occasionally bitter, or merely dulled. New methods, child guidance, and psychological study in various ways are doing much to help this group, though such measures are perhaps less accepted as a matter of course among 'public-school parents' than among those in other walks of life. But twenty or thirty years ago no such aid was thought of, and 'rebels' there had to be in most of the big communities. They were not necessarily 'rebels' in the accepted sense of one who made trouble merely by obstreperousness and breaking the rules. Good schools have generally known how to deal with this type, and the troublesome Middle School girl who turns out an admirable prefect or hockey captain, though she sounds like the product of a story-book, is a common enough phenomenon. The child, however, who is 'difficult,' who fails either to get on with the rest in general or to make a

P   225

particular friend, who hates games and takes no interest in her work, who, without being ill, is generally just sufficiently below par not to be quite well—is it to be wondered at that she finds the school as much a problem as it finds her? There are two ropes that may pull her out of the Slough of Despond: a hobby or line of action in which she can successfully find herself, and a sympathetic person who she feels can understand her. Often this is some one quite unexpected, not necessarily a popular or even an experienced person—a young music mistress, a house matron, even a quiet older girl who has been passed over for the prefectship—but for the 'rebel' to feel that there is just some one on her side, or some interest in which she can be absorbed, softens the hard, deadening feeling and straightens the warping mind. Lacking these, she will go out thinking, not necessarily that she is a failure (and it is possible that a streak of undiscovered talent for writing or art, later recognized, will go to strengthen her own good opinion of herself), but that the school is. For the mind turned in on itself fails often to see the merit of both adaptability and humour, and the misfit whose heart is set on roundness may not appreciate that squareness is sometimes as important a quality.

There are probably fewer misfits now in the public or high schools; perhaps more have found salvation from themselves through the increased interests provided or through contact with teachers trained to think sympathetically. But one cannot always tell. For the real trouble with those whom I have called rebels is that they are not necessarily 'naughty' nor even 'difficult'—outside. Perhaps they do not 'let on,' either at school or at home, how unhappy they are. They store it up—and then write books about it. That the second decade of this century did produce a crop of bitter grain from all kinds of schools is undeniable; witness the collection of retrospective essays published under the title *The Old School* (But is it too material to remind readers of this that the majority of these writers were at school during or just after the War, and that had it been possible to feed and warm them better they might have looked on school life with a less jaundiced view? Spiritual warmth and mental food no doubt count for most, but maize pie, cold pipes, draughts, and "that empty feeling" are a very depressing constant background to a child; and these things were, and doubtless could not be helped.)

As the idea of education both in public and in high schools was, materially speaking, "to fit a girl for either marriage or a career," it is worth following the girls out of their school life to see what in fact actually happened to them. It is not possible to get a complete record over a really long period. There are some 'old girls' who always drop out of an association, and there was a considerable time-lag before these associations or unions, which in modern times are so much taken for granted, began to collect news of past and leaving members of the schools. Curiously enough, there was quite considerable objection to any such associations being formed in some schools. The reply from an old girl of one of the first schools was, "I keep in touch with girls I liked; others I never want to see again"—which shows that the writer had not been overwhelmed with the spirit of the Old School Tie. Another objection was that they would be merely modelling themselves on old boys, who "only meet once a year to carouse at dinner"—which was apparently no attraction. However, the St Leonard's Seniors, the Cheltenham Guild, the Old Roedean Association, the Sherborne Old Girls' Union—these and dozens of others were formed, and their records do provide us with some guide of what 'the old girl' is doing to-day, or has been doing for the last forty or fifty years.

The following are among the careers taken up by the St Leonard's Seniors. They have become missionaries, barristers, editors, journalists, secretaries, photographers, dispensers, nurses, warders, doctors in all branches, assistant mistresses or headmistresses, lecturers, authors, musicians, dressmakers, milliners, and public speakers. Some have taken up farming, gardening, dairy-work, weaving, embroidery, and work in stained glass. And this remarkable list dates only from their jubilee, in 1927; we should probably add to it a dozen new professions recently made available. Cheltenham Guild, also, at a comparatively early date had members who had taken up medicine, nursing, law, agriculture, accountancy, art, literature or stage work, commerce, horse-breaking. The management of a mill is mentioned, and partnership with father or husband in a firm, besides a great deal of voluntary or social work, including Scouts or Guides at home or overseas.

It is no wonder that one of the smaller boarding schools announces, "About 30 per cent. of the girls take university courses after leaving school, and about 95 per cent. take some definite training to fit them for a career." A casual remark in the history of a big high school shows that it was not unusual for two-thirds of a Sixth Form to go on to the university, of whom some years later half were married. To take, equally at random, a reunion of fourteen girls within two years of their leaving a G.P.D.S. Trust school—their doings showed an amazing variety. Two had got places at the university (Oxford and London), two were studying music, and one more, after working for a year as a school secretary, had determined to do the same; one was at the Froebel Training College, another training for nursery-school work under the L.C.C.; one was taking a three years' domestic-science course; one though at the moment engaged on another job, had her mind set on dramatic art; one was working for a Civil Service examination; two were in the Civil Service as typist and clerk; another had a secretarial job in the B.B.C.; while the fourteenth, having only lately left school, was still at home. To these should be added a librarian and a child's nurse who were unable to join the party. It is rather remarkable that none was taking physical training, and that none was—or admitted to being—engaged.

The variety of occupations taken up has not been seriously studied, and it would be interesting to see whether one school or type of school encouraged, or at least produced, a particular form of career. At a guess I should say they did so much less than do boys' schools of the same grade. Yet the public schools themselves each had a strong individuality, and most of the early ones had their lines marked out by the founders. We have seen that Cheltenham was from the first a proprietary school (a day school originally) "for the daughters of gentlemen"; the following classes are mentioned as comprising the parents, in descending order of number, by 1864— Army officers, private gentlemen, clergy, medical, Civil Service, lawyers, bankers, Naval officers, merchants. The Ladies' College was, on the whole, started for the sisters of the boys who went to the recently founded Cheltenham College. The St Andrews school (later taking over the name, as it took over the grounds, of the old St Leonard's College) was founded in 1877 by a local company, primarily with the object of educating their own daughters, but arrangements were from the first made for taking boarders. Pupils came from a distance, and it was not difficult when Miss Dove retired from the headship for her to organize a number of parents and others to found a school on the same lines in England—Wycombe Abbey —in 1896. Wycombe, however, differed from St Leonard's and Cheltenham in having no day girls, having but a small town to draw on, lacking the university or social background of St Andrews or Cheltenham. Perhaps for this reason more attention could be paid to the school buildings and grounds; Wycombe Abbey was certainly fortunate in having from the very start plenty of dwelling-room and wide open spaces, though, of course, it now holds more than three times the original hundred for whom the first building was intended. The same stress was laid as at St Leonard's on a high and energetic standard of work and games, the house system, and prefectorial discipline.

Before Wycombe Abbey and not long after St Leonard's another school had been founded under quite different auspices. A large and remarkable family, the Lawrences, had, partly through an accident to their father, fallen on difficult times. To help the family income and to assist the education of the younger members Mrs Lawrence, attended by two of her daughters, ran a small school of day pupils and boarders at her large house in Wimbledon. The eldest daughter, Penelope, who had taken the Natural Sciences Tripos at Newnham, worked first as a demonstrator at Cambridge and later in other capacities, while the charge of the school at their home lay more and more heavily on Dorothy and Millicent Lawrence. It was to Dorothy that the idea is said to have first occurred (at the age of twenty-four) that the three sisters might found what afterwards should become a public school for girls—a school for the sisters of the boys who went to Eton or Winchester. It was an ambitious enough thought for 1884. The eldest sister joined what became known in the family as "the Firm," and the three young women started in a small way a boarding school at Lewes Crescent, Brighton. Even in this rather inappropriate *milieu* some of the public-school ideas were put into force almost from the beginning—the playing of games and the division of the school into houses. With these was combined remarkably good teaching, including science, languages, and music; these subjects, as also art, were in the beginning taught by one or other of the large family of sisters, some of whom began as pupils while their elders were running the school.

Owing, no doubt, to the very remarkable personality of its founders the school prospered and increased, moved into larger premises, without at first being able to attain their wish of being in the country, and then, by good management and financial courage, the present site on Roedean Brow was acquired, and the present school buildings erected in the last few years of the century.

It was said of Miss Lawrence by a younger sister that "she had a breadth of view and character that is generally associated with a man," though without being a "mannish" woman.

> It was never to be forgotten that while girls were to have the same training in sportsmanlike behaviour, self-government, and simplicity as their brothers, they must be fitted to become good mothers and housewives.

Yet to the outsider the emphasis seemed to be laid on the first of these characteristics, and the tradition of sport was as firmly rooted in Roedean by the energetic Miss Lawrence as in St Leonard's, 'officered,' as it was to begin with, by young women from Girton.

North and south were the foundations laid, also east and west. There was a revival of the old Godolphin foundation at Salisbury, which was approved in 1886; there was Sherborne, founded in the last year of the century with a council both of local interest and general distinction, a school of "true religion and sound learning," which under Miss Mulliner, herself a student of Miss Beale's, reflected in some ways, but not all, the characteristics of the pioneer. There were various Church Trust schools, Low, Middle, and High, and there were a few like the Royal School, Bath, which corresponded to those public schools which took chiefly the sons of one profession or class. The East Coast was comparatively thinly populated with schools, in spite of its bracing atmosphere; but even in the last century there was St Felix, Southwold. Enumeration becomes tedious, but it is interesting to notice how vast was the army of schools that sprang into being between 1877 and 1900.

One last may be said to belong in spirit, if not by three years in date, to the nineteenth-century girls' public

schools—St Paul's Girls' School. This was founded out
of the funds left originally by Dean Colet in the trust of
the Mercers' Company. Under their wise management
the estate left for the upkeep of the boys' school had
increased tremendously, and the governors of St Paul's
School, having the money in hand, decided to endow a
girls' school which should be in all respects on the same
footing as the older institution.

The first head was Miss Gray, who came there from
the headship of the Junior Department of St Leonard's.
She laid down very clearly what was to be the chief end
of education at the new school—it was to educate home-
makers. As it was perhaps unique in being a public
school (in the sense in which this is used of Eton and
Winchester) and a day school—Cheltenham having by
this time grown on the house side till this overshadowed
the day element—it could be admirably planned to Miss
Gray's ideals. These she put before a conference of staff
and parents at an early occasion; and her description of
the ideal mistress of a home is so complete and definite
as to be worth quoting:

> The mistress of the home must be capable of securing as far
> as possible the comfort and the enjoyment of all those in the
> home. She must have good health, equable spirits, a good
> judgment, a quick intelligence, courage, firmness, and patience.
> She must be motherly even if she is not a mother, and must be
> both able and willing to give all necessary care to those of her
> household who are weak or ailing. Whether she is what the
> world calls rich or what the world calls poor, she must be un-
> ostentatiously liberal. She must use her means so wisely that
> the pinch of poverty is eased if she is poor, and wealth is not felt
> to be a burden if she is rich. The pleasures of the home must be
> her special care; she must provide some enjoyment, and not
> merely food and warmth. She must learn the art of drawing
> others out and making them show the best of themselves—the
> secret of every good hostess; she must study the equally difficult
> art of concealing many a care that would obtrude but for her
> self-control.
> Nor are her interests confined to her own home and its

dependents. As she is in her home, so she is in the community—a beneficent presence, cheerful, helpful, encouraging, ready to take a share in whatever good work is going forward. Wider still I should like her sympathies to extend; let them embrace some of the great causes which are being pleaded before her country; it will be all the better for her home if she have some opinion about the politics of the day.

There is a moral dignity in the ideal mistress of a home that comes in part from self-respect, in part from the respect of those whom she rules. And, whatever be her creed, there will be no long spaces in her life when she cannot spare a thought for the unseen and the eternal.

In one respect at least the scholastic and academic women of the nineteenth century proved their detractors the falsest of prophets. Much learning and great exertions neither made them mad nor drove them into early graves. Miss Beale in 1864 had studied 'statistics' which showed that the average age of 'literary ladies' (at their decease?) was over sixty, but she was gravely understating so far as the latter half of the century was concerned. If we look at the founders of the G.P.D.S. Trust, for instance, we find that the redoubtable Lady Stanley of Alderley lived for eighty-seven years, Miss Shirreff (who was, besides, an early mistress of Girton) to eighty-three, and her sister, Mrs Grey, to ninety, while Miss Gurney died in 1917, at a mere eighty. Of the two great headmistresses Miss Beale died in harness at seventy-four, and Miss Buss, after nearly fifty years of work, at sixty-eight. Miss Davies, who went to record her vote in 1919 (though not upon crutches, as Mme Bodichon in 1865 had prophesied), died in her ninety-second year. If it is argued that these ladies were not themselves scholars, though the cause of scholarship in others—one can turn to some of the earliest Girton students, of whom Miss Lumsden lived to be over ninety, Mrs Bryant carried on at the North London Collegiate School till after the War, when she was sixty-eight, and Dr Sara Burstall, of a later generation, put in forty years of teaching, and has been retired for several. The loss of Miss Rogers at Oxford, by a motor accident, at the age of eighty-one is but recent.

It has been said, with perhaps more poetry than obviousness, that the girls' public schools of the last century were as different, to begin with, as flowers in a garden, for they were the expressions of the personalities of their first heads. And it is not only heads of schools and colleges, but all those who worked for women's education who seem to have this vivid personality. Even more than in their portraits it is seen in their letters and other writings; a book like Lady Stephens' account of Miss Davies, with full quotation, makes most racy reading. Remarkable also is their wisdom. When a kindly and helpful head advises, reproves, or cheers a young assistant mistress, when an experienced one lays down the reins and writes a book, in nine cases out of ten she is saying or writing just what, *mutatis mutandis*, had been discovered and enunciated by Miss Lawrence, Miss Dove, or Miss Burstall, even by Miss Beale or Miss Buss. And the more one hears and reads of these vital women, absorbing and absorbed, the more one becomes aware of their power, their rich and glowing personalities: Miss Buss, direct, public-spirited, with perhaps a touch of the dictator; Miss Beale, driving forward her immense work, with a personal interest in each member and her contribution; Miss Davies, vigorous, persistent, undismayed in the face of opposition, and almost equally so by that far more difficult trial, cleavage of opinion among friends; Lady Stanley with her dignity and her shrewdness; Mme Bodichon with the corn-coloured hair and independent artistic judgment; Alice Marks (Hertha Ayrton, the scientist); Dr Sara Burstall; and dozens more. Without being in all respects *laudatrix temporis acti* one may say, "We shall not look upon their like again."

CHAPTER X

OFF THE BEATEN TRACK

THERE were during the period of the high-school and public-school foundations two other important types of school for the better-off child. Both had been in existence for a long time, and they represented, one on each side, the two great religious sections outside the Church of England. These institutions were the Nonconformist academies— among which the Friends' schools were outstanding for girls—and the Roman Catholic convents. Perhaps it was because both types of religion felt themselves 'in opposition'—and were, in fact, at the beginning of the century under severe political and educational disabilities—that their schools developed very definite tendencies and outlooks. The Anglican Sisterhood schools, founded under the approval of Dr Pusey from 1848 onward, such as the Clewer and Wantage Sisters, though important in themselves, do not differ in kind, but only in degree, from the schools founded under High Church trusts.

As far back as 1695, not many years after the beginnings of the Quaker movement, it was the advice of the Yearly Meeting

> that Schools and School masters who are Faithful Friends and well qualified be Plac'd and Encourag'd in all Countys, Citys, Great Towns or Places where there may be need, and that such School masters as much as maybe sometimes correspond one with another for their help and Improvement in such Good and Easy methods as are most agreeable to the Truth and the Childrens advantage and benefit.

Not all schools either of the Quakers or of the other Nonconformist bodies took girls, but among the Friends the idea of spiritual equality between men and women— the logical outcome of the belief in the value of personality

235

—is very marked, and they have long had both co-education and schools for girls. By the end of the eighteenth century Quaker schools were established in different parts of the country (a few only in London), particularly in Yorkshire, where there were many Quaker families. The schools were carefully graded according to the fees that the parents could pay. One type—the farm schools—took girls of twelve to sixteen for the cheap rate of about £14 per annum, and, like the German *Landerziehungsheim*, insisted on mixing a good deal of practical work with sound education. As a result the daughters of the poorer Friends were able to receive a considerably better education than those of other families with approximately the same income.

But the most interesting point about the Friends' schools was the modern spirit of the teaching. The idea of awakening the interest of the child and of encouraging her to pursue her studies intelligently rather than as mere memory work is a commonplace in these days, but that the early schools should have realized such a thing in the days of Rousseau, or even of Pestalozzi, is remarkable indeed. The announcement to-day in the prospectus of a school that "stress is laid on preparation for citizenship and education for leisure" shows that Quakerism still considers itself in the fore of educational progress. 'Domestic science' also was early taken as a subject in girls' schools, either as an adjunct to 'formal science' or as an equivalent to the manual training which is such a marked feature of their boys' schools—for instance, Leighton Park.

However, 'book-learning' was not overlooked. The Schools Inquiry Commissioners, in their tirade against the "phrenzy of accomplishments," which had but increased since Hannah More's day, and especially against the hours assigned to piano practice, noted that in Friends' schools music was sometimes replaced by Latin, German, and Euclid—"I could not but think with

advantage," said one of them. It is true that one Commissioner reported that he could not examine the girls of
a certain Quaker school, the reason given being that this
was too exciting a process, and that "to rouse the spirit of
emulation overmuch is dangerous." Nevertheless two of
the first six Girtonians (Miss Woodhead and Miss Lloyd)
seem to have been Friends, or at least taught in Quaker
schools, which speaks well for the standard of these.

The liberal tradition with regard to women is shown,
for example, in the feeling of equality between men and
women teachers that one gets from the accounts of the
Friends' Teachers' Guild meetings, inaugurated at the
end of the last century. Both in the addresses and in
the debates at conferences the opinions and ideas of the
women seem to be accepted entirely on their merits in the
easy manner of a people accustomed to take account of
the work, not the sex, of the worker. (This is merely the
opinion of an outsider on reading the reports.) Such an
attitude is bound to tell on the education of girls and their
ideals.

The best known of their schools for girls is The Mount,
York, which has been in existence for over a century. As
often happens with Quaker schools, not by any means all
the children are connected with the Society of Friends,
though no doubt the case was different at an earlier period.
By 1908 it was said that in not more than two schools
were the Quakers in a great majority. In fact, it is probably true to say of others besides Leighton Park that they
came into being not merely to educate the children of
Friends, but to express through education the Quaker
view of life. Either way, the Friends' schools are regarded
as "a precious inheritance."

The connexion between Unitarianism and distinguished women has been suggested; for an example of
education among 'Orthodox Dissent' we may turn to the
Wesleyans. The education of children was a special care

in the eyes of their founder, who, though his advocacy of strict discipline has earned him a reputation for severity (not undeserved when we consider the early rules for Methodist school-children), was himself in practice a lover of the individual child. But in the development of Methodist education three points stand out. First, the very distinct line of cleavage between ministers' children and the children of the laity. The most famous Wesleyan school, Kingswood, was to begin with designed for the sons of ministers. Ministers had the right to send their sons there for six years, as an alternative to getting a grant for their education. Trinity Hall, at Southport, founded in 1864 as a day school, became the equivalent school for girls, and though now by no means a small proportion are children of the laity, it was an understood thing in the last century that ministerial children came into a different category from other daughters. (They even began at an early stage to take external university degrees, though higher education was very restricted among Methodist girls.) The second distinctive point is that in the early part of the nineteenth century the Methodists concerned themselves chiefly with elementary education, and it was when this branch became more and more a matter for the State that they turned to the secondary schools, other than Kingswood. In the first elementary schools boys and girls alike shared the benefits of religious and primary education. There was a school near Bristol in 1741, before the foundation of the present Kingswood, in the charge of one master and one mistress. Mr A. H. Body points out:

> As the teaching staff was unpaid, there was obviously no monetary advantage to be gained by employing a mistress, and her appointment appears to have been made solely because it was more suitable that the girls should be taught by one of their own sex.

A subtle comment on modern distinctions of sex in teachers.

But this excellent precedent was not followed in the

more advanced field, for the third point must be noted—
that for a long time the secondary education of girls,
excepting always ministers' daughters, was ignored as far
as schools were concerned. They were educated at home,
and the ideal was not far from the 'shirt-and-pudding-
maker' type. It must be remembered that Wesley's own
sisters had suffered under the same disabilities, and the
bad tradition of drudge-daughters was not broken. One
reason for keeping it was doubtless the difficulty of
expense. Methodists as a whole had little to spare until
wealth developed with trade. The first and most obvious
procedure was to spend on the boys and keep the girls
at home or send them to private schools, about the prevailing inefficiency of which no more need be said.

Nevertheless, to this condemnation exceptions must be
made, and one that was striking—the school at Clapham
which has become Queenswood, near Hatfield. It is now
of the proprietary public-school type, having a board of
governors, but was started privately. Like so many
educational institutions for girls, the present school is in
its fourth decade. The Methodist Council were swept up
with the tide of new educational foundations, though not
perhaps on the crest of that wave, and after 1885 we get,
for example, Kent College at Folkestone, Farringtons at
Chislehurst, and the Jersey College for Girls.

To some extent the curriculum and ideals of such
schools were those of the G.P.D.S.T., but on the whole
it was only in the later foundations, such as Hunmanby
Hall, in Yorkshire, that a definite training for professions
was emphasized. Elsewhere the ideal has been rather to
prepare the girl for home interests and voluntary social
service. That the tide is now running in the opposite
direction may be gathered from an address delivered at
the Speech Day of the West Cornwall School in 1932.
Sir Harold Bellman assumes that his audience has sat
uneasily under the oft-repeated advice of the "Be good,
sweet maid, and let who will be clever" type. He suggests

that it is desirable for them to exercise cleverness and still be good—a new idea, apparently, outside the tradition of previous generations of speakers. He points out:

> Doubtless most of these gentlemen dictate notes for their speeches to clever girl secretaries; they are fortunate if clever girl journalists are present to report their utterances with charitable lucidity; and if they appear in print it is below such major news items as the latest epic of a woman aviator, a woman explorer, or another of that regiment of women whose conduct is distinguished. Their homes are adroitly managed by women; during their leisure their daughters drive them cleverly through traffic-crowded streets, or their nieces run them to a standstill at tennis; while if they seek entertainment in drama, music, films, ballet, art, or literature it is inevitable that they will be cleverly served by a great deal of feminine talent. In short, this world is full of clever girls doing clever things.

"In short," what he advises is a break-away from the old Methodist idea, and an acceptance of the standards of a twentieth-century world.

At the other end of the religious scale come the convents. The education of girls has for a long time been taken in hand by the Roman Catholic Church, though of the teaching orders the earliest concerned themselves with boys only. But in the seventeenth century there were various communities of women who regarded teaching as a part of their vocation. Naturally this did not apply to Protestant England, and it is to France that we must look chiefly for the full development of such educational societies as the Cistercian *abbayes* and the Ursuline convents; there was also that remarkable foundation La Maison de St Louis at St Cyr, so carefully watched over and encouraged by Mme de Maintenon. It was that country and that century which saw the production of some of the most famous Catholic books on girls' education. The subject had since the earlier days of the Renaissance been neglected or illiberally regarded. But now came works by Mme de Maintenon herself, Fénelon's treatise *De l'Éducation des Filles*, Père La Chaise's *Instruc-*

tion Chrétienne pour l'Éducation des Jeunes Filles, and a number of others.

Since the teaching orders, from the days of Les Filles de la Congrégation de Notre Dame, founded by Pierre Fournier in 1597, to the Order of the Sacred Heart at the beginning of the nineteenth century, were either founded in France or, like the Ursulines, early introduced there, the French tradition in education has persisted wherever their schools have sprung up. Such characteristics as a training in fine needlework and the domestic arts, and a rigid system of 'surveillance,' were to be found in English convent schools even at the time when the public schools for girls showed their most vigorous growth. Characteristically, French also was the idea of an education founded on philosophy, and a form of moral philosophy tended to be the basis of education for girls also, attended, however, by the warning, "The best safeguard of both their faith and good sense is intellectual modesty." *La morale* had been a lesson at St Cyr in Mme de Maintenon's time, and "the elements of Catholic philosophy" are said to form part of the training of the Catholic girl to-day. It was suggested by Mother Stuart twenty-five years ago, in discussing the ideal curriculum, that the study of logic could be introduced by the study of grammar—"even English grammar"—and it is interesting to see that one of the most up-to-date educational handbooks, entitled *Thought and Expression*, makes use of a combination of these same studies in the teaching of language.

The plan of studies of a teaching order in modern times is developed from innumerable editions dating back to its foundation. Mother O'Leary has given some details of the curriculum of the French schools of the Order of the Sacred Heart in 1805. It includes Bible history, Church history, French grammar and language, literature, and arithmetic, including book-keeping. These are all to be taught by the class mistress. There are also geometry, mythology, history, drawing, music, and writing, by specialists—the last subject nearly always taught by a master. Geography and domestic science seem to have been optional. Later, foreign languages and natural history (science?) were added.

Testimony to the intellectual side of convent teaching seems to be favourable. "In my own experience it was at least as good as the [education] I received later at the best type of English high school," wrote a pupil who left in 1914. Public examinations were at first regarded with disfavour, but when it became educationally expedient that Catholic girls should take them to qualify for teaching posts they did so. The same applied to the university courses. Catholic schools have long had training colleges for their own teachers; moreover, attendance at a university was discouraged. One reason given was that the woman who came up in pursuit of the degree only, without sharing the full life of the community, was missing what the university had of most value to offer. But when the position of women was assured Roman Catholics took advantage of it, and provision was made for the woman student, as at Cherwell Edge, Oxford, where a hostel for home students was founded by the Order of the Holy Child. And amid considerable applause from undergraduates a Reverend Mother carried off the Chancellor's Prize for English in 1933, with an essay on *Coffee-houses of the Eighteenth Century*.

But it was not primarily for nuns that the girls were being trained. This is a description of, I believe, the Convent of the Sacred Heart at Roehampton.

The Order . . . was founded by a saint. But she was a French saint and a woman of the world. The first object of the Order had been to provide a good education for the daughters of the French aristocracy. Certain formal graces still clung to our manners. Nuns in the higher positions had to be greeted, wherever we met them, with a deep curtsey. When we saw our parents in the parlour on Sundays and Thursdays we had to wear our Lisle thread gloves. The parlour had once been a ballroom in the big eighteenth-century house, and a certain faded elegance still clung to its parquet floor and stiff lace curtains. On entering it we made no less than three curtseys—one to our own relatives, one to the other children's, and a third to the *surveillante* in charge.

At the back of our Mother Foundress' mind had been the idea that many of us would one day marry. She had great faith in the influence of good wives and mothers and a great sense of social dignity.

Two novelists of to-day—rebels both—have left striking, though far from pleasant, pictures of convent schools, drawing, presumably, on their own experience. Both testify to the extraordinary skill with which the nuns play on the emotions and imaginations of their pupils and to the sureness of their psychological technique. It is not to crush the spirit of the child that those in authority intend, but to mould her will and to direct her sentiments.

One thing was severely stamped out of us—any tendency towards a dangerous independence of mind. Through years of training the nuns had learnt to recognize the faintest signs of such an attitude, and it was severely repressed. They could detect it in the slightest thing—a straying curl, an inclination to 'answer back,' and, most of all, in the faintest hint of speculation in matters of faith. The world was waiting for us outside with its Satan-set traps of heresy, free thought, and easy morals, and the whole object of our education was to arm us against its snares. Mental pride and physical vanity were considered the most dangerous of all our temptations, and our mistresses were always on the watch for their appearance. I do not agree that their sharp way of dealing with them was due to any sadistic impulse. Given the Catholic way of looking at things, there was no more personal cruelty in it than in the drawing of a poisoned tooth.

This is from an account of the school by Miss Antonia White, who acknowledges her debt as a writer to "Lippington," and whose autobiographical novel *Frost in May* gives a devastating account of the system—a system in which she had been so deeply rooted that it was almost impossible to tell from her book whether she was or was not still a Catholic.

The other writer, Miss E. M. Delafield, stresses rather more than Miss White the physical austerities of her convent school, but brings out as clearly the shrewdness and power with which, for example, the Reverend Mother deals with a superficially devout child in *Zella Sees Herself*, or with a girl who has a vocation, like Frances in *The Pelicans*. It is remarkable how both authors seemed to be under a compelling necessity to write their own experiences of school with the utmost vividness, drawing on them over and over again. (Miss Delafield, of course, has for some years ceased to do this.) It seems as if a real catharsis were necessary before they could free themselves of the convent influence; no doubt the intended effect of their training.

Because of the prohibition laid on Roman Catholic teaching in this country it was for at least two centuries necessary to educate in their homes girls of Catholic families, unless they were sent abroad. The English tradition in those families is therefore against the boarding school; many of them also belong to that class of society which in the nineteenth century was not in the habit of sending girls to school. But as girls' schools in England improved and became more popular, so the importance of providing something to meet the needs of Catholic girls became apparent. The first English foundation of the Order of the Sacred Heart dates from the forties, though there were other teaching congregations at work before this, such as the Canonesses of the Holy Sepulchre at New Hall, Chelmsford, and the Faithful Companions in Somers Town. The Catholic boarding schools aimed at combining good teaching and corporate spirit with a preparation for life in a particular sense—life regarded as a warfare between the Faith and the World.

Ideas of corporate life with its obligations and responsibilities are gained; honoured traditions and ideals are handed down if the school has a history of its own. There are impressive and solemn moments in the life of a large school which remain in the memory . . . those deep impressions belong especially to old-established schools, and are bound up with their past. . . . The schoolroom at home is always the schoolroom; it has no higher moods, no sentiment of its own.[1]

Together with this reverence for tradition, which might, of course, be paralleled with that of public schools, both girls' and boys', goes the feeling of the need for carrying it on, even in the teeth of opposition.

What do we want to bring up? . . . Not good nonentities who are merely good because they are not bad. . . . We want integrity of character, steadiness, reliability, courage, and thoroughness, all the harder qualities that serve as a backbone . . . The gentler qualities which are to adorn the harder virtues may be more explicitly taught. It is always more easy to tone down than to brace up . . . there must first be something to moderate before moderation can be a virtue, there must be strength before gentleness can be taught, as there must be some hardness in material things to make them capable of polish.

This sounds at first unlike the subduing of independence referred to above, but the two ideas are not really contradictory. For the Catholic ideal is quietness of mind and firmness of will, but a quietness and a will based on faith. It must be a will "great in self-discipline, and in this is found its only lasting independence." Catholic schools have for some time felt that their religion holds in the world to-day a position more akin to that of Christianity in the first century than to that of the medieval church. The idea of persecution, or at least opposition, expected in a non-Catholic country is bound to make them regard education as a part of their armour, offensive sometimes, but as a rule defensive. (The methods of their educators are influence, vigilance, correction, and discipline.) Hence the stress laid on the stronger qualities; hence also the strengthening of links with a great past. Many educators are wise enough to distinguish between what is essential and what is 'accidental' in their heritage.

[1] J. E. Stuart, *The Education of Catholic Girls.*

> We to-day try to do, not what St Madeleine Sophie did in 1850, but what she would do to-day were she facing the problems which are ours. . . . Accidentals may, indeed must, change to meet changed conditions, but truth is not relative.[1]

It is this spiritual continuity with the thinkers of old, rather than the literal interpretation of it, which convinces us that, whether we admire the system or not, Roman Catholic schools possess an 'education with a tradition.'

It is curious that of those 'typically English' institutions the girls' public boarding schools, the first, if we except the pioneer, Cheltenham, was founded on the Scottish soil of St Andrews. Yet it was only in accordance with the tradition of Scotland that she should be in the forefront of educational development, and both as teachers and as pupils her daughters had been generally excluded from the scathing comments on the upbringing of women in the worst period. Schoolmistresses protesting to the Schools Inquiry Commission of the "unfathomable ignorance" of the girls who came to them would make an exception in favour of Scots, and T. H. Green, Commissioner for the district which included Birmingham, says that on the whole the only competent teachers are the Government-trained women (reported, however, to be defective in manners) and the Scots, who are accustomed to teaching large classes.

There was certainly in the mixed schools north of the Border a very different outlook from that of the ladies' seminary. Mixed they were in every way, for the country tradition was that the laird's son and the minister's daughter should learn at the same school as the village children. And even in the dame-school merit told, irrespective of sex. In some charming memoirs of Mary Louisa Cannan, who was young in the eighteen-twenties, is told how she was sent to a dame-school to learn sewing, but how her precocious literary ability was employed by

[1] M. F. M. O'Leary, *Education with a Tradition*.

LAWN TENNIS, JULY 1880

By courtesy of "The Illustrated London News"

her companions for reading them stories while the girls did her sewing and the boys threaded her needles. And at a later stage, at the academies in small towns up and down the country, boys and girls were educated together (though they played separately, sometimes having little intercourse out of school) under the same dominie, and shared in the discipline of the same tawse or a slap in the face for misbehaviour.

Even when education was 'private' it did not necessarily exclude girls from sharing the same studies as boys. At the manse, for instance, where pupils would often be taken to share lessons with the minister's own sons, a girl might well learn the classics along with her brother and the rest. It was because of this participation in the boys' curriculum that Scottish governesses were often so successful in a mixed schoolroom—they could give their small boy charges a good grounding in the sterner subjects, arithmetic and especially Latin.

But though the tendency through the nineteenth century was still towards co-education, there had been schools for girls founded as far back as the seventeenth century. The first important foundation 'for lasses' was the Merchant Maidens' Hospital in 1694, for the daughters of Edinburgh burgesses, ministers, and nominees of the founders. Their curriculum included the domestic arts, English, writing, arithmetic, and music, to which were later added modern languages and mathematics. For recreation is mentioned "the Lawn Tennis." It will be seen that this is not by any means the boys' curriculum, yet is a very fair one in its way. Not all 'proprietary' schools, however, were successful, and there are tales of a school for ministers' daughters which rival *Jane Eyre*.

At the nineteenth-century revival of learning, when in 1870 the Merchants' Company's School, now named the Edinburgh Ladies' College, was opened, and in 1871 the George Watson's Ladies' College, there was a reversion to the old idea: teach them all that boys are taught. Actually the curriculum, as in English girls' schools, was more flexible than that for boys; little if any Greek was learnt by most girls, but otherwise the full academic course was taken, to which were added cookery, needlework, and dancing. (The domestic subjects suffered an eclipse towards the end of the century, but are now revived.) Music had been a 'subject' from the first, including the teaching of the piano, for the 1200 girls.

The academies and ladies' colleges were for the most part day schools, but the idea of grouping girls in towns for the benefit of their education is mentioned by Miss Davies in 1864. It was the practice for girls to be collected in boarding-houses in Edinburgh, kept by ladies who took the place of private tutors, and to go out to classes in the course of the day. Miss Davies agreed that it was a plan "favourable to Scottish education generally." We have seen that at St Andrews the school was designed both for local children and for girls coming from a distance to board: two years later the Girls' School Company founded a school in Glasgow, and others followed. One of the chief differences made by the founding of the boarding school was that women began to replace men as heads, and, indeed, as teachers generally in girls' schools. At the opening of the Edinburgh Ladies' College most of the teachers there were men. The realization that a headship is not out of the question (as it would be in a mixed academy) has doubtless encouraged women in the teaching profession.

Nevertheless it continued in Scotland later than in England to be customary to educate girls at home, rather than to send them to boarding schools, unless some reason like the absence of parents on foreign service made the latter course desirable. It was not only in the highest class of society, such as that depicted in Lady Frances Balfour's memoirs, and among those who, like the Haldanes, were accustomed to a regular season in London, but in many families less well-off, that the tradition of home education lasted up to at least the last generation. And we can trace it back to the beginning of our period in the *Memoirs of a Highland Lady*. Sometimes, as in the nineteenth century in England, it was combined with a year at a finishing school, generally in Edinburgh, or with a rather longer period at some English school like St James's, Malvern. But the chief educator was the governess—often more cultivated than scholarly—or even, where money was scarce, the village schoolmaster, who would come to give lessons. Where there was a London season or travel abroad, languages, music, drawing, and perhaps some form of gymnastics or dancing would be added, and the lack of training in the exact sciences was often compensated for by a background of literary or political conversation at home or in the society in which those few months were spent. Classes or schools might be attended in London or Edinburgh, while the governess remained to supervise preparation and continued the good work when the girls went 'home.' There is something of a Miss Yonge atmosphere about some of the reminiscences of the late nineteenth- and early twentieth-century Scots ladies.

Two characteristics of girls' education in Scotland (apart from the tradition of co-education) strike the outside observer: independence and liberality. There is a Scottish Education Department, corresponding to the Board of Education in England, but though there may be, and may have to be, attempts at unifying, there is no uniformity. It is true that circumstances in Scotland, as in England, have led to the decay of the private school, but the ideals of freedom in organization and curriculum are firmly held. There had been even in the early days more freedom for the 'young ladies' than in England, at a time when it would have been unusual there, for instance, to see girls walking in groups unsupervised in the public gardens; this is said to have been allowed in

Edinburgh in the seventies. The idea of encouraging girls in their own pursuits, even to allowing them without much difficulty exemption from their classes, shows the width of the Scottish conception of education. Even now in the prospectus of Scottish schools one may see some such announcement as "They wish to avoid any system of examination which unduly presses or hurries the pupils," or "It is the aim . . . to avoid overwork and to evoke interest in study." It is good to realize that just because there is such a fine tradition of the value of education in Scotland such statements can be put forward without lowering the high standard for which the country has long been admired.

CHAPTER XI

PRIMARY EDUCATION

IF a foreigner suddenly asked whether English children were brought up under a system of co-education, many people would unthinkingly answer 'No.' Yet this would be a wrong reply as far as four-fifths of the population are concerned. So apt are we to ignore or take for granted the system which provides for the large majority of our people all the education they ever get. Or do we, by thus tacitly ignoring it, acknowledge that we are not turning out the elementary-school child at fourteen years old as 'educated' at all? Anyway, for the bulk of our people co-education is the rule, at any rate till 'ten-plus' or eleven years old. After that age, as anyone realizes who has read the Hadow Report, or even the letters in *The Times* on this controversial subject, children in increasing numbers are being drafted off to senior, central, or technical schools (and the scholastic cream skimmed off for the secondary schools) to conclude, if not complete, their education. Whether these are separate or mixed depends on the size of the school, the bias of its curriculum, the policy of the local education authority, or some other fact. But quite a number even of these children continue co-education till the leaving age.

It seems amazing, when one thinks of all the controversy about girls' education in the upper classes, not to mention the higher education of women, and all the ink spilt in pamphlets, newspapers, and commissioners' reports, that when it came to elementary education (with one exception) no difference should have been made between the curriculum for boys and girls, and no attempt to educate them separately. Whole families of boys and

251

girls were packed off to the local Board schools, and there on forms or at double desks they sat in and out (one square yard per child was the floor space originally allowed by the L.C.C. for the whole school building), learning what they could, or would, take in, and what the teacher had time and energy to give them, before the inspector came. The story of the tremendous task before the elementary schools and their attempts to cope with it has been lately told by Mr G. A. N. Lowndes in *The Silent Social Revolution*, but the very fact that nine-tenths of what he says is applicable to boys and girls alike shows that the educationists appeared hardly conscious that up to the age of twelve, and later fourteen, a 'child' could mean one or the other. Perhaps the fact that the leaving age was at first so low obscured a difference which is presenting itself more obviously now that children are at school till fourteen, or, under some progressive local educational authorities, till fifteen.

There was one exception to the similarity of curriculum. As far back as 1864 (but no doubt before also) it is stated that

> in inspected schools under the Privy Council [*i.e.*, the Education Committee, later to become the Board of Education] the same instruction, with the single exception of sewing, is given to children of both sexes, and the same examination under the Revised Code is applied to all.

Actually some authorities—Yorkshire, for instance—made the appearance of sewing on the time-table (did they ask to see the products or inspect the classes?) a condition of receiving the grant. The time devoted to teaching the subject in this county (not the class time for each child) was to be three hours a week. It is not very clear what happened to the boys during these three hours. It seems unlikely that they were taught the later equivalent for needlework—carpentry, for carpentry means wood and tools, far more expensive materials than flannel and needles, and unlikely to be provided by the authorities.

Possibly they did extra arithmetic, as suitable for masculine brains, or organized games. In the syllabus designed by the London School Board Committee, under the chairmanship of Thomas Huxley, the alternative subject for boys was "mensuration."

Since there was, for the most part, no difference made in the nineteenth century between these boys and girls, both being looked on merely as the offspring of the labouring classes—young rustics or even so much factory fodder—the same theories of education fitted both. So in tracing very briefly the outstanding developments of elementary education during the last century we shall come upon the ideas—they can hardly be called ideals—deemed suitable for girls of the 'lower orders.'

The first idea, carried over from the eighteenth century, was, in a word, docility. Schools were promoted by several educators with the openly avowed object of taming the rough lads and girls who would otherwise have inconvenienced the lives and damaged the property of those better off than themselves. No doubt Robert Raikes and Hannah More had higher things than this in mind, when he started his Sunday school movement in Gloucester in 1780, and she some ten years later began her work in the Mendips, but they certainly justified themselves to society as being its protectors in this respect. Raikes alleged:

> Farmers and other inhabitants of the towns and villages receive more injury in their property on the Sabbath than all the week besides; this in a great measure proceeds from the lawless state of the younger class who are allowed to run wild on that day free from every restraint.

Three years after the schools were started he claimed:

> The behaviour of the children is much civilized. . . . Gloucester is quite a heaven upon Sundays, compared to what it used to be.

Hannah More's view of the benefit she was conferring on society went beyond the immediate relief:

My plan for instructing the poor is very limited and very strict. They learn of weekdays such coarse works as may fit them for servants. I allow of no writing. My object has not been to teach dogmas and opinions, but *to form the lower class to habits of industry and virtue*.[1]

Hannah More's contemporary, the didactic and active Mrs Sarah Trimmer, expounded much the same view:

It is consistent with sound policy to bestow education upon children in the lowest classes of life. . . . The Sunday schools . . . furnish a sufficient portion of learning (except in the articles of writing and accounts, a little of which one could wish all the poor might obtain, though the Sabbath day is not the proper time for these acquirements) for such as cannot be spared on weekdays from the labours of the plough, or other occupations by which they contribute to the support of families.

She also insists that "persons of superior abilities"—*i.e.*, the upper classes—must themselves visit the Sunday schools if these are to have full effect. This shows either a well-developed sense of responsibility or some shrewdness in playing on the snobbery of the 'lower orders'—perhaps both.

The early attempts of these educational philanthropists were often Sunday schools only—or else a distinction was made, as by Mrs Trimmer, between weekday "schools of industry" and Sunday learning. Similarly, under Miss More, what we might call technical work occupied the week, and the Sabbath was distinguished by being reserved for reading and religion. These last two objects combined excellently, as the most usual text-book was the Bible. It may be remembered that the S.P.C.K. had been in existence for nearly a century.

Though these schools belong to the eighteenth century, the spirit which prompted their foundation lasted on into the nineteenth, becoming, if anything, less kindly as opinion hardened against liberal theories, owing to the reaction against their expression on the Continent and

[1] Italics mine.

the French war. Education, if properly controlled, stood as a line of defence against the 'unparalleled blasphemy' of complaining against the natural order of things as they were. The effectiveness of the Sunday schools in this particular was exploited in a peculiarly revolting manner by the factory-owners of the North, who encouraged the movement and became patrons of the schools—at least that was the accusation of one witness from Stockport before a commission in 1832. Six days a week should the people labour and do all that they were told to do, and on the seventh they were given lectures on how to behave and to be reconciled to their lot—for the benefit of their employers.

This is not to say that the movement as a whole was tainted with hypocrisy—only with condescension. After all, if children were taught to pray, in effect,

> God bless the Squire and his relations,
> And keep us all in our proper stations,

then why not substitute for "the Squire" "the manufacturer," who was rapidly taking his place and more than his power?

Yet the Sunday schools were the first attempt at any spread of literacy among those whom they affected, and as such were extraordinarily important in England, and even more in Wales.

> However inadequate their work, however imperfectly they were equipped for their task, they showed that universal education was possible, and they made the Bible the centre of their instruction—two facts of enormous importance in later developments.[1]

Both these points were stressed in the work of Joseph Lancaster, popularizer of the now despised 'monitor system,' by which what a child had just learnt was immediately passed on in the form of instruction to the more ignorant. Of course, this meant that the one man in

[1] F. Smith, *A History of English Elementary Education.*

255

charge of the school could superintend an enormous
number of scholars, and, crude as was the method, a great
number did in fact learn to read. The desire to get at
books had become a real passion with numbers of working
men, who sent their children to his school in Southwark
to have a chance which they themselves had never got.
In the early days of the century philanthropy and self-help
were doing what they could to stay this hunger. Dickens
describes such a school in *Our Mutual Friend*. Charley
Hexam is a 'volunteer boy' who began his schooling in
"a miserable loft in an unsavoury yard"—for which not
much can be said. But

> even in this temple of good intentions an exceptionally smart
> boy, exceptionally determined to learn, could learn something,
> and having learnt it, could impart it much better than the teachers
> as being more cunning than they, and not at the disadvantage in
> which they stood towards the shrewder pupils.

Owing to his success as a monitor Hexam is received
into a better school.

Lancaster, who was a Nonconformist, had an opposite
number in the Church—Dr Bell—and the monitor
system because of its cheapness and apparent practica-
bility was adopted in the two societies which sprang from
these men's efforts—the Nonconformist British and
Foreign Schools Society and the National Society for
Promoting the Education of the Poor in the Principles of
the Established Church throughout England and Wales.
In brief, what was aimed at in these schools was instruction, which consisted, as before remarked, of Reading and
Religious Principles.

Of the two objects of education so far noted—docility
and literacy—were both or either applicable to girls?
And how many girls were in fact partaking of the education which offered these? It is extremely difficult to be
sure, as the figures of the total number of children said
to be taught in any kind of school are, according to
modern authorities, "completely unreliable and often

ontradictory." In any case, such figures are considerably
n excess of the number of children at any time actually in
ttendance on any one day. Nor is the distinction often
nade between girls and boys. But when, in 1805, Lan-
aster's school in Southwark was said to have held eight
undred pupils, less than two hundred of these were
irls (under the supervision of his sisters); he wished to
ncrease the number to a thousand boys and three hundred
irls. These proportions sound credible. It is clear,
owever, that neither were girls as a whole so rough as
o make their taming imperative, nor was it regarded as
o necessary for them to become literate as for boys.

The charity, Sunday, and 'society' schools existed
hiefly in towns or, like Miss More's, in thickly populated
istricts. In the villages old traditions lingered longer.
n the rare cases where the cottager could afford the time
nd had the knowledge there might be home education
r self-education, like that of Stephen Duck, the agri-
ultural labourer who became "the fortunate court
oet." (He read, with the help of a dictionary, such
vorks as *Paradise Lost*, *The Spectator*, Dryden's *Virgil*, and
hakespeare; he himself wrote poems such as *Thresher's
Labour*, and eventually got a pension from Queen Char-
otte.) But the common means of education in the
illage were the dame-schools. These survived with
arying degrees of efficiency, generally attempting very
ttle, but often effective in 'the art of reading and
pelling' and probably on the whole a stabilizing and
indly influence. We must not forget the old woman that
'om in *The Water Babies* found at the bottom of Hartover
ell, who gave him the milk and cried when he wandered
ff into the river. But these schools were mostly small,
nd did little to solve the educational problems of a
apidly enlarging population. Moreover, they went
eadily downhill during the next century. At no time
ere the qualifications of the 'singleton' teacher very
ood—often the teaching was combined with some other

R

trade, and was merely an additional means of livelihood for some quite unqualified person. In an agricultural district a schoolmaster wrote in 1867:

> There are three dames-schools in the village, but the children come to me knowing next to nothing at about eight years old. I get some at six and seven; those I get at six would read, write, and cipher easily at ten, but those I get at eight could not. These small schools destroy the power of the national school. If I could get all children at six they would be able to get as far as the compound rules of arithmetic at ten. . . . There is no infant school, and the dames-schools are of no use.

One must make allowance for the tendency of every teacher to think the child has been mismanaged by his predecessor, but there is a good deal of evidence against the later dame-schools. In the seventies, after Forster's Elementary Education Act, they died out rapidly.

That a few educationists had more vision and humaneness than the introducers of the 'mechanical' system is seen by the schools of Robert Owen, Wilderspin, the Scots reformers Wood and Stow, and some others. Probably these men would have hesitated to state outright that they were working for the happiness of the child—the age for this had not yet come in England; the writings of Rousseau were regarded with suspicion, in spite of M Edgeworth's attempts to popularize them, and the work of Pestalozzi was in general unknown. But there was real spirit of charity in the best and not the degraded sense of the word behind some of those who tried to deal with the education of the poor. Owen had worked out theories for himself before he travelled on the Continent and saw Pestalozzi, Oberlin, and Fellenberg—to the last of whom he sent his own sons for education. He believed in the effect of environment on the formation of character improve the environment and you will improve the child —particularly if you can begin young enough. His work, therefore, and that of the philanthropists whom he influenced lay chiefly with infants. These began in

Owen's New Lanark school at the age of two. Dancing was taught to the youngest, and singing from four years old; free movement was also encouraged at Wilderspin's school in Spitalfields, where it was recommended that half the scholar's time should be spent in the playground under supervision. But the eighteen-twenties were not favourable to the ideals of happiness, interest, and comparatively small classes—*i.e.*, not more than a hundred and forty infants under a master and mistress, or eighty under one teacher—it was the passive obedience and mechanical memorizing of the monitor system which was to set the tone of the next sixty years.

One advance, at least in theory, was made during the third and fourth decades. Harried by Whitbread (who proposed a Parochial Schools Bill, to deal with pauper children, rejected in 1807), by Lord Brougham (who succeeded in having a committee appointed to inquire into the education of the lower orders, and introduced a Bill for promoting parish schools, defeated in 1820), and by Roebuck (who moved that the House proceed to devise means for universal and national education), Parliament began grudgingly to admit that the education of its citizens was in some slight degree the responsibility of the State. Not that this was allowed in so many words, but educational historians are inclined to consider the granting of £20,000 "for the erection of school-houses for the education of the poorer classes" in 1833, and the subsequent appointment of a Privy Council Committee on Education, as the first hesitant step in acknowledging the necessity of State support and State control. And in so far as no distinction was made in the sex of the children who attended such instruction as was forthcoming it may be said that the girls of 'the poorer classes' were allowed a place in the State, as Mary Wollstonecraft would have wished, and this some time before their wealthier sisters.

The Committee was fortunate in its first Secretary.

Dr Kay (later Sir James Kay-Shuttleworth) is one of the few—is perhaps the only known figure—in the history of English elementary education who can be described (but seldom are) as heroic. His name and traces of his work crop up not only in this department, but in every field of nineteenth-century education. A history, or even a panegyric, of him would be out of place, but Sir Michael Sadler's words and the comment of his biographer, Mr Frank Smith, may be given:

> To him more than to any one else we owe it that England is supplied with schools for the children of her people, and that this costly work has been accomplished without a breach between Church and State.

And

> What had seemed impossible in 1839 was by 1849 almost achieved in its main outlines, and the victory was on the side of tolerance and reason. . . . His attitude was scientific; the aim was clear, but the means had still to be found, and when found they had still to be tested before they were applied. He did not expect quick returns; he spoke sometimes of a generation and more passing before certain results could be established. This attitude was unique in his day. . . . England was fortunate in that the Committee of Council was guided in the critical years by a man of so wide a vision and so wise a method of application.

One of Kay-Shuttleworth's most difficult problems, referred to above, was, in Cobden's words, "the task of inducing the priests of all denominations to agree to suffer the people to be educated." The rift between Church and Dissenters in the matter of schools, going back to the previous century, and becoming marked by the personal differences of Bell and Lancaster and the rivalry of the societies that subsequently followed up the work of these two, developed into the bitterest kind of denominational struggle when the question of grants and privileges arose The struggle must be remembered as a background in all discussion of elementary education, but need not be

followed up here. So anxious was each party for the right
to propagate its doctrine—the question being further
complicated by the Secularists, who came to the fore in
the fifties, and wished to disassociate 'national' schools
from any kind of religious teaching unless specifically
demanded by the parents—that in their ideals of education
the child itself seems to have played very little part. The
girl or boy appears less as an individual than as the
recipient or the material for teaching, doctrinal or otherwise. The controversy which continued with the non-
payment of educational rates by Nonconformists in
Church-school areas right into this century became a
battle for ideals of freedom and of social duty, but ideals
in education seem to have been excluded.

One piece of work was started by Dr Kay, as he then
was, in the face of a flat refusal of Government to take any
share in or responsibility for it. This was the training of
teachers, as opposed to monitors, for the extension of the
work of educating 'the poor.' The first idea of what
became the 'pupil-teacher' seems to have grown up
almost accidentally when in a Poor Law school one of
the older children was found taking a class in a master's
absence. At an institution in Norwood containing over
a thousand children the system of 'learning to teach' was
begun—chiefly for boys from the workhouses—and the
success of this and other schemes there was marked.

> Half the time at Norwood was devoted to handicrafts . . .
> and the girls were taught practically the whole of the duties
> of household management as well as sick-nursing.

In 1840, however, a real training college was established
at Battersea, for which the practical working-ground was
found in the local school. Students from the age of
thirteen to thirty were inspired and helped; a genuine
enthusiasm was caught for an education that should not
only instruct but enlighten the people. The idea was a
success; in the next year a new training college was

opened for men (St Mark's, Chelsea), and the well-known Whitelands soon after, for women teachers.

However, the great number of schools were still staffed with children, for we should count them as no more, who were in training as pupil-teachers. They worked in charge of big classes when they were perhaps themselves not much over thirteen, and they spent their evenings over such work as they took home from pupil-teaching centres, or what their headmaster could spare time to give them. Their apprenticeship in a school lasted about five years; they could then attend the training college or continue working by themselves till they passed the examination and became certified teachers. Many took the examination as they were working. It is no wonder that a headmistress who had been through this apprenticeship in the sixties called it "the hardest period of life a girl can possibly know," and later put forward very strong objections to the whole system. She complained partly that the girls were "robust and healthy" at the beginning of their five years, were no longer so at the end, and also that in her district—a very poor one—they had to meet with "many things which should not be brought under the notice of young girls." But, provided they did not break down, the girls themselves kept on with the apprenticeship, their parents encouraging them, and the elementary schools of the last half of the century must have been largely staffed with these young people. It seems quite incredible when one reads of their conditions (in the evidence given before the Cross Commission, for instance, 1886) that they should have had any kind of spiritual or intellectual ideals left.

For from the middle of the century elementary education went, according to our modern standards, back rather than forward. The only improvement was in the number of children 'under instruction,' and even this did not grow with anything like the rapidity that increased population and increased grants warranted. The Newcastle Commission, whose report in 1861 emphasized the need for increased efficiency in instruction, but wished it kept strictly to the three R's ("with sewing for girls"), led to the limitation of scope in elementary schools, and to the Revised Code. Under this Robert Lowe (who promised Parliament that education should be *either* efficient *or* cheap, as the grants would depend on payment by results) instituted what the Commission called

> a searching examination by competent authority of every child in every school to which grants are to be paid, with the view of ascertaining whether these indispensable elements of knowledge are thoroughly acquired.

The state of things produced by this system—the system being grafted on to the degrading poverty of much of the population, and intensified by the pressure which compulsory attendance, secured in theory by Mundella's Act of 1880, brought on the school—this combination of circumstances could hardly have been worse. The elementary-school child was still regarded by the public at large as the working man or woman in embryo, and the purpose of the school was therefore

> to give the vast mass of the children of the nation who could not aspire to be anything but labourers, artisans, domestic servants, and laundry girls the minimum mental equipment necessary to launch them upon life.[1]

On the other hand, the school managers and the teachers whom they employed were led (or tempted) to regard every child as "a little grant-earning machine," for each was individually examined by the inspector, and it was only a storm of protest that raised the age for this individual examination from *three* to six years. An inspector reports:

> For one manager that asks me if his school is going on well there are twenty who now say, "How much shall we get?" and the expression on a child's failure to pass any subject is not regret at his ignorance so much as indignation at his stupidity and the consequent loss.

---

[1] G. A. N. Lowndes, *The Silent Social Revolution.*

The teachers were regarded "as if the earning of money were the only motive which impels them to give of their best." They were also found, inexcusably but not unnaturally, falsifying the registers of attendance, on which the grant might partly depend, and were therefore looked upon with all the more suspicion. (The rule was made that registers must be marked in ink, and no erasures were allowed; the rule still exists, with its ban on that friend of teachers the ink eradicator "A. & B.," but its purport is now happily lost in obscurity.) Of the inspectors it was said by teachers that they gave neither sympathy nor encouragement,

> since we had in full force what we should call a system of payment by results. Before that period I think they were very sympathizing; a few of the inspectors who were appointed before 1860 showed in every way all the sympathy they possibly could. . . . Now they come simply to see what the so-called results are, and they go away perhaps without making an observation to you.

The whole atmosphere was clouded with suspicion, of behaviour and of motive. It was hardly wonderful that the children did not thrive in it. Besides there was the over-pressure which was attributed to this payment by results, a system described as "injurious to the teacher and the taught." Intellectual teaching did not pay, and so great was the fear of being blamed on the day of trial that a headmistress explained, quite sympathetically, that her own assistant was worried when she, the head, took over a lesson because "these discursive remarks of mine do not tell in the examination as brilliantly as the hard-and-fast line she would have worked upon." Stories are frequently heard of children learning their reading book by heart that they might appear to know how to read, and only being discovered because they held it upside-down, and the illuminating comment is made in evidence that in needlework "cutting out is like a piece of arithmetic— the child *learns it off by heart* and cuts according to the number, 1, 2, 3, or 4."

It is true that the promoters of this system had begun to change their minds about its object; an alteration was visible as early as 1867—after the passing of the new Reform Bill. It was Robert Lowe himself who said, "We must educate our masters" (not "We must instruct

LAMBETH "RAGGED" SCHOOL (GIRLS'), 1846
By permission of "The Illustrated London News"

them"), but he admitted that "the mass are growing up in vice and ignorance." And a circular of the seventies sent to inspectors explains that the object of education was "to promote the development of the general intelligence of the scholars rather than to seek to burden their memories with subjects"—about as blatant a piece of lip-service as was ever perpetrated when one considers the state of things. Though as far as 'subjects' went, it was true that, since at first only the three R's paid, there was a complete slump in any other form of teaching. Even the text-books claimed to be "specially adapted to the requirements of the Revised Code" without going a step beyond it. (I saw a similar advertisement in an Indian paper in 1938 of a text-book suitable for examinees, as giving "no unnecessary details." No doubt the experience could be paralleled elsewhere.)

Yet if even so much as lip-service was done to the idea that intelligence as well as instruction was desirable in 'the lower orders,' that was some kind of advance, though one must admit very little was done to put this ideal into practice. It is an improvement on Lowe's earlier attitude to "Primary and Classical Education":

> The lower classes ought to be educated to discharge the duties cast upon them. They should also be educated that they may appreciate and defer to a higher cultivation when they meet it, and the higher classes ought to be educated in a very different manner in order that they may exhibit to the lower classes that higher education to which, if it were shown to them, they would bow down and defer.

Comment is unnecessary.

There was this in common between Lowe and the more liberal-minded of his contemporaries, who included Matthew Arnold, Huxley, and Ruskin: all were agreed that the great purport of the schools besides providing instruction was to train character, though they would have differed very considerably on what line this training was to take. Anyway, one of the duties of the inspectors was to inquire into the moral tone of the school, and the Cross Commission asked more than once whether inspectors *were* in the habit of making such inquiries— which apparently they were not. "I have never heard of the least attempt to do such a thing." "They can only tell by examining the scholars."

But after all, grant or no grant, the raising of the tone in a school depended almost entirely on the teacher, generally on the head teacher. This is true to-day, especially in the country. "The factor that more than any other determines the nature of a school is the head master or mistress," comments a report on rural education of a few years ago. And if the schools became, as they did, 'humanizing centres' of the districts in which they were placed, the credit is due almost entirely to the generation of elementary-school teachers who worked in the surroundings and atmosphere described above, but who refused to allow mere mechanical instruction to become their aim, but insisted that the ideal was civilization. Mrs Burgwin's words have been often quoted; she was a teacher of some twenty years' standing who had for thirteen years been in charge of the girls' department of a school near the Mint, containing 870 children in all. She was asked whether the existence of the school had left any mark on the condition of the people around. Her answer was:

> Yes, very much so indeed. You could hardly in years gone by bring a person down that street without a blush of shame; the people did not think of putting window blinds up; they pitched everything out of the windows into the street regardless of passers-by, and made, in fact, the street the dustbin of the place; and certainly their language was shocking. Now I can frankly say that, provided the people are sober, whatever quarrel there may be going on, and they will be using bad language, if they see a teacher coming up the street it is instantly stopped, and they would not give me a vile word as I pass them. Some Christmasses ago I sent a new short curtain to every house to give it a bright appearance for Christmas Day, and now the people feel a sense of shame in various ways. If they attempt to come near you dirty they would even apologize. I know that in many instances a woman will borrow a neighbour's apron to come up and speak to me so that she may come up looking clean. I felt it my duty, if one came up to me dirty, to tell her that she should have enough self-respect to wash her face before she came to see me.

Influence of this kind only came through her very strong personality and the care she took of the individual child. She said, regarding an assessment on one subject with which she was not satisfied, "I know every child in

267

my school; I know what every child can do, and I could not at all account for that assessment." She found out that two girls "belonged to the darker side of human life" from their "unchildlike" manner, and the fact that they did not talk or play with the others. She knew that one child of twelve was getting exemption because she went round with her one-armed father, who played the cornet (a borrowed instrument), and collected the pennies for him. These details slip out casually in her evidence, showing quite remarkable sympathy and care for each child. It is no wonder that she was able to inspire them with self-respect and that, as another witness said:

> I feel most strongly that the girls that I turn out of that school will never be content to live the same kind of life as that which their mothers have led.

In a word, the standard she set herself was "not merely to turn out an educated, but a good and happy woman."

It is true Mrs Burgwin was exceptionally able, and perhaps exceptionally idealistic. And it has been put forward in favour of the system of payment by results that it was necessary at the time to deal with the army of totally ignorant and undisciplined children that was pouring into the schools, unwillingly coerced or with difficulty extracted from their jobs as child-workers and household drudges. Naturally enough, considering their home circumstances, they were sadly wanting in health, and pressure on the attendance sheet as well as on the minimum attainments was necessary to keep them in school at all. But as far as the woman teachers were concerned, I think they would undoubtedly have been better off without the Code; their energy and devotion would have been not a whit less, and the strain might have been relaxed. "I cannot imagine a teacher who would willingly let a child go," is Mrs Burgwin's reply when it is suggested that some might be willing to get rid of a backward child who would do the school no credit —*i.e.*, not earn a grant. Possibly, however, the need of earning the grant was some inducement to the managers to pay more than the minimum attention to the schools for which they were responsible.

It quite strengthens one's faith in Providence to see how the higher view has prevailed over the lower. The practical improvements came perhaps even before the old idea faded, that the elementary school was "a kind of waiting-room—very much third-class—for life." [1] Of the benefits of this century three perhaps are outstanding —provision of free meals to necessitous children, medical inspection, and the widening of the curriculum. Free dinners had been found necessary in Mrs Burgwin's district in the eighties; she had found the children so restless and tired that they could not learn; and when a doctor remarked, "These children are decidedly hungry" she set herself to collect subscriptions to provide cheap or free dinners. It "made a vast difference." The extension of the system, with the implied admission that the State is responsible not only for the instruction of children but for seeing that their condition reaches a minimum standard such that they can profit by this instruction, continues to-day. The medical examination of every school child which should take place at the beginning, middle, and end of its school career is the undertaking of another responsibility—though, of course, it still rests with the parent to say whether the treatment advised shall be carried out. In these matters the girl and boy are treated alike, and always have been. The insistence that at least twenty minutes of every school day have now to be devoted to physical exercises foreshadows our new ideals of health. An elaborate syllabus was issued in 1919, and more has been done since. In fact, one hears the criticism that country children who often already have a long walk, and a good many outdoor duties, are none the better for the extra exercise. Open-air life and constant, unhurried work produce a co-ordination of muscles

[1] Lowndes.

unrivalled by the more conscious physical training. Mr Grisewood says of "Our Bill" that to watch him walk across a ploughed field was an education, and there is no exercise like housework for keeping the figure. However, attention to the physical side of the girl or boy's education has come to stay, and National Fitness is now one of our National Ideals.

The extension of the curriculum brings up for perhaps the first time the question of differentiation between girls and boys. When only the three R's were concerned the teaching applied to both alike—though it was suggested in 1886 that girls might be exempted from learning the tables of area and capacity, on the ground that these were not much good to girls. But even in drawing—one of the first 'special subjects'—the idea began to appear that two schemes might be allowed. Mrs Burgwin suggested a more mechanical one for boys and a more artistic for girls, who, "if I may put it so, like pretty things." As the range of subjects increased, most of these could be taken in common, such as geography, history, elementary science, singing, and some kinds of handwork, while in country schools gardening was added for the boys to correspond with the girls' inevitable needlework. The widened curriculum of the Board schools met with a setback in 1900 ("the Cockerton Judgment"), but the average elementary-school time-table now contains all the above subjects, though the 'science' is often termed 'nature study.'

The desirability of one branch of study for girls has been felt more and more as the view of the elementary-school child's future has changed. The same difficulty arises with the girl here as in secondary and public schools, though it has been less subject to discussion. In towns at least a very great many of them will 'go to work' on leaving school; on the other hand most of them will marry after a varying number of years. We therefore have the 'dual aim' again in their upbringing. If girls were looked on 'from above' as merely potential factory workers, laundry girls, and domestic servants (beginning in this 'trade' very definitely as apprentices, and learning under experienced women in large households) the question of teaching *them* to be good wives and mothers, whatever may have been said of the better-off girls, seems to have been ignored. A beginning in education with this aim was made in the last century. Instruction in cookery might be regarded as "an excellent thing for girls," and domestic economy was required as the first special subject to be taken by girls. By 1902 there were 4700 departments (schools) taking domestic subjects (cookery, laundry, household management). But the difficulty was the provision of equipment and teachers where either the money was scarce or the girls were too many.

> At one extreme the inquirer would find a slovenly classroom, as often as not unswept, filled with the fumes of uncovered gas-rings. Disposed about the various desks, he would discover groups of girls from four to six in number, under their ordinary class teachers, interfering with each other's efforts to make beef tea, rock cakes, and pancakes, or to recook cold meat cooked by the previous class. At the other extreme he would encounter large classes of girls drafted to cookery centres fitted with elaborate stoves and appliances of a type which they could never hope to see in their humble homes, and by sheer weight of numbers compelling their harassed teachers to set them to endless rubbing of flour through sieves, and the picking of every single stalk from every single currant.[1]

And early 'lecturers in cookery' complain bitterly of the places in which they have to teach or demonstrate—a schoolroom, a public hall, a cottage kitchen, or even "a kind of outhouse." The same disadvantages applied to the teachers of other domestic crafts, when such lectures began to be given not only to the girls at school, but to the older women who had not had the chance of learning them at school. Classes in cooking, upholstery, lectures

[1] Lowndes.

271

on hygiene and nursing, were given under the auspices of various societies, and have continued and advanced, particularly since the War, as a part of the great movement of women's institutes. This, of course, is adult education, but the learner is generally the ex-elementary girl, and it is natural that the teaching in these schools, especially in the senior departments, should move in the same direction. The modern aim is to make the girls

> realize the value of the home as a social and national asset, and to provide a model which will stimulate the desire for improved conditions in their own homes; to help them to appreciate the importance of domestic and personal hygiene, well-balanced, economical meals, and labour-saving methods in home organization.

Apart from instruction, the best way of measuring the distance run in the last forty or fifty years is to contrast with the 'moral tone' aimed at by the nineteenth-century authorities and so succinctly described by Lowe, as above, the Board of Education's present ideals for the primary school—*i.e.*, one giving education up to the age of eleven, after which all education will, it is hoped, be of a secondary grade. The primary school is regarded as the chief nursery of character, and in a very fine phrase the Board suggests the aim of teaching "how to behave in a manner consistent with self-respect and a sense of honour." The purpose put at greater length is

> to form and strengthen the character, and to develop the intelligence of the children entrusted to it, and to make the best use of the school years available, in assisting both girls and boys, according to their different needs, to fit themselves, practically as well as intellectually, for the work of life.

Primary education, in so far as it meant elementary education in a 'Board school' or charity school, certainly had a very poor history in the nineteenth century, and attained its comparatively good standard in the present century almost entirely through the persistence and devotion of the school teacher, male and female. But, so

far as 'primary' is used to denote the first stage of the
education for the upper- and middle-class child, it is one
of the brightest patches in the female education of our
period. Little girls brought up together with their
brothers under the authority of mother, sister, or governess, with not so much attention paid to 'lessons' as to
prevent enjoyment, and, as a rule, anything from a very
fair patch of garden to a large park for playing in, ought
to have had a pretty good time. And to judge both from
children's books and from memoirs, in the latter half of
the nineteenth century at least, they did.

Of course, this statement might immediately be chal-
lenged with the charge of repression and moralizing so
often brought against nineteenth-century parents. The
inevitable 'rightness' of Papa seems a distinctly unnatural
phenomenon in these days, and the impossibility of trans-
gressing certain fixed moral or conventional codes with
impunity was made abundantly clear to children—as,
indeed, it was in society when they ceased to be children.
And the gallows episode of *The Fairchild Family* will
doubtless be quoted as 'typically Victorian'—especially
by critics who do not realize that that part of the book
was written before Queen Victoria was so much as born.

The same remoteness of date applies also to Miss
Edgeworth's works and to *Mrs Leicester's School*—that
delightful production of Charles and Mary Lamb. But
even if we take the children of *The Parent's Assistant*, they
do not appear to have received such particularly depressing treatment. It is true that when Rosamund has chosen
the purple jar in preference to a new pair of shoes her
father will not take her with him "walking slipshod," to
teach her, in effect, that you cannot have your cake and
eat it. True, also, that when Lucy goes into the dairy
she sees in one bowl a rich, yellowish liquid such as her
mother has with her tea, and in another a thin, bluish
liquid such as she and her brother have with their breakfast in the mornings, whereas in these days the children

would have had the cream. (But now Lucy would never see these two dishes; the milk would appear in bottles on the doorstep.) And, of course, the children regard the privilege of receiving instruction from Papa and Mamma with perhaps almost unnatural delight. But then it is very good instruction—their father's explanation of the workings of the thermometer and the barometer is remarkably clear and interesting.

Children's books of the first years of Queen Victoria's reign do not seem to have survived in great variety,[1] but from the middle of the century there are numbers of 'stories.' Such publications as *Aunt Judy's Magazine* give very vivid pictures of family life—large families with many friends, a general liveliness shown in games, competitions, charades, or theatricals, and an atmosphere of affection and good humour. I hesitate to refer again to Miss Yonge and Mrs Ewing, but there are the less-known names of M. and C. Lee, there is L. T. Meade (though her girls suffer from enlarged consciences), there is Mrs Molesworth, and later the unrivalled genius of E. Nesbit.

In trying to justify the Victorian upbringing it would be a mistake to over-paint it. Those who did not have a happy childhood have been only too prone to record its miseries, and a good many reminiscences show at least one grim shadow. Eleanor Acland's (in *Good-bye for the Present*) is Barley, their nurse—"a kind of evil genius" who filled their minds with terrors and blighted their lives by petty tyrannies. Looking back, she wonders whether their mother did not notice, or whether she decided that it could not be helped, or that the woman's obvious merits (she was competent in the physical care of her charges) outweighed her defects. She points out that "the vogue for intensive child-study had not set in,'

---

[1] Of course, against these happy families must be set *Dombey and Son* but as a rule Dickens's children belong to a less 'privileged' class o society.

nd that the children were seldom in their mother's
nd their nurse's company simultaneously. Out of sight
pparently meant out of mind, for when they were down-
tairs Barley could be forgotten.

And even this nurse-beridden childhood of the eighties
ʼas far from unhappy, and the account of their early
essons shows no dissatisfaction. Their family was taught
y the mother, evidently a cultured woman with wide
nterests who enjoyed making things interesting—from
ʼnglish poetry to astronomy—apparently not "the use
f the globes." She could even teach arithmetic clearly,
iving over and over again *explanations* of why you should
carry one,' and similarly in spelling. It is true that the
nodern teacher might think little of their early lesson
ooks, which included, for Sundays, *Peep of Day* and
ine upon Line—but at least they were allowed to paint
ne pictures of these, while the modern child can only
dorn its pages surreptitiously. And the list of books
ʼhich "Mother" read to them differs very little from the
st that Lady Acland's own daughter was reading in the
wenties of this century. They include *The Water Babies,
vanhoe* and other Scott, *Pickwick, Treasure Island, Kid-
apped*, and *The Little Duke*. To the modern list can be
dded *The Jungle Book* and Arthur Ransome's stories.
Miss Harrison, who condemns Victorian education as
ingeniously useless," adds:

But for some things I am devoutly thankful. I was made to
learn for some fifteen years three verses of the Bible every day.
I might choose what poetry I wished. In this way I learnt
impartially great quantities of Milton, Wordsworth, Mrs
Hemans, and Gray's *Elegy*. . . . I learnt *The Prisoner of
Chillon*. I learnt them all lying on a backboard, and to this day
my flat back is the admiration of dressmakers.

Nowadays it seems you learn only what is reasonable and
relevant. I went to Rome with a young friend educated on the
latest lines and who had taken historical honours at Cambridge.
The first morning the pats of butter came up stamped with the
Twins. "Good old Romulus and Remus," said I. "Good old
who?" said she. She had never heard of the Twins, and was

much bored when I told her the story; they had no place in constitutional history, and for her the old wolf of the Capitol howled in vain. "Great God, I'd rather be . . ."

Up to the age, then, when the brothers went off to school, when, we hear, "elementary Latin and algebra were cut out of the curriculum, as being unnecessary for a purely feminine schoolroom," and the plague of "tiresome propriety" descended on her, the girl's life was often a very happy one. There is an impression of vigour and enjoyment: lessons seem to be taken in the stride, illness not made much of; children are let alone a good deal, and they know how to use their imaginations. One of the saddest sights in modern life is a child unable to play by itself, whether because its circumstances are too confined or because it has not the necessary richness of mind to draw upon, or even because it has so little practice in solitude that it has not mastered the art of being alone. It has lost the sturdy independence of the little girl who, in answer to her brother's "Come here, Dora! I want you!" could answer, "Thank you, Eric; but I want myself!"

It is on belief in the personality and independence of the child that the educational reformers of the last two centuries have founded their systems. Rousseau's idea, as we saw, was to treat the child as a person to be by education as fully developed as possible—at least when child meant 'boy.' Pestalozzi, regarding the home as the best 'school of infancy,' treated the family as the ideal unit of education and the mother as the chief educator. His theory, following Rousseau, that familiarity with the thing must precede description of it, his way of educating through the experiences of the senses, form and number coming before words—these are methods rather than aims, but the description of his institution—"It is not a school you have here but a family"—is the best comment on the spirit of his work.

Froebel, who was his disciple but yet evolved for

himself much that was different both in theory and in practice, has become far better known in this country. His ideal for the child grew from his belief that life must

EGOISM

"Come here, Dora! I wants you!"
"Thank you, Eric; but I wants myself!"

Drawn by George du Maurier

By permission of the Proprietors of "Punch"

be considered as being but one in all its phases, a belief expressed sometimes in a rather confused mystical form. But since each phase must be perfectible if the whole is to be complete, the child is capable of perfection in all the

different stages of its development, and need not be regarded merely as an embryo man or woman. The infant
has a perfection of its own, and is not merely an incom-
plete boy or girl; the child is and should be different from
the adolescent with a difference of character, not merely
of ability and brain-grasp. Here is a change of attitude
towards children's minds rather like the change towards
their clothes which we see in the eighteenth century. The
portraits cease to show us the miniature dress of man or
woman, and give us instead really charming children's
dresses.

Here is Miss D. M. Stuart's description:

> No longer were infants tortured with whalebone stays and
> padded petticoats; the baby-sister of the sculptor Flaxman has
> a roomy, easy frock, and the engaging child in Walton's *Fruit
> Barrow* wears a simple white dress with a shady blue hat,
> though her pretty mamma boasts an uptilted hat nodding with
> plumes and a tight-waisted gown encumbered with vast panniers.
> The Augustan girl-child, as painted by the great artists of the
> time, is a real child, with her locks unfrizzed, with a loose frock,
> usually white, and no finery more gorgeous than an azure ribbon
> or a pair of coral-coloured shoes.[1]

In the same way the children, real or imaginary,
educated by the reformers were not to be forced into a
curriculum so inflexible that it was torture to their minds,
nor were their brains to be padded out with unnecessary
facts. They were to develop their imaginations and their
reason freely—and there was no suggestion by Froebel
and his followers that the latter quality was lacking in the
girl-child.

Froebel lays particular stress on two points: the need
of spontaneous activity in a child and the value of play.
The child *wants* to be doing things, and the educator
must see to it that such occupation as would be the very
thing that the children would choose if left to themselves
is the next progressive piece of work. Similarly, without

[1] *The Girl through the Ages.*

278

going into the theory of recapitulation—*i.e.*, that the child in play lives through the various phases of the human race: hunting, trading, home-making—the teacher should encourage the expression of the child's imagination and activity in play. Froebel's use of what he called 'gifts,' which correspond roughly to 'apparatus' in other systems, was an attempt to bridge the gap between the child's mind and the universe around by making it familiar with the sphere (ball), the cube, and other shapes. The whole basis of his scheme is that the child should not be moulded to the form desired by the teacher any more than a plant is moulded, but must grow naturally like a flower in a garden—hence his name *Kindergarten* for the school of the very young.

While Froebel regards natural development of the child as of the first importance, yet it is to him that the teachers of to-day look for much of their training. For Froebel laid great stress on the work of the teacher, as apart from the home influence. He himself instituted a course in method for women teachers; although their office is to make use of suggestion regarding the children's occupations, and not commands, to superintend their play, but not direct it, they are not the less important. His emphasis on training has been recognized, and the Teacher's Certificate of the National Froebel Union has now become the normal passport to a junior school or kindergarten post in a secondary school.

The insistence on the child's individuality, and on respecting this by individual education, is developed even further in the Montessori method of education. Dottoressa Montessori, who was born in 1869, about thirty years after Froebel achieved recognition of his ideas, began, as is well known, with work on the feeble-minded, and on a *crèche* for working women's children in tenements in Rome. She insists on a training through the senses and muscles, to accustom the child to objects and situations that must be dealt with later in life. The child should develop self-reliance, through being always 'on top of' the situation, and able to *do* things with the material at hand. To bring this about the material and situation (environment) must be carefully prepared, and the apparatus graded to advance in difficulty only with the powers of the child. Successful efforts like the matching of colours, the putting together of complementary shapes, the fastening of buttons or hooks, and so on, lead to counting, by numbers of balls, to reading by the use of letter blocks—when the child desires to do so. That is to say, all education should be self-education; the stimulus must be the child's will, not the teacher's drive. In fact, the teacher as such is abolished, even in name, and the person in charge of the children is called a directress. There is no class teaching, for a room full of 'Montessori children' will contain a collection of individual units, each child working at its own rate which it attains by individual effort. One advantage of this can be gathered from a comment made by the Board of Education Consultative Committee in a report on the primary school: that very young children are not naturally co-operative; in work or play, or even talk, there is a real barrier between one child and another, and they enjoy going about their own business. At a later stage the idea of co-operation grows up, and can be developed in team games and class-work, but this is a stage to which the child should not be pressed.

But to make this 'work' there has to be one safeguard.

> If Madame Montessori advocated vigorously the claims of the child to individual freedom, she guarded herself by the limitation that such freedom could be exercised only in so far as it is consistent with an equal degree of freedom for other people.[1]

And the one who must see that "other people" have this equal degree of freedom has, in the last resort, to be the person in charge, whether called a teacher or not. There-

[1] T. Rayment, *Modern Education.*

fore her strain and responsibility is not lessened but increased by the fact that each child is working independently, and one is inclined to remember that a good teacher will make almost any system work, but that no system will work well without the good teacher.

However, the line of thought in Dr Montessori's system is clear; one can see the connexion between the method used and the ideal of self-reliance, spontaneity, and controlled activity which should be produced. And the dissatisfaction which is sometimes felt with her methods can for the most part be traced to two causes. One is that any scheme which requires patent and expensive apparatus *must* be confined to the few. There *are* local authorities who encourage the use of the actual apparatus employed by the Montessori Society, but as a rule elementary-school teachers know they have no chance of getting the actual stuff, and set about working in the spirit rather than the letter, composing their own 'didactic material' as the only solution of this difficulty on the large scale. The other objection holds for many schemes of child education; that they are so simple as to be unnecessary for the averagely intelligent child, who will pick up in the ordinary nursery (still better, the garden) methods of coping with materials and situations whether the environment is prepared or not. This becomes increasingly true as the child grows older. It is an old criticism, perhaps somewhat Philistine. But, as Dussault put it, "Pestalozzi gives himself much trouble to teach children that their nose is in the middle of their face."

In addition to the National Froebel Union and the Montessori Society there is another organization that has done much good work—the P.N.E.U. (Parents' National Educational Union). Miss Charlotte Mason built up this society for the co-operation of the parent and teacher in the interest of the child, with a view particularly to helping the private governess. It is interesting to find 'the lady with a profession' taking a share in the organization and progress of education like her opposite number in a school. The P.N.E.U. helps her with training, books, 'refresher' courses, and a sense of union with others who have the same object—governesses, parents, and teachers in P.N.E.U. schools. The name of the Ambleside Training College is a mark of distinction for those who are looking for trained governesses or teachers of young children. The scope of the P.N.E.U. goes beyond primary education, but starts from the same principle of individual work and development, while combining it with a general scheme which enables progress to be continuous.

To return to the first stage of education on the larger scale, progressive authorities tend to begin the children's training before it is possible or advisable to teach them any kind of formal lessons. One might ask, "If you are not to begin with the three R's with children of three or four, what are you to do with them?" Here is the answer of the nursery school:

> The children learn decent bodily habits, including the cleaning of teeth, the use of a handkerchief, the use of soap and water, and where necessary the use of a bath. They learn the elements of social behaviour, and anyone who has watched the table manners of children in a nursery school and who knows how such children feed at home must appreciate what such learning means. They learn to take care of the schoolroom, of flowers and animal pets, to prepare the tables for meals, to wash plates and mugs, to prepare for sleep, and afterwards to fold blankets, put away beds, and put on boots or shoes. They learn to don and doff their out-of-door clothing. Very young children do not take readily to co-operative activities, but they gradually learn to work in groups, to take part in games and singing and rhythmic exercises and conversation.[1]

In fact, they are becoming persons capable of receiving an education which has for its ideal the development of the individual and the training of the citizen. They progress through the junior school—girls and boys alike,

[1] Rayment.

for the report referred to above says, "Sex differences in educable capacity up to the age of eleven appear to be negligible"; and it advises separation only for games and physical training, in which special exercises are considered appropriate for girls. In the senior or secondary school there may be scope for differentiation either between boys and girls or between different types of mind and abilities in the same sex. True, the ideal career for the elementary-school child is far from being always realized, but it is now recognized that there is an ideal for her just as much as for her better-off sister.

CHAPTER XII

THE TWENTIETH CENTURY

The following paragraph by Mr Lyn Harris, taken from *The Modern Schools Handbook*,[1] may be considered a statement of an aim widely acknowledged in this country for both boys and girls:

> As the old Persian proverb says, "The ways unto God are as the number of the souls of the children of men," and a school, if it is to be a preparation for life, should contain a great variety of souls, and, if they are left comparatively free to develop, a great number of ways will result. It was the practical mystic George Fox who emphasized that something of God in every man which, if it could be given opportunity for development, would lead the individual towards a way of life in which his neighbour's welfare would be his first consideration. We have altered our terms. We speak now of the individual's contribution to the corporate life, of social responsibility, of social and anti-social action, but we mean what has been meant by the great teachers throughout the ages, and expressed for most of us, at any rate in the West, by the simple teachings of Jesus. . . . Individualism alone is not enough, nor is the common pattern of a common service. The highest development of the individual compatible with the good of the community, for the service of his fellow-men, would present our aim.

It is only fair to say that Mr Harris adds a plea for an appreciation and application of psychology which would not be so generally acknowledged, but this is as a means, not an end in itself. During the first ten years of the century, however, two influences in particular helped to swing girls' education in the direction of "the good of the community" as an aim, rather than, though not exclusive of, "the highest development of the individual."

These two influences were the growth of the public-

---

[1] Gollancz (5s.).

school spirit, already referred to, and the Suffrage movement. The former meant the cultivation of loyalty to a
group—albeit a small group—and, being an outward
turning of the mind, it helped and educated the larger
loyalty to 'the Cause' of Women's Suffrage. That is not
to say, of course, that the Suffrage leaders came chiefly,
or even largely, from the public-school classes—though
one can see the connexion of the two loyalties pretty clearly
in such a book as Viscountess Rhondda's *This was my
World*. Many of the foremost fighters had learnt in a
harder school, such as the trades unions. But it was an
unexpected characteristic to find in women—that they
were capable of interesting themselves so deeply in something often outside their own sphere and to many of them
an abstract principle. They had begun to break through
the vicious circle whereby women were denied the rights
of citizens because they were uneducated and therefore
unfit, and refused the education, general and particular,
that would fit them for participating in the general
concern of citizens or for a particular profession on the
ground that this was unnecessary on account of their
position. They began, as we saw on looking back into
the last century, a kind of dovetailing, by which the
demand for further civic rights went alternately with a
training in citizenship.

Far back in the days of Mary Wollstonecraft had been
born the idea of woman as a citizen. But perhaps one of
the earliest statements showing that to be public-spirited
might be regarded as a virtue in a woman was the epitaph
of John Stuart Mill's wife, who died in 1858:

> As earnest for all public good as she was generous and devoted
> to all who surrounded her, her influence has been felt in many
> of the greatest improvements of the age, and will be in those
> still to come. Were there even a few hearts and intellects like
> hers this world would already become the hoped-for heaven.

There had been experiments too in fostering this
quality. In 1864 a course of twenty-five lessons on

political economy given in a girls' school had produced the following comments from the "young ladies" taught:

> I should not now be inclined to look down on those who are obliged to earn their own living [a lesson, as the directress of the school notes, which this young lady and her companions had great need to learn].
>
> I have learnt that neither wasteful expenditure nor inconsiderate almsgiving is likely to do anything but harm.
>
> We should also meet our engagements and pay our debts punctually. It is not quite honest if we do not, and it is thoughtless to keep shopkeepers and others waiting for their money.
>
> I seem to have learnt to look at things in a broader and less selfish way. . . . There was less gossip in the school, as we had in the lessons an interesting subject for conversation and thought.

Allowing for a natural desire to be "pleasing and pleased" and to fall in with the directress's views, one cannot but see here the beginnings of a feeling for education in citizenship which makes 'economics,' 'civics,' or 'general affairs' such a popular subject, as a rule, in a girls' school.

These lessons were mostly theoretical, though it is to be hoped that they had a practical result, at least so far as to the payment of bills. But the Suffrage leaders of a later generation were to acquire a more practical education, which was besides a training for a career—a political one. Miss Eleanor Rathbone says:

> These developments [of Suffrage work] did provide for those who took part apprenticeship to the arts and crafts and qualities of the political engineer—organizing, canvassing, speaking, pamphleteering, drafting, team-work, compromise, submitting to authority and wielding it, keeping your temper and profitably losing it; above all, tireless industry and indomitable perseverance; refusal to allow rebuffs or failures to cause the least outward sign of discouragement.
>
> Perhaps this kind of training developed also some of the politician's characteristic faults—partisanship, opportunism, superficiality, and triteness of thought. The quantity and kind of work demanded left little time or freshness for constructive thinking.[1]

---

[1] *Our Freedom and its Results*, edited by Ray Strachey.

However, the insistence on *The Common Cause* (so one of the Suffrage newspapers was named), and on responsibility towards a community in a large sense, has played an ever-increasing part in education since those days. And the idea of 'training for citizenship' both determines the orientation of many newly founded schools and also affects the outlook, and even the curriculum, of some already established.

In following the history of post-primary education during this century one finds for the first ten or fourteen years little violent change, but rather a wide and steady development of ideas already established. High schools and other secondary schools, public schools and women's colleges all flourished. Of the first a reviewer of Dr Sara Burstall's *English High Schools for Girls* says in 1907: "The girls' high schools are among the healthiest institutions this country possesses." She herself says that the first years of the century were a most happy period of consolidation and vigour in the life of her own school. Secondary schools were being organized under State control, receiving grants, but not yet excessively burdened by outside authority. Of the public schools the veteran, Cheltenham, celebrated its jubilee in 1904; the others were rapidly increasing in numbers and efficiency, as any school record will show. At the universities full advantage had been taken of the concessions where they had been given. At Oxford so many women were taking the full degree course that the Association for the Higher Education of Women gave in 1906 a diploma (as was already given at Girton) as an equivalent of a degree, and the 'halls of residence,' for the most part now 'colleges,' were flourishing under the Delegacy for Women Students, presided over by the Vice-Chancellor. A great deal of new building was also undertaken during this period both by schools and by colleges.

There must have been some survivals of the old inefficient private schools of the last century. Miss Dorothy

Whipple, for instance, had the bad luck to go first to one "kept by two sisters, maiden ladies with no other qualification for setting up school than the possession of a house and the necessity for earning a living." She tells how the smallest pupils did pot-hooks on slates to keep them quiet, in a cramped and dingy room.

> No sooner had I filled my slate than Miss Sophy with scarcely a glance would efface my labours with a sponge and command me to fill the slate again.

The poor ladies had a desperate struggle (no wonder, for efficiency was the order of the day), and "they slowly starved." Miss Sophy caught a chill, had no strength to resist it, and died; her sister was taken to a charitable institution for the aged poor. Unfortunately their pupil went on to a second school also kept by maiden ladies; these, however, had degrees, and were therefore known as MA and BA respectively. Miss Whipple's comment is that they were too anxious to make young ladies of their charges, too critical, too reproachful.

> No doubt we were young hoydens and in need of discipline. But there was too much of it. We must come and go in gloves and keep our hats on, never run, never jump, never raise the voice or eat sweets in the streets.

(Other schools would probably have forbidden this last habit; perhaps it was the manner of the prohibition that rankled.) Miss Mannin, to take another example at random, also had distasteful experiences of a private school; and doubtless these could be paralleled. But the general impression is of vigorous development in every type of school, and a sense of ease and increase in education, as in many other departments of life during the years preceding 1914.

"And then came the War."

The branch of education which felt its influence most strongly was, of course, the highest. The War had two contrary effects on the women's colleges. On the one hand, the employment of women in all kinds of official and Government posts gave an impulse to training. It also made the way easier as far as the long-lingering prejudices against higher education for women were concerned. When every young woman was leaving home and 'doing something' it became quite natural to send a girl to the university; in fact, instead of being any longer 'daring' a college career became, by contrast, considerably more sheltered than a great many of the jobs or professions that girls were taking up. And forthwith the universities were crowded, and the colleges had waiting lists, which continue to this day. Then the same impetus that had broken down the barriers of prejudice in the minds of parents and dons succeeded in flinging open the doors of the last stronghold—Oxford University, where, immediately after the War, Congregation carried the decree conferring full membership of the university on women, and degrees, some retrospectively to those who were fully qualified, some by decree to those who had earned them by worth, if not technically by examination. This took place about the same time as the Representation of the People Bill, passed in another male assembly, gave votes to women over thirty years of age.

Yet a curious reaction was taking place against the academic life and training for women. It was due to the other types of work that had been taken up—on the land, in hospitals, canteens, and factories, or even nearer the Front. It was impossible to avoid the feeling, unjustified as it may have been in the long run, that a woman was not making so effective a contribution to the country's cause by studying Greek as by driving an ambulance. (The cause of civilization was not regarded as a separate thing.) And, indeed, the lorry-driver, if Miss Vera Brittain has correctly interpreted the mind of the practical worker, was of the same opinion. Academic honours were at a discount—and have remained so to some extent ever since. Whether we are now to be hustled into the belief that it is more important to learn Air Raid Precautions than history or literature the very near future will show. But certainly the War has helped to give our schools a practical bias—and perhaps our academic women an inferiority complex.

As an answer to those who advocate an almost complete abandonment of academic training for children at an early age, in favour of a 'practical' education, and to whom the word 'academic' is merely a term of abuse, I would quote the following justification, by Dr Brock, of the 'grammar school' against the vocational or technical school:

> The lovely furniture made by the boys of a senior school, the gay weaving done by the girls—these things get across to the public at once. They may even become 'news.' [1] But many of the things which all schools are trying to do and which are the characteristic activities of the grammar school cannot be photographed or exhibited—a young mind, for example, learning to think its way through a mass of evidence, fairly and with humility, to an independent conclusion. Day in and day out we are striving to train young minds in independent thought, through science and Scripture, through history and mathematics and everything we teach; and such independent thought is the only safeguard against the dictator or the mob. . . . You cannot photograph a mind learning the difference between knowing and nearly knowing. But a nearly known declension or geometry proposition shows up the essential difference, and there is need of something clear-cut and exact and austere in this modern world which has eliminated the difference between right and wrong in other realms besides morals.

It is only fair to say that some people emphasize this very point on the side of handwork—the moral effect:

> In nothing else does slipshod work so obviously bring its own punishment. The disadvantage of a slurred and blurred idea of the causes of the monsoons is by no means evident to an average school-girl; she cannot look into her own mind and see the result of shirked thought; but the result of a carelessly drawn right angle when binding a book is only too patent to her disgusted self.

---

[1] The writer had been told by a journalist, " Education is never ' news.' "

ST SWITHUN'S SCHOOL, WINCHESTER

Above, main entrance. *Below*, architects' model showing the whole of the
projected buildings.

By courtesy of the architects, Messrs Mitchell and Bridgewater   230

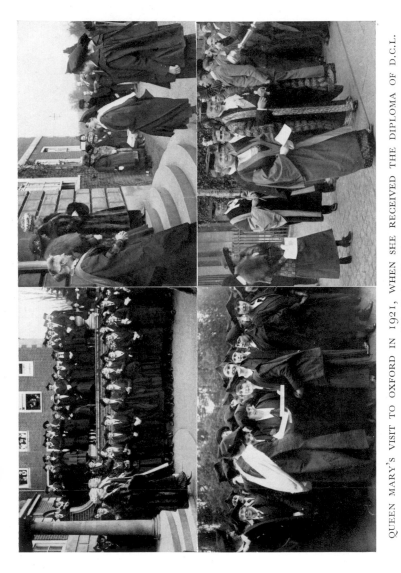

QUEEN MARY'S VISIT TO OXFORD IN 1921, WHEN SHE RECEIVED THE DIPLOMA OF D.C.L.

Photos Sport and General

A very potent remark; but one would think that the admission that the "average school-girl" cannot look into her own mind and see the result of shirked thought would be, more particularly in these days of propaganda, the justification for emphasizing that that is what education should teach her to do.

The two quotations above are from what the evening papers would call a 'symposium' of headmistresses' thoughts (entitled *The Headmistress Speaks*)—a series of independently written essays of 1937. But the problems they discuss are continually with us. It is interesting to see how the thirteen writers, almost all in charge of big secondary day schools with children of "comfortably-off but not well-off " parents, and including a greater or less proportion of free-place scholars from the elementary schools, with grants from central and local Governments, and therefore acknowledging a certain dual control—how these headmistresses have stressed much the same values, and have even followed much the same pattern in their contributions. Nearly all begin with some statement of an ideal of which the following are fair examples:

> As every child is a spiritual being, potentially creative and good, the most vital and responsible part of her training is to keep alive and develop in her the instinctive realization of her spiritual heritage, and through worship and work to help her to enter into it and use it ever more fully. Education should liberate the creative faculties and integrate the spiritual, intellectual, and physical into one indissoluble whole.

Or:

> The school-girl's proper activities are those which train her to be a thoughtful person with the power to enjoy living a civilized life during her schooldays as well as afterwards.

Or, more briefly, "to foster in the growing child the public and private virtues."

To the attainment of these ends half a dozen points are made on which the contributors are in general agreement: the need for co-operation with the parent to foster individual development, the advantage of a wider curriculum ("Ideally a special course should be planned for each child"), the use of modern inventions, wireless, films, and so on, not necessarily in school, but as a recognized part of the child's environment; the encouragement of co-operation rather than competition, because "a good co-operator is a better person than one who believes it his mission in life to devote *himself* to the service of others." They are, perhaps naturally, in favour of day (as opposed, or at any rate complementary, to boarding) schools; they hold that it is a disadvantage for a school to take 100 per cent. free-place scholars, as the mixture of those who have had a more 'leisurely' type of preparatory education does much for both; and they have a definite desire that in the training of the girls the married life and care of a family should be looked on as the most natural and appropriate aim.[1] (One of them, indeed, would like to run a matrimonial agency: a curious swing-back to the arrangements of a past century, with the teacher taking— as she often has to take unwillingly—the part of the parent.) The relation of the girl to the community occupies a good deal of thought, and the dual aim of the general education of a citizen and the particular training by which a girl is to earn her living. Of course, not all these points are dealt with by every headmistress, but there is a consensus of opinion on what comes as the conclusion to nearly every essay, that the aim of the school must be a spiritual one, and that spiritual ideals must animate the headmistress and her staff if the girls are to be in any true sense 'educated.'

There are specific suggestions, some of detail, such as the addition or extension in the curriculum of speech training (in this connexion dramatic work might be, and

---

[1] "It is still women's work to create an environment for other people, and the quality of life is their constant preoccupation. They must give out to other people without becoming exhausted, and deal with a mass of trivial detail without themselves becoming trivial."

often is, mentioned); the adoption of domestic science or vocational courses; the substitution in certain forms or at certain times of 'free' homework for set preparation. As against too great freedom of this sort there is the statement that the important function of the school is to give serenity; "a school life that is a series of experiments on the part of authority fails as much in its duty as one too closely hemmed in by tradition"; and a very necessary plea for the 'slowing down' process in education: "the value we put on activity is too great." On the question of examinations—or their abolition—and on compulsory subjects these doctors disagree.

I have quoted these views at some length, because the secondary school is such an important part of our English educational system, and is still increasing in importance, that its ideals affect an immense number of English girls. They show, too, the kind of problem with which the headmistresses and staff are dealing, and which is occupying their minds for forty weeks in the year. The fundamental one is the same as that which met Mrs Bryant at the North London Collegiate forty years ago:

> We do not suppose—we are far from desiring—that the girl from the high school is, on the average, to spend her life in some professional career, but we do hold that she should be brought up so as to be able to earn her own living if necessary. . . . We recommend to her choice those occupations which are most in harmony with the requirements of the womanly life. It is the same wisdom that makes the agricultural labourer prefer 'service' for his girl, and determines the middle-class parent to have his daughter trained as a teacher. Nevertheless, we hold that when a girl shows a marked taste and ability for any kind of work it is fair to the work and to her that she should go to it. All sorts are wanted to make a vigorous and interesting world.

Well and good—but in fact she admits that the majority of girls leaving the Middle school, at fifteen or sixteen, go out to work for a living, and that "shorthand, typewriting, book-keeping, clerks' work of all kinds" (not "in harmony with the womanly life"), "with good knowledge of languages, if possible, bound the immediate horizon of work for many." The one word 'business' sums up the prospect of life for the typical secondary-school girl. And for many years this charge was made against the secondary, county, and municipal schools—that they only succeeded in turning out typists with mechanical brains—just as the elementary schools were accused of turning out brainless factory hands. The obvious reply—that if that is all the employment they are likely to get, why should they be trained for more, and that to increase their powers and develop their sensitiveness is nothing but a cruelty when one considers the environment into which they will be thrust on leaving school—is only sometimes made in bitterness of spirit. As a rule headmistresses are not defeatists. Many of them believe, like Sanderson of Oundle, though with far less scope, in making the school "a miniature copy of the world as we would love to have it."

One cannot neglect the rise during this century of the technical school, which is the passage-way for many children from either the elementary or the secondary school to 'the job.' It takes the place presumably of the old apprentice system, and deals with the child at the difficult period when the restraints of the ordinary class teaching of book and desk are over and the more subtle hold of the job has not yet begun. There are also, for the same type of girl, the commercial schools, though in the rush of modern competition it is difficult to see what meaning the word 'ideal' can hold for them. Yet they come at an important point in a girl's life, and it may be that there she is working for the first time with those of the opposite sex. A good deal of responsibility for friendships, tone, and the ultimate placing of girls in jobs lies with the heads and teachers of such 'colleges' as Pitman's. There are a few schools too which train chiefly for a special career; such is St George's, Red Lion Square, which has for many years specialized in training for the clerical grades of the Civil Service. The problems in all these places are connected with competition, stress of modern life, employment, and straitened means, which, though not necessarily the same as poverty, can be as bitter.

At the other end of the scale of means there is the rise of new public boarding schools for girls. A number of these were founded in the twenties—Benenden, Wadhurst, and those of the Allied Schools Trust, of which Westonbirt is probably best known. The aim of the latter at least was to provide an education for a class of girl who in the last century would not have gone to school at all, but who would have been brought up in the social and probably cultured atmosphere of her home, with the additional training of a 'season' in London, when she might come into contact with some of the finest minds of the day, and a period of travelling or residence abroad. The school education aimed at cultivating manners and a certain poise which, it was felt, was sometimes lacking in the older schools, where more emphasis was laid on the side of work and games. The idea was to combine this with a sense of responsibility towards a larger community —responsibilities of Empire being specially stressed— and a training which would enable girls on leaving to take a part in the administration of local affairs, or social work, should their circumstances give the opportunity. With this purpose an experiment was inaugurated by Miss Popham, now headmistress of Cheltenham Ladies' College, of having a house for older girls who had either left the school or come specially for the training in citizenship which it offered.

The school has gone through too many vicissitudes in its short life for the ideal to be fairly judged. There is no doubt that girls given as much freedom and individual choice as is made possible by very large grounds and a personal time-table, as well as by the delegation of a good deal of authority to the responsible seniors, do gain a self-confidence and an ability to cope with a situation which is extremely desirable. They also have a real sense of manners and dignity when the school is in contact with the outside world. There is always, of course, a natural pride in any school which creates the desire that it should be shown off to advantage on speech-days and such, and that its members should do it credit in manner as well as in distinction; the present emphasis on natural good manners and self-control is only a swing-back from the time when, artificial good behaviour having ceased to be demanded, the result was a certain off-handedness and a lack of grace in the school-girl. But whether the new schools have been so successful as they had hoped in developing the social feeling of the upper-class girl, using 'social' in its wider sense, is by no means certain.

In the flourishing days of the landed gentry the squire's daughter was almost bound to inherit or acquire some of her father's feeling for his tenants and villagers. It is true that just as his attitude might have more than a touch of Sir Roger's patronage, so hers may have been that of an embryo Lady Bountiful. But there was a kindliness and an individualness that took much of the sting out of patronage or out of that much misused (and abused) word 'charity.' Generally the girl liked doing kindnesses, and was willing to go to a good deal of trouble to help those whom, in rather simple and obvious ways, she could help. The gardener's wife, the keeper's baby, the postmistress's invalid sister—these were people whom she knew, and often had always known, and she felt towards them as she grew up a responsibility and neighbourliness, just because her father and mother were wealthy and lived at 'the Place.' And, as from the days of Mrs Trimmer it had been recognized that 'persons of quality' could give encouragement by their presence and interest in the schools, she was not infrequently found taking a Sunday class, and she was familiar with most of the children in the parish. This applied with even greater force to the parson's daughter, but any girl of good family in the country might feel the same. The motto *Noblesse oblige* would very seldom be on her lips, any more than on her brother's, but it was in effect part of her daily life. Her motive, however, was not an abstract one, but generally sheer kindness and good feeling and the desire to help the individual woman or child that she came across who was not so happily placed as herself.

There was a rather different expression of the feeling of responsibility among girls of a particular—and quite common—type of upbringing. The Evangelical church-man and -woman were very much their brothers' keepers —especially so far as the matter of example was con-cerned. The idea of behaving circumspectly so as not to scandalize—in the Gospel sense of 'causing to stumble' —the less well-taught members of society and those who had had fewer advantages than oneself is one that easily attracts the charge of hypocrisy. But it was reasonable. You went to church when you did not feel like going partly to encourage your servants to do so; you refrained in the parish from doubtful or 'advanced' behaviour which might have been allowed in London, where your example would not be 'shocking.' We may consider this attitude mistaken, but it was, consciously at least, sincere, and the loss of this feeling of responsibility helps to explain the disappearance of a certain code in the modern generation of the 'well-off.'

To return to the encouragement of social service in schools, the daughters of the wealthy—now so much less wealthy—are in danger of slipping between two stools. The home training in village service no longer exists to the same extent, and in any case, if a girl is at school for three-quarters of the year from the age of, say, twelve to seventeen, the contact is broken. And though many hundreds of girls from public schools do go back to their homes and parishes and give themselves to the voluntary work of running Guides, Scouts, women's institutes and clubs, there cannot be the same closeness of touch, and there is not at first the real interest of having known these people and their habits and difficulties for years.

Of course, there is far more presentation to girls than there used to be of the social need. They hear at school a great deal about girls' clubs, settlements, camps, and other forms of social work; they are taught, often, something of the different forms of State assistance and the part played by voluntary effort. And there is undoubtedly a type of mind that responds to this call—sometimes the most sympathetic spirit, the 'born leader,' or the finest brain. Such girls do take up some form of organized social work, are trained for it, and, of course, have much more scope than they would ever have found in a quiet country existence or a busy parish life of fifty years ago. But—as far as it is true that the 'average woman' responds rather to personal needs than to abstract principles—talks and lectures on social work in general, or even particular stories (unless the lecturer has an exceptional personality), fail to touch the school-girl deeply, and too much of it rouses a dull, rather shamefaced resentment. "She wants to drive us all into settlements," was a comment more outspoken than most after a careers lecture that had not been a success.

It is only fair to add that a good deal of work is successfully undertaken by schools in the way of school camps, holiday outings, and, particularly by old girls, school missions or their equivalent. Towards the end of school life, or on leaving, a girl's energies and enthusiasms do turn outward to a larger world, and there is plenty of opportunity for her both to hear and to do. There is also an excellent tendency to give younger girls an idea of the connexion between a real interest and the sums which they subscribe on occasions or by the term to 'some charity' by letting them have the opportunity to discuss its disposal in regular school meetings held for the purpose. The result is most often that it goes to children or animals; these needs are most real to them.

298

The belief behind the Summerhill system is that education must concern itself primarily with the instinctive side of the child. The unconscious is infinitely more important than the conscious mind. Our theory, then, is that the child must be free to express itself in the manner that its dynamic driving force demands. We may call that driving force the *id*, the unconscious, the life force, what we will. It is a force that will find an outlet for its energy in one way or another. If left free it will express itself in love and creation; if suppressed it will find a way out in destruction, hate, illness of soul and body.[1]

This is an extreme form of the 'modern' school theory. It is only too obvious that, like headmistresses of secondary schools, the principals of the new schools have ideals, some more and some less definite, which they are fond of expressing. Not many go as far as the perhaps logical conclusions of Mr Neill in "abolishing adult authority" and substituting—when it was found that "any community must have laws"—a system of self-government. One junior school states candidly:

> We believe that even at twelve and thirteen years children cannot be trusted to exercise authority wisely, and that responsibility of this kind puts on children of this age an unfair burden and one of which they themselves are grateful to be relieved.

Some advocate a diarchy, but chiefly on the principle of expediency and responsibility to parents.

> Situations will therefore fall into two main groups; those which can be resolved by the children and those which must be resolved by the school authorities.

(Most schools of any kind would now allow this; where they disagree is at what point to draw the line.) Often the practical co-operation of the children in school discipline is expressed in some form of advisory council; it is certainly one characteristic of the 'modern' school that there is a great deal more free discussion between pupils and staff, both individually and as groups, than was usual at the beginning of the century. A few harassed members

[1] *The Modern Schools Handbook* (Gollancz, 5s.).

of staff in less modern or less well-to-do schools would murmur, "Where do they find the time for all this discussion?" It would be interesting, too, to know whether, when they reach undergraduate age, the pupils of such schools begin discussing things all over again, or whether the fundamentals have by then been fully explored.

The difference in attitude towards authority is certainly one of the main changes that have taken place during the century. Of course, the change has come gradually, and is not the prerogative of those schools which term themselves 'modern' or 'sane.' Thirty years ago a headmistress could speak of the relation of staff and girls in a big high school as follows (though she is referring to the social life of the school in clubs and games outside the class-room):

> They meet as friends, and while proper respect is paid to the superior, the older and abler woman, there is not the great gulf fixed that there was in earlier days.

In 'modern' schools the relation varies from a friendliness due to increased consideration for and study of the child to an utterly informal attitude, with a deliberate ignoring of outward respect, the staff being called by their Christian names or nicknames, while the responsibility for school affairs is considered to rest not on the staff, but on the community at large. As the wiser heads point out, however, an attempt to make the children consider themselves entirely responsible for the running of the school ('complete self-government') is humbug, as in point of fact they are not, economic conditions making this impossible. Their world does not exist under the conditions of the adult world, but is a model in artificial conditions of "the world as we would love to have it." And if children mistake the model for the real thing, the process of distinguishing between the two once they leave school must be a painful one.

But the real advantage of the new attitude is that put so well by Homer Lane—the children feel that the grown-ups are on their side. Once this friendliness and confidence is achieved—usually as much by the personality of the individual teacher as by any free-and-easy system—Authority has gone most of the way to solving its problem.

Homer Lane achieved his solution in dealing with his own colony, the Little Commonwealth, for 'difficult children,' and it is the pride of the 'modern' school that it meets the problem of the unhappy child, the misfit, the rebel—and through sympathy and experience finds it no problem. The means are often psychological, including, in one school at least, definite psychoanalysis of an unhappy or neurotic child; the aim is that the child's personality should develop untrammelled, and "the children are encouraged to be themselves."

Health management and exercise must be among the greatest practical difficulties that a school which allows 'complete self-government' has to face; one girls' school (Maltman's Green), otherwise very free in outlook, roundly declares:

> In the matter of health, and especially when young, the girls may not have that freedom which they enjoy in other directions, and are in this respect in the hands of the matron and the housemistress.

Generally the pitfall of 'fussing' girls is avoided.

> There is in the school [Badminton] a sturdy attitude towards health, which is encouraged by keeping thoughts of illness in the background, and not drawing attention to its possibility by the presence of nurses in uniform, or by the daily taking of temperatures at the beginning of term.

But on the prevalence of illness in some schools the ex-headmaster of "Churnside," [1] Mr J. H. Simpson, makes

---

[1] "Churnside" is the name he uses in describing a boarding school where a number of fee-paying boys are educated together with boys from the county and neighbouring towns who have received their primary education in elementary schools and pay little or nothing. Of course, this is made possible only through the generosity of an endowment. The experiment appears very successful, and it is to be regretted that no such benefactor has yet endowed a school for girls on similar lines.

a penetrating remark. It is to the effect that a small boy cast into the mass of others, among whom he finds himself ignored, realizes that if he complains of some ailment he will get the undivided attention of a matron and perhaps a doctor for a few moments at least—and he unconsciously plays up to the desire for significance. If he is given attention in other ways his health will show a remarkable improvement. The same probably applies with greater force to girls. At any rate, most schools now, whether 'modern' or otherwise, give the greatest care to the children's health, diet, rest, etc., and where this is not done it is financial incompetence rather than lack of feeling which as often as not causes the neglect. In matters of health boys' schools are undoubtedly learning from the standard set by girls' schools. The same is true of physical training, of which one headmaster says, "English girls are half a century ahead of their brothers." Compulsory games are becoming less taken for granted, the emphasis being laid on the practical value of other kinds of physical labour and the training it gives both in manual exactness and mental perseverance, rather than on 'exercise' and the team spirit. In co-educational schools where games are the rule boys and girls generally play separately, and the games are different ones, except for tennis. In work, on the other hand, it is found that the difference between one boy and another, or between one girl and another, calls for such differentiation in the curriculum that this covers the tastes and abilities of children of both sexes. This applies also in handicrafts— if all the girls automatically learn needlework and the boys woodwork, obviously that is not co-education. But at a 'free' school where either there is no compulsion to attend classes or the time-table of each pupil is arranged individually no difficulties of this sort can arise.

On the question of examinations 'modern,' like other, schools are divided. Some quite definitely approve of the specialized work which an examination renders necessary.

302

It tends to encourage effort and concentration, and can be accomplished without undue pressure and without too much interference with the curriculum.

There is the wholesome feeling that an examination should be taken in one's stride, though this is more likely to occur when it is regularly taken. A very ingenious method of encouraging a good attitude is that of Hurtwood, a junior school.

A notice appears now and again on the notice-board stating that an examination will be held in a certain subject on a certain day, and anybody wishing to enter for the examination is asked to sign below.

Naturally schools add as a rule that their procedure leads to the children's passing examinations when they need to, or want to, in a particularly short time, and with the benefits of 'real' education thrown in.

The question of examinations is clearly bound up with compulsory subjects, and very often these are anathema, particularly mathematics. Why, asks one head, should children be made to learn a subject of which Bernard Shaw, or Mussolini, or Charlie Chaplin possibly know nothing. On the same principle he might have added that Sherlock Holmes did not know whether the earth went round the sun or *vice versa*, and refused to 'lumber up' his brain with such useless knowledge. Unfortunately there are more potential Watsons than potential Sherlocks, and one does not know which child will be which. All the same, Mr Neill would find himself in agreement, about the uselessness of compulsory subjects, with the ex-head of St Paul's Girls' School, Miss Gray:

Throughout my teaching life I have never wavered in my belief that no subject should be made compulsory for entrance to a university, because no subject has any educational value unless it can be learned with some intelligence. There are a few minds, and they are not necessarily to be envied, that are equally intelligent in all directions. Some find algebra difficult and Latin easy; some find history unforgettable; others, like Mrs Disraeli, cannot remember which came first, the Greeks or the Romans. I am not thinking of mere ordinary difficulties; they are made to be surmounted. I am thinking of difficulties so great as to be all but impossibilities.

Miss Gray's account of passing the Little-go in mathematics shows how a really intelligent person had to cope with a subject for which she had a 'blind spot':

> I did not reason during those critical hours; that would have been too dangerous. I *remembered* as well as I could ; I tried on one model sum that had been shewn me after another.

For what it is worth, my own experience leads to a similar conclusion. I spent what must have amounted to weeks in a year over mathematics at school. I was not resentful about this at the time, because the teaching was good, and I wished to please the mistress who so patiently tried to make me see light. But, looking back, I maintain that the effort was not worth while, when I remember the way in which I 'skimped,' for instance, history and geography, which I considered easy subjects. I now wish I had given more time to these, as algebra is the one subject I was taught for which I have found no manner of use during my post-scholastic life.

Whether examinations are taken or not, whether or no there is a compulsory time-table, a movement is afoot for much greater freedom in the planning of school time. I suppose, in fact, girls have always divided their preparation time as seemed most expedient. Certainly our time-tables had forty- or thirty-minute periods as carefully marked out for each subject as they would have been in the days of Miss Buss, when a time-slip had to be signed by the parent, or are to-day, when the child takes home a time-table displaying such words as: "If the time taken over any lesson is in excess of that allowed, parents are asked to inform the headmistress." But actually some very different arrangement takes place, even in a boarding school, and it may be as well to recognize this and to allow a free disposal of time—though, of course, this makes things much more difficult for the class teacher. The adoption of the Dalton Plan, in which the year's work is from the first divided into 'assignments' which are given weekly or monthly to the pupils, who carry them out independently, and can thus work at a different pace in different subjects, is also said to entail very hard work for the subject teacher. This criticism of the Dalton, the Project, or other modern methods is not necessarily a reason for ignoring them, and against the difficulty and labour involved in preparation must be set the omission of much laborious marking. In many schools marks have had their day. Where they exist they have as a rule assumed what should have been their original function, that of a record, not a stimulus. There is a convenience in measuring a girl's progress—or the opposite—by some definite scale, and, particularly in younger forms, the children like to know how they have done. But much marking is a weariness of the flesh, and the struggle of deciding whether to award a 'half' or a 'plus' for the sake of encouraging the child or spurring her to a higher standard comes hard on a young and conscientious teacher. The theory that work should be done for its own sake and the interest that the child finds in it is (after the change in attitude to authority) responsible for the greatest difference in the working out of the school 'business'—the old name for curriculum. No doubt the theory was held by the great teachers of the last century, but the boys' schools had to contend with a long and bad tradition in this respect,[1] and the girls took over that tradition, along with much else that was of value.

Delight in 'doing things' has been the means of educating children, as we are so often asked to do, 'for leisure.' Many schools now have periods of 'organized leisure,' 'free preparation,' or time for out-of-school activities. Of

---

[1] "It doesn't matter what you teach a boy, provided he doesn't like it"—*Old saying*. Compare: "Go and see what Tommy's doing, and tell him not to."

course, this is not in itself new—there have always been school societies (sometimes too many), and for a long time facilities for crafts have been increasing. The present tendency is shown in the names given to the product of these leisure or non-scholastic hours—'projects' or 'creations.' (Sometimes, however, they are called 'books,' presumably on the principle that a book is not a dead thing.) Where the work is as a rule carried on in formal classes experiments in the use of leisure are continually being tried, and where 'leisure' is difficult to come by classes are sometimes abandoned altogether for a period, and the time given to 'creative work.'

Such are a few 'modern ideas.' What do they amount to? On the whole they are the development and putting into practice of the old truths which the real educationists have always known, at which they have aimed, and for which they have struggled, being held back by lack of money, by force of convention, by their own inexperience in applying them. Each generation has more experience, and on the whole more freedom from convention, though other pressure counters this advantage; the difficulties of money are unfortunately little better—in some ways worse. But as a rule the 'modern' school is doing in an extreme form very much what the less modern school is doing in a restrained way, and has tried to do for some time. If there is any great change in outlook it is based on the fundamental belief which most teachers hold, and in the main act upon—that a child is really 'good.' This was a startlingly new theory to many in the days of Rousseau. Of course, it was not entirely unknown even in the eighteenth century; it has always been implied in the Quakers' doctrine of the inward light and in the great value they set on personality, to go back no farther. But the idea of original virtue was undoubtedly obscured by the belief in original sin. The fact that psychology supports the former is not necessarily an argument against it.

Yet it is not even a new idea that educators should

DR M. D. BROCK, O.B.E., M.A., LL.D.
From the painting by Harold Knight, R.A.
By permission of the Governors of Mary Datchelor Girls' School

concentrate on the complete development of every child. "The only safe course is to hold up individual perfectness as the aim of education," is not an extract from the prospectus of a school founded last year; it is from the pen of Emily Shirreff, who wrote on *Intellectual Education* and helped to found the Girls' Public Day School Trust, over sixty years ago.

Modern ideals may seem when scanned to be but the old writ large, but do we in twentieth-century education find anywhere the factors which were common to the upbringing of the great Victorian women? What has become of the balance between freedom and discipline, between solitude and the social life, of the religious impulse and the strong male influence? Looking at modern life, we must admit that, in their original form at any rate, most of these are disappearing. Yet in a new guise the first of them, the combination of freedom and discipline, remains. Freedom, especially a freedom of thought in politics, religion, and even morals, is hardly ever in these days denied by parents to their children. Freedom from the herd mind becomes more difficult for any of us to attain every year. But in schools, if anywhere, an attempt is being made to combat mental slavery by means of mental discipline. Children, as every teacher will proclaim, are being taught to think, to judge, to decide for themselves. It is a tremendous task, a David of mental integrity against a Goliath of prejudice and propaganda, and even the best weapons may turn in one's hand. Reading, for example, which should make the child's mind wider and more flexible, may merely become a means of assimilating so much dope. But, hampered as she is by examination requirements, by lack of means, by an overloaded curriculum, the teacher is attempting to give her pupils a disciplined freedom of thought, to enable them to cope with the increased physical and mental liberty which has come into their lives. Discipline too there is in their lives, but of a different kind from formerly

—a discipline of circumstances. It is a discipline of straitened means and of competition, of responsibility and sometimes of affection, very seldom in these days a discipline of prohibition. A large community, for example, has to make its own discipline, but the tendency is more and more towards principles evolved from within, rather than rules imposed from without.

A far more complete disappearance is that of the single male influence. How many fathers to-day have leisure or inclination to bring up their daughters between the ages of eight and eighteen? One of the chief planks of the day-school advocate is that the girl is left in a partially male environment for at least some hours of the day. But a breadwinner who returns as his child is settling down to her homework, or who spends the week-end at golf, is in a very different position towards her from the leisured Victorian parent, with his questions and answers, his encouragement and authority. And the modern father, however sympathetic his relationship with his daughter, very seldom undertakes her instruction. The attitude of the elder brother too, when he exists at all, has altered considerably. He also is much away from home, and during a considerable part of the childhood of either his avocations and those of his sister are distinct. She rarely shares his studies or is taught by him, and though she may in holiday times see a great deal of him, may dance, play tennis, and generally go about with him, it is as a companion and an equal, not as a dependent.

There is a similar difference with menfolk outside the family. The man tutor is not unknown, but uncommon for a woman, except perhaps at a university, and though the modern girl has probably more occasion for and more freedom of acquaintance than her predecessor, this very diversity makes one prevailing influence the more unlikely. As for the husband's part in forming her character—it would be absurd to generalize. But it is safe to say that because of both the later age for marrying and the wider experience of life, often including a job in which she keeps herself, a girl's character is much less likely to be moulded after marriage than it used to be.

If the pressure on a girl's early years of a man's directing mind must be said to have waned, what of the directly religious influence? In many schools, though in proportionately fewer homes than during the last generation, there is a definitely spiritual background to education. It is generally a Christian, and frequently a Church background—Confirmation marking a very definite development, as a rule, in a girl's adolescent life. But on the whole the stress is on the second great Commandment and not on the first, and even then it is less an abstract idea of duty than a deep sense of justice that leads girls from sheltered homes to undertake work for the less fortunate neighbour.

As for the balance between solitude and the social life, that has been badly upset. Solitude is hard enough for any of us to come by in these days; for the child of school age it is particularly rare. The cry of "too many distractions" is heard on every side, and with justification. It needs a good deal of will-power for a girl to withdraw from the attractions of school and family environment sufficiently to make for herself that inner solitude which seems so necessary for all great lives. It is not that daydreaming has ceased—often it happens that the greater the pressure without, the more desperately the child will creep away into a world of her own—but the empty space and time in which the Victorian girl might spread herself is simply non-existent. The days are filled with varied occupations, just as the big estates are filled with little houses; the girl living under a crammed school time-table has the same confined existence as the girl living in a flat. Hence the complaint that when solitude or leisure comes her way her resources are few; she does not know what to do with her time. Against this it is only fair to put the attempts of educators to teach her this.

The numerous 'ploys,' from the nursery school upward, are designed to teach her self-occupation. (And, setting aside the purely æsthetic value of the product, is the modelling of clay animals very different from the modelling of wax fruits, or the tooling of leather purses from the netting of bead ones? Or are we circling round towards the production of the 'accomplished young lady'?) Yet it is evident that a deliberate pause for thought is what many girls must either make for themselves or do without.

On the other hand, in one sense the modern child *is* more solitary; her brothers and sisters are fewer, if any. A good deal has been written about the only child, or the child to whom the addition of a new small member to the family is a remarkable and perhaps disturbing event, not one which in the regular course happened every few years. The compensations for the well-filled schoolroom are two—an earlier school-going age and a new and more familiar relationship with the parent, especially the mother. On the adequacy of these compensations it is, again, impossible to generalize.

If then these or similar factors in education are necessary to produce great women of the Victorian type, we shall not find such women in the coming generation. But it may be that the characteristics of our modern education —freedom, responsibility, companionship, public spirit, and an ideal of social justice—are producing a type that is as fine and in accordance with the age. As a nation we are paying far greater attention now than formerly to the ideals of women's education. A much larger proportion of English girls receive their education in schools which, whatever their limitations may be, are at least endeavouring to foster

> the free growth of individuality, helping every boy or girl to achieve the highest degree of individual development of which he or she is capable in and through the life of a society.[1]

---

[1] Report of the Consultative Committee (Board of Education) on Secondary Education (Spens Report), 1938.

Even if some of us are critical of the methods or the products of these schools, we may believe with Emily Davies that the very fact "that somebody cares" will

"HUSH, MRS HUNDRED, HUSH!"
Drawn by G. L. Stampa
By permission of Messrs Ernest Benn, Ltd.

improve the result. And it is possible that the great women of our day are obscured, not because their personalities are less forceful than those of the pioneers, but because there are more of them. We may have among us in this or the coming generation social workers as devoted as Josephine Butler, novelists as powerful as the Brontës, poets as spiritual as Christina Rossetti, organizers as vigorous as Florence Nightingale, but they are not notable

> as a star when only one
> Is shining in the sky,

because the firmament is already crowded.

We have heard much of the greatness of the pioneers. What of the girl of to-day? She too has her tribute, though a light-hearted one. For the modern girl is not as bad as she is painted.

> And she can ride and she can swim,
> And she can dance till the stars grow dim,
> And, waking fresh as violets,
> Play eighteen holes or seven sets,
> Or paint, or cook,
> Or write a book,
> Or fence, or vote,
> Or sail a boat,
> Will run a mile or run a man
> (And run the office if she can),
> Defend a burglar, drive a 'plane,
> And in the evening dance again; . . .
> Hush, Mrs Hundred, hush!
> Your song is sung;
> But not so long ago
> You were the Modern Young.[1]

---

[1] From A. P. Herbert's *Hush, Mrs Hundred, Hush!* (Reprinted by the special permission of the Proprietors of *Punch*.)

EPILOGUE

THE history of the past hundred years in women's education seems a tangle. Yet through the confusion we can trace certain stages—perhaps rather round a circumference than along a line, for it seems almost as if the wheel were to come full circle. But what has been gained is never utterly lost, and if the phases recur it is with brighter and stronger ideals. For the education of girls at the beginning of the last century was, by and large, designed to get them husbands. Little matter what sort of wives they would make, the point was to "marry your sons when you will, and your daughters when you can." The idea of educating them to be good wives developed during the century—it was still a *sine qua non* that the girl was to be married, but there was some glimmering of the idea that she might be a companion, and, indeed, actually a more valuable one if she had a certain trained intelligence. Thus came the development of personality and the education of the individual girl so as to bring out whatever was best in her—an ideal that, curiously enough, was often found most strongly in the larger communities like Newnham College, or the G.P.D.S.T. schools. But, personality once allowed, what could its education lead to but to woman's work outside her home, voluntary, perhaps, at first (as on the school boards), but in due course why not professional? And when, as a working individual, a woman took her place in the social community her education must fit her for this, and we get among girls, for better or for worse, the growth of the public-school spirit. Emphasis is laid on the responsibility of every girl for her house or school, as representing the community—"that each may live for all and all may care for each" can be not less an aim in little than a prayer at large. Yet lately, as if to balance this education for citizenship, there seems a swing towards training the girl for the individual home, through the stress laid on domestic science and physical training. Anyone who studies that most sensitive barometer of educational employment *The Times Educational Supplement* cannot fail to see this. Compared with general academic posts, the number of jobs listed under domestic science between about 1934 and 1937 was out of all proportion. For the year 1938 the stress was on physical training.

True, there has probably never been a time when it was the ultimate aim of the majority of educators to produce among girls characteristics other than those suited to an ideal home life. Here speaks a schoolmistress who was looked on as rather old-fashioned in the sixties:

> I think a girl ought above all to be fitted for her domestic duties, even to scrubbing and scouring. I make all my girls do plain needlework and devote one evening a week to needlework for the poor. The girls do their own mending; I do not keep a lady's maid for them. I would teach cooking if that were possible. The girls learn to keep house and help me to keep the books, receive the goods sent home by the tradesmen for the use of the house, check the tradesmen's bills, weigh out the materials for puddings, make tea, etc., etc. When out shopping I take one or two of the girls with me and accustom them to calculate the value of the articles bought and make out the bills. . . . I think it is very important that girls should be taught how to converse properly. Every evening we meet in the drawing-room and discuss historical subjects or the news of the day. When I can manage it I get a few friends to meet them or take them to a friend's house.

The Schools Inquiry Commissioner who quotes this merely adds, "I had no opportunity of testing the mental attainments of these young ladies."

Emily Davies, writing in 1866 on *The Higher Education of Women*, has collected a magnificent though contradictory set of Victorian ideals, of which, unfortunately, she does not as a rule give the context. But "Mr Anthony

Trollope" is quoted as saying, "We like women to be timid," against which "Mr Helps" complains that

> Women are not taught to be courageous . . . yet there are few things that would tend to make women happier in themselves and more acceptable to those with whom they live than courage.

Miss Nightingale and the "heroines of the Crimea" are applauded, yet there is also "an admiration for the commonplace, unambitious kind of old maid, who is content to do good in her own neighbourhood, and among the few persons whom she really knows—who takes a lively interest in the welfare of her nieces, and who regales herself with tea and gossip"—a position which would *not* have suited the Lady with the Lamp. Another writer urges that, as "the common sense of the world has long ago settled that men are to be pleased and women are to please," girls should continue to cultivate the accomplishments as "instrumental to the successful exercise of this power"; while another says:

> Accomplishments are quite a secondary matter. If men do not get tired of the songs they soon get tired of the singer if she can do nothing but sing.

(The speaker might have been the creator of Clive Newcome's Rosey; this heroine's songs numbered five in all.) Still, this is only divergence as to the means; the end is the same, that she should be a pleasant companion. More definite views are expressed in the following:

> That they should be trained to be good and generous is by far the first thing. The next thing is that they should be well-mannered and healthy.

Surely not an inevitable combination?

> The third requisite is that they should know how to express themselves—should have a right standard in judging books and men. . . . The fourth is that they should know how to bear rule in a household.

Tennyson's "Isabel" is contrasted with Coventry Patmore's "Jane," whose husband

> Feels 'twould do him good to scold his wife a little . . .
> Till soothed in mind by meat and rest,

the woman's patience demanding, by complement, a man's sulkiness to practise upon.

Miss Davies sums up the ideal presented to a girl, as late as the middle of the century, in often quoted words: "To be amiable, inoffensive, always ready to give pleasure and to be pleased."

To ardent spirits like Miss Davies herself and Miss Buss such an object is false and degrading. Yet, as one of Miss Buss's pupils says, "To be deeply pleasing to a husband and widely pleasing to other men seems to me as good an ideal as a woman can have," and she complains that these pioneers failed to see all its possibilities. They ignored to a great extent what one may call the Ruskin ideal, the ideal of *The Princess*, that of the intelligent feminine mind trained to appreciate and be a companion to a husband, but without ambition to stand by itself.

> O we will walk this world
> Yoked in all exercise of noble end. . . .
> Yield thyself up; my hopes and thine are one;
> Lay thy sweet hands in mine and trust to me.

The chief quarrel that the reformers had with the otherwise admirable education which might be devised for such an ideal was that it ignored the economic side of the woman's position. Miss Buss from the first, and Miss Beale, with more caution, later, put forward the vital importance of fitting a woman for earning a sufficiently good living to become independent of her family or a loveless marriage. Miss Beale determined to have it both ways: marriage was the highest profession, but all knowledge could be used for the development of a good citizen of God, our citizenship being in heaven; therefore every girl was being educated for a profession. Miss Buss's determined attitude to this question is expressed in a letter:

> But as I have grown older the terrible sufferings of the women of my own class, for want of good elementary training, have more than ever intensified my earnest desire to lighten, ever so little, the misery of women brought up "to be married and taken care of," and left alone in the world destitute. It is impossible for words to express my fixed determination of alleviating this evil—even to the small extent of one neighbourhood only—were it possible.

It is a short step from this to a positive exultation in a career as such, and in the self-expression which the professional life at first brought to women. Mrs Strachey shows that the idea of "a career" called forth an almost ecstatic appreciation:

> Work, indeed, came to seem almost an end in itself to some of them, and they attached a value to earning their own livings which that somewhat dreary necessity does not in reality possess. The feminists of two decades before the War saw the employment problem in an artificial and slightly propagandist light. They thought of work as a satisfaction of personal needs, an outlet for gifts and powers, a fulfilment of personal individuality. If a woman could have an independent career, they felt, she would be safe in the certainty that she was justifying her existence, as well as safe in the fact that her own ways of living would be decided by herself and paid for by her own exertions. She would be really free.[1]

Much talk of this kind was mere exaggerated nonsense, and is very justly taken off in, for example, the early plays of Bernard Shaw—*You Never Can Tell* and the less-known, because more 'dated,' *The Philanderer*. But the effect on the schools was anything but nonsensical —as one young woman put it: "The thing that mattered was that we should know our work, and to our lasting good we realized this, and got to know it so as to save time." That is from a high school. The same spirit is shown in a public school, where the aim was "to learn

[1] *Our Freedom and its Results.*

how to learn and teach oneself." This rather sober spirit has continued; we see it in Miss Beale's successor, Miss Faithful, who says, "The aim of the school should surely be to encourage life to be lived for the glory of God and the relief of man's estate," and in the *St Leonard's Jubilee Book* (1927): "What the school must give to-day to meet the uncertainties of the future is training and resourcefulness, efficiency, the power of honest work and the spirit of service."

The ideal of training for service is continued in higher education, but there is also the expression of a rather different point of view. Miss Jane Harrison contrasts the individual life with the life of the race, from which, as she says, the unmarried and childless cut themselves off. The individual life she calls "a side-track, a blind alley . . . yet surely a supreme end in itself." On the whole, she is glad she escaped marriage.

> For a woman [it] hampers the two things that made life to me glorious—friendship and learning. In man it was always the friend, not the husband I wanted. Family life has never attracted me. At its best it seems to me rather narrow and selfish; at its worst, a private hell. The *rôle* of wife and mother is no easy one; with my head full of other things, I might have dismally failed. On the other hand, I have a natural gift for community life. It seems to me sane and civilized and economically right. . . . I am content to have lived many years of my life in a college.

She ends: "Old age is a good and pleasant thing."

This is an ideal very rarely expressed, yet I believe it to be true for a certain number of women, as it is for perhaps an equally small proportion of men. Miss Harrison has put down courageously and sincerely what is not easy to describe; most women of the 'single' temperament either do not trouble to define their outlook or they keep it to themselves, in the belief that they will be misunderstood or not credited; that their ideal will, by the majority, be regarded as a *pis aller*.

Granted, then, that there are some women who definitely

318

prefer life either on their own or connected with communities of their own sex; that there are others who have chosen such a life because, though not ideal, it seems on the balance to offer the best that, on account of some circumstance or other, they are likely to get; and that yet another section must needs for the sake of dependents or other cause join the ranks of permanent workers (as distinct from home-makers)—granted, too, that these classes form by no means the majority, but quite a considerable proportion of the women who are now, as girls, to be educated in this country—what can the educators do about it? The difficulty has perhaps never been put more briefly and clearly than in a report of Mr (Sir Michael) Sadler:

> Another cause of unsettlement of thought about girls' education is that the training of many girls suffers, often unavoidably, from a divided aim. It would be comparatively easy to frame a curriculum and a course of school training which would fit a girl for the duties of home life. Again, it would be comparatively easy to plan curricula which would give at the least expenditure of time and effort a sound preparation for professional or business life. But the difficulty lies in the fact that the future of so many of the girls is uncertain. They may not eventually decide or need to earn their own living in a professional calling. Their work may lie in domestic duties at home with their parents or in a home of their own. But during their school days it is necessary, in a large number of cases, to prepare them, so far as may be, for either event.

It may seem presumptuous to add even a pebble to the mighty pile of ideas which increases voluminously every day. But I would try to explain what seems to me the crucial word in the remarks quoted above and in so many others: 'prepare.' The educationists sometimes seem to forget that the child or young woman is actually living while she is being a subject for educating; that the 'preparing' must take into account her ideas and her character *at the moment*, and not only mean 'moulding' or 'drawing her out' for the time to come. Of course, an appeal to the future is sometimes justified, but it should not be felt as a tacit plea in so much of Authority's attitude as is common now. There is too much stress on "when it comes to the examination," "when you become a senior girl," "when you have a home of your own," "when the time comes for testing your character." It is not that these thoughts are not latent in the child's mind; indeed, the very fact that the young tend to look forward with such desperate eagerness to the time

> When we are grown and take our place
> As men and women with our race,

should make us beware of encouraging them to grasp at the shadow in such a way as to lose the substance.

Perhaps we are beginning to act, consciously or unconsciously, on the idea of vivifying the present. The child should delight in Shakespeare *now*, in the form-room or in her own private reading, because 'it is fun,' or because something in the poetry or in the situation stirs her, not in order that in the examination she may write a note on the pun, or produce an essay on the character, or even go to see the plays acted in the holidays or when she leaves school. She should feel that a problem in mathematics is worth solving, and that the act of solving it is in itself a joyful one; it is not enough to do the work in order to "get on to the next." A piece of handwork is a delight to the craftswoman while in the doing; a play is enjoyed in rehearsal, not only at the performance. The virtue of a bit of self-discipline, the delight in the company of your friend, the understanding of a point of view in some one or some subject uncongenial —these things are 'good' in themselves, not only good because they help to form the admirable school-girl character—or even the Perfect Woman. That we are beginning to realize this, in practice at least, seems to me a discovery, or rather a rediscovery, of one of the greatest truths, whether we learn it from Lucretius, or Kipling, or the Sermon on the Mount.

Life itself must have aims—or an aim; but to educate is to enable anyone to find these aims, not to find them for him or for her. Of course, there must be help—argument, encouragement, sympathy—in fact, 'teaching.' But the end of teaching, as every one realizes when the child leaves school, is to produce self-education, and self-education is the power of defining one's aims and reaching towards them, a clarifying and a progression unending.

"It seems absurd to waste life in preparing to live," wrote poor Mary Wollstonecraft, but many educationists would have about a quarter of it wasted in this way. The preparing has been best carried out when the girl or boy, the young man or woman, knows how to enjoy the thing done, and looks on it as worth doing for its own sake, not only with a view to getting on to the next. We have seen again and again how the 'object' of education has been this or that, the training has been 'for' one purpose or another. True education is not 'for' anything. To be educated is to be made aware of the fullness of life, moment by moment, and to be enabled to live well.

BIBLIOGRAPHY

ACLAND, E.: *Good-bye for the Present* (Hodder and Stoughton, 1935).
ADAMSON, J. W.: *English Education* (Cambridge University Press, 1930).
ASHBY, A. W., and BYLES, P. G.: *Rural Education* (Oxford University Press, 1923).
AUSTEN, JANE: *Sense and Sensibility* (1811).
—— *Mansfield Park* (1814).
—— *Emma* (1815).
—— *Northanger Abbey* (1818).
—— *Persuasion* (1818).
BEALE, D., AND OTHERS: *Work and Play in Girls' Schools* (Longmans, 1898).
BELLMAN, SIR CHARLES HAROLD: *After School* (Sampson Low, 1936).
BENSON, E. F.: *Queen Victoria* (Longmans, 1935).
BODY, A. H.: *John Wesley and Education* (Epworth, 1938).
BOSANQUET, THEODORA: *Harriet Martineau: A Study* (Oxford University Press, 1927).
BRITTAIN, VERA: *The Testament of Youth* (Gollancz, 1933).
BRONTË, CHARLOTTE: *Jane Eyre* (1847).
—— *Shirley* (1849).
—— *Villette* (1853).
BROWNING, E. B.: *Aurora Leigh* (1856).
BURSTALL, SARA: *English High Schools for Girls* (Longmans, 1907).
—— *The Story of Manchester High School for Girls* (Manchester University Press, 1911).
—— *Retrospect and Prospect* (Longmans, 1933).
—— *Frances Mary Buss* (S.P.C.K., 1938).
BUTLER, ELIZABETH: *From Sketchbook and Diary* (Black, 1909).
Cheltenham College Magazine, The.
Child's Guide to Knowledge, The (1861 edition).
CLOUGH, B. A.: *Memoir of Anne Jemima Clough* (Arnold, 1897).
COBBE, FRANCES POWER: *Life of Frances Power Cobbe* (1904).
COOK, SIR EDWARD T.: *Florence Nightingale* (Macmillan, 1925 edition).
CRUSE, AMY: *The Englishman and his Books in the Nineteenth Century* (Harrap, 1930).
—— *The Victorians and their Books* (Allen and Unwin, 1935).
CUNNINGTON, C. W.: *Feminine Attitudes in the Nineteenth Century* (Heinemann, 1935).
DAVIES, E.: *The Higher Education of Women* (1866).

DAVIES, E.: *Thoughts on Some Questions relating to Women* (Cambridge University Press, 1910).

DAVIS, R.: *Four Miss Pinkertons* (Williams and Norgate, 1936).

DICKENS, CHARLES: *Nicholas Nickleby* (1838–39).

—— *Dombey and Son* (1848).

—— *Our Mutual Friend* (1864–65).

Dictionary of National Biography, The.

EDGEWORTH, MARIA: *The Parent's Assistant* (1796–1801).

—— *Moral Tales* (1801).

ELIOT, GEORGE: *Silas Marner* (1861).

—— *Middlemarch* (1871–72).

EWING, J. H.: *A Flat Iron for a Farthing* (Bell, 1873).

—— *Six to Sixteen* (Bell, 1876).

FAITHFUL, L. M.: *In the House of my Pilgrimage* (Chatto, 1924).

FAUCIT, HELEN: *On Some of Shakespeare's Female Characters* (1885).

First College for Women, The (*Queen's College Jubilee Book*, 1899).

FITCH, JOSHUA: *Lecture to the Social Science Association.*

Founders of Roedean (Roedean Memorial to Miss Lawrence, 1935; Farncombe's, Brighton).

Fraser's Magazine.

Friends' Teachers Guild pamphlets.

GARDINER, D.: *English Girlhood at School* (Oxford University Press, 1929).

GASKELL, MRS: *Cranford* (1851–53).

—— *Life of Charlotte Brontë* (1857).

—— *Wives and Daughters* (1864–66).

GIFFORD, M. J.: *The Diary of an Oxford Lady* (Blackwell, 1932).

Girlhood of Queen Victoria (edited by Viscount Esher; Murray, 1912).

Girls' Public Day School Trust Jubilee Book, The (Cambridge University Press, 1924).

Girls' Public School Year Book, The.

GOLDSMITH, OLIVER: *The Vicar of Wakefield* (1766).

GRANT, ELIZABETH: *Memoirs of a Highland Lady* (Murray, 1911).

GRAY, FRANCES: *And Gladly Wolde he Lerne and Gladly Teche* (Sampson Low, 1931).

GREER, LYNDA: *Winifred Mercier* (Oxford University Press).

GUNN, J.: *The Infant School* (Nelson, 1904).

GURNEY, MARY: *Are we to have Education for our Middle-class Girls?*

HALDANE, ELIZABETH S.: *Mrs Gaskell and her Friends* (Hodder, 1930).

—— *From One Century to Another* (MacLehose, 1937).

Handbook of Suggestions for the Consideration of Teachers and others concerned in the Work of Public Elementary Schools (Board of Education; H.M. Stationery Office, 1937).

BIBLIOGRAPHY

HARRISON, JANE: *Reminiscences of a Student's Life* (Hogarth Press, 1925).

HAVERGAL, M.: *Memorials of F. R. Havergal* (Nisbet, 1880).

Headmistress Speaks, The (edited by E. Philips; Kegan Paul, 1937).

HODGSON, W.: *The Education of Girls and Local Examinations.*

HUGHES, M. VIVIAN: *A London Girl of the Eighties* (Oxford University Press, 1936).

HUTTON, R. H.: *Lecture to the Social Science Association.*

INGRAM, JOHN: *E. B. Browning* (Eminent Women Series; Allen, 1888).

Josephine E. Butler, an Autobiographical Memoir (edited by G. W. and L. A. Johnson; Arrowsmith, third edition, 1928).

Lady Margaret Hall Jubilee Book (1928).

LODGE, E.: *Terms and Vacations* (Oxford University Press, 1938).

LOWNDES, G. A. N.: *The Silent Social Revolution* (Oxford University Press, 1937).

LUMSDEN, L. T.: *Yellow Leaves* (Blackwood, 1933).

MEAKIN, A. M. B.: *Hannah More* (Murray, 1911).

MEYNELL, WILFRID: *Lady Butler* (*Art Annual*, 1898).

MILLER, F. F.: *Harriet Martineau* (Eminent Women Series; Allen, 1884).

Miss Weeton (edited by Edward Hall; Oxford University Press, 1936).

Modern Schools Handbook, The (edited by T. Blewitt; Gollancz, 1934).

NEFF, W. F.: *Victorian Working Women* (Allen and Unwin, 1929).

Old School, The (edited by Graham Greene; Cape, 1937).

O'LEARY, M. F. M.: *Education with a Tradition* (University of London Press, 1936).

Our Freedom and its Results (edited by Ray Strachey; Hogarth Press, 1936).

PENNELL, E. R.: *M. Wollstonecraft* (Eminent Women Series; Allen, 1885).

PREEDY, GEORGE: *This Shining Woman* (Collins, 1937).

Quarterly Review, The.

RAIKES, E.: *Dorothea Beale of Cheltenham* (Constable, 1900).

RAYMENT, T.: *Modern Education* (Longmans).

Report of the Consultative Committee (Board of Education) on the Differentiation in Curricula between the Sexes in Secondary Schools (H.M. Stationery Office, 1923).

Report of the Consultative Committee (Board of Education) on the Education of the Adolescent (H.M. Stationery Office, 1926).

Report of the Consultative Committee (Board of Education) on the Primary School (H.M. Stationery Office, 1931).

Report of the Royal Commission on Elementary Education, 1887 (Cross Commission).

Report of the Royal Commission on Endowed Schools (Taunton Commission) (1868).

RHONDDA, VISCOUNTESS: *This was my World* (Macmillan, 1933).

RIDLEY, A. E.: *Frances Mary Buss* (Longmans, 1895).
Robert Browning and Julia Wedgwood: A Broken Friendship as Revealed in their Letters (edited by R. Curle; Murray and Cape, 1937).
ROUSSEAU, J.-J.: *Émile* (1762).
RUSKIN, JOHN: *Sesame and Lilies* (1865).
St Leonard's School Jubilee Book (1927).
Saturday Review, The.
SHARP, E.: *Hertha Ayrton* (Arnold, 1926).
SHERWOOD, MRS: *The Fairchild Family* (1818–47).
SHILLITO, E. H.: *Dorothea Beale* (S.P.C.K., 1920).
SHIRREFF, EMILY: *Intellectual Education* (1858).
SHORE, EMILY: *Journal* (Kegan Paul, 1891).
SITWELL, EDITH: *Victoria of England* (Faber, 1936).
SMITH, FRANK: *A History of English Elementary Education* (University of London, 1931).
Some Modern Artists and their Work (edited by W. Meynell; Cassell, 1883).
STEADMAN, F. C.: *In the Days of Miss Beale* (Burrow, 1931).
STEPHEN, B.: *Emily Davies and Girton College* (Constable, 1927).
STUART, D. M.: *The Girl through the Ages* (Harrap, 1933).
STUART, J. E.: *The Education of Catholic Girls* (Longmans, 1911).
SWANWICK, H. M.: *I have been Young* (Gollancz, 1935).
SWIFT, JONATHAN: *On the Death of Mrs Johnson* [*Stella*] (1728).
TENNYSON, LORD: *The Princess* (1847).
THACKERAY, W. M.: *Vanity Fair* (1847–48).
—— *The Newcomes* (1853–55).
TOMKINSON, W. S., and PHILLIPS, M.: *Englishwomen in Life and Letters* (Oxford University Press, 1926).
WALLAS, ADA: *Before the Bluestockings* (Allen and Unwin, 1929).
WHIPPLE, D.: *Other Day* (M. Joseph, 1936).
WHITE, ANTONIA: *Frost in May* (Harmsworth, 1933).
WHITNEY, JANET: *Elizabeth Fry* (Harrap, 1937).
WILSON, BARBARA: *Dear Youth* (Macmillan, 1937).
WRIGHT, E. M.: *Life of Joseph Wright* (Oxford University Press, 1932).
YONGE, C. M.: *The Daisy Chain* (1856).
—— *Hopes and Fears* (1860).
—— *Womankind* (1876).
—— *Countess Kate and the Stokesley Secret* (1892).
YOUNG, ARTHUR: *Autobiography.*
YOUNG, G. M.: *Victorian England* (Oxford University Press, 1936).
ZIMMERN, A.: *The Renaissance of Girls' Education in England* (Longmans, 1898).

INDEX

INDEX

Governesses' Benevolent Institution, 43, 122

Grammar, study of, 33, 62, 93, 191

Grammar schools, justification of, 290

Gray, Frances, 167, 232, 303–304

Greek, study of, 44, 48, 64, 66, 71, 74, 103, 191, 289

Green, T. H., 175, 197, 246

Grey, Josephine (Mrs Butler), 28, 49, 50, 135, 141, 142, 144, 310; upbringing of, 35–38

Grey, Mrs William (Maria), 77, 127, 142, 143, 196, 198, 233

Griffiths, T. (lecturer to Queen Victoria), 31

Grisewood, F., 270

Grove, —, 143

Grundy, Mrs, 137, 142

Gunns, the Miss (*Silas Marner*), 14

Gurney, Catherine, 31

Gurney, Elizabeth—*see* Fry, Elizabeth

Gurney, John, 33

Gurney, Mrs Russell (Mary), 127, 158, 200, 233

Gurney, Samuel, 33

Gurneys of Earlham, The, 32

HADOW REPORT (1926), the, 251

Hall, Mrs S. C., 142, 148

Hare, Augustus, 32

Harrison, Jane, 11, 140, 160, 318; education of, 65, 103, 112, 275

Hastings, Lady Elizabeth, 15

Havergal, Frances Ridley, 48

Haworth Parsonage, 34–35, 51

Headmistress Speaks, The, 291

Headmistresses' Association, the, 203, 213, 220

Hebrew, study of, 67, 103

Héger, M., 95

Heraldry, study of, 67, 191

Hexam, Charley (*Our Mutual Friend*), 256

Hill, Octavia, 28, 48, 51, 96

History, study of, 56, 60, 64, 66–67, 73, 165

Hitchin, 148, 159, 183

Hoare, Samuel, 31

Hodgson, W. B., 17, 149 *n.*, 155

Holloway College (Royal), 181

Holy Child, the, Order of, 242

Home and Colonial (Training) School, 171

Hopes and Fears, 76, 101–102

Hospitals, 151–152; Middlesex, 43, 152; Salisbury, 45; Westminster, 186

Howe, Julia Ward, 45–46

Howe, S. G., 45–46

Hughes, Mrs M. Vivian, 91. See also *London Girl of the Eighties, A*

Huldah, 12

Hullah, John, 126, 148

Hume, David, 33

Hutton, Richard Holt, 15, 16, 147, 156, 185

Huxley, Thomas, 253, 266

Hygiene, 202; need for instruction in, 85

Hypatia, 126

IMLAY, GILBERT, 21

Inchbald, Elizabeth, 16

Ingelow, Jean, 126

Inspectors, 263, 264

Italian, study of, 44, 62, 66, 68, 91, 103

Ivanhoe, 61, 275

JAMESON, ANNA BROWNELL, 102, 116

Jane Eyre, 93, 95, 117, 130, 247

Jebb, Sir Richard, 146

Jeune, family, 55–57, 59, 61, 62, 76, 84

Jex-Blake, Sophia Louisa, 126

John Grey of Dilston, 37

Johnson, Esther ("Stella"), 16–17, 18

Johnson, Mrs Arthur, 173, 177

Jowett, Benjamin, 126

Jungle Book, The, 275

KAISERSWERTH, Deaconesses' Institution at, 45

Kay-Shuttleworth, Sir James (Dr Kay), 123, 260, 261

Kensington Palace, 30, 31

Kent, Victoria Mary Louisa, Duchess of, 29, 30, 31, 49

Kenyon, John, 40, 76

Kindergarten, 279

Kingsley, Charles, 126, 148

Kingswood School, 238

Kipling, Rudyard, 223, 320

Knightley, Mr (*Emma*), 53

Kyberd, Miss, 96

331